PUBLISHING

GW00598897

THIS EXAM KIT COMES WITH
FREE ONLINE ACCESS
TO EXTRA RESOURCES AIMED AT HELPING YOU PASS YOUR EXAMS

IN ADDITION TO THE OFFICIAL QUESTIONS AND ANSWERS IN THIS BOOK, GO ONLINE AND EN-gage WITH:

- An iPaper version of the Exam Kit
- Articles including Key Examinable Areas
- Material updates
- Latest Official ACCA exam questions
- Extra question assistance using the Signpost icon
- Timed Questions with an online tutor debrief using the Clock icon

And you can access all of these extra resources anytime, anywhere using your EN-gage account.

How to access your online resources

If you are a Kaplan Financial tuition, full-time or distance learning student

You will already have an EN-gage account and these extra resources will be available to you online. You do not need to register again, as this process was completed when you enrolled. If having problems accessing online materials, please ask your course administrator.

If you purchased through Kaplan Flexible Learning or via the Kaplan Publishing website

You will automatically receive an e-mail invitation to EN-gage online. Please register your details using this e-mail to gain access to your content. If you do not receive the e-mail or book content, please contact our Technical Support team at engage@twinsystems.com.

If you are already a registered EN-gage user

Go to www.EN-gage.co.uk and log in. Select the 'add a book' feature and enter the ISBN number of this book and the unique pass key at the bottom of this card. Then click 'finished' or 'add another book'. You may add as many books as you have purchased from this screen.

If you are a new EN-gage user

Register at www.EN-gage.co.uk and click on the link contained in the e-mail we sent you to activate your account. Then select the 'add a book' feature, enter the ISBN number of this book and the unique pass key at the bottom of this card. Then click 'finished' or 'add another book'.

Your Code and Information

This code can only be used once for the registration of one book online. This registration will expire when the final sittings for the examinations covered by this book have taken place. Please allow one hour from the time you submitted your book details for us to process your request.

QI4Y-VPoW-Zlob-QU7L

Please be aware that this code is case-sensitive and you will need to include the dashes within the passcode, but not when entering the ISBN. For further technical support, please visit www.EN-gage.co.uk

For technical support, please visit www.EN-gage.co.uk

Paper F4 (ENG)

CORPORATE AND BUSINESS LAW

EXAM KIT

KAPLAN

PUBLISHING

British Library Cataloguing-in-Publication Data

A catalogue record for this book is available from the British Library.

Published by:

Kaplan Publishing UK

Unit 2 The Business Centre

Molly Millar's Lane

Wokingham

Berkshire

RG41 2QZ

ISBN: 978 1 84710 987 3

© Kaplan Financial Limited, 2010

Printed in the UK by CPI William Clowes, Beccles, NR34 7TL.

The text in this material and any others made available by any Kaplan Group company does not amount to advice on a particular matter and should not be taken as such. No reliance should be placed on the content as the basis for any investment or other decision or in connection with any advice given to third parties. Please consult your appropriate professional adviser as necessary. Kaplan Publishing Limited and all other Kaplan group companies expressly disclaim all liability to any person in respect of any losses or other claims, whether direct, indirect, incidental, consequential or otherwise arising in relation to the use of such materials.

All rights reserved. No part of this examination may be reproduced or transmitted in any form or by any means, electronic or mechanical, including photocopying, recording, or by any information storage and retrieval system, without prior permission from Kaplan Publishing.

Acknowledgements

The past ACCA examination questions are the copyright of the Association of Chartered Certified Accountants. The original answers to the questions from June 1994 onwards were produced by the examiners themselves and have been adapted by Kaplan Publishing.

We are grateful to the Chartered Institute of Management Accountants and the Institute of Chartered Accountants in England and Wales for permission to reproduce past examination questions. The answers have been prepared by Kaplan Publishing.

CONTENTS

Section

Features in this edition

In addition to providing a wide ranging bank of real past exam questions, we have also included in this edition:

- An analysis of all of the recent new syllabus examination papers.

- Paper specific information and advice on exam technique.

- Our recommended approach to make your revision for this particular subject as effective as possible.

- Enhanced tutorial answers packed with specific key answer tips, technical tutorial notes and exam technique tips from our experienced tutors.

- Complementary online resources including full tutor debriefs and question assistance to point you in the right direction when you get stuck.

December 2009 – Real examination questions with enhanced tutorial answers

The real December 2009 exam questions with enhanced "walk through answers" and full "tutor debriefs", updated in line with legislation relevant to your exam sitting, is available on Kaplan EN-gage at:

www.EN-gage.co.uk

You will find a wealth of other resources to help you with your studies on the following sites:

www.EN-gage.co.uk

www.**acca**global.com/students/

INDEX TO QUESTIONS AND ANSWERS

INTRODUCTION

The style of current Paper F4 exam question is different to old syllabus Paper 2.2 questions and significant changes have had to be made to questions in light of the legislative changes in Companies Act 2006.

Accordingly, some of the old ACCA questions within this kit have been adapted to reflect the new style of paper and the new rules. If changed in any way from the original version, this is indicated in the end column of the index below with the mark *(A)*.

Note that the majority of the questions within the kit are past ACCA exam questions, the more recent questions (from 2005) are labelled as such in the index.

The pilot paper is included at the end of the kit.

KEY TO THE INDEX

PAPER ENHANCEMENTS

We have added the following enhancements to the answers in this exam kit:

Key answer tips

All answers include key answer tips to help your understanding of each question.

Top tutor tips

For selected questions, we "walk through the answer" giving guidance on how to approach the questions with helpful 'tips from a top tutor', together with technical tutor notes.

These answers are indicated with the "footsteps" icon in the index.

ONLINE ENHANCEMENTS

 Timed question with Online tutor debrief

For selected questions, we recommend that they are to be completed in full exam conditions (i.e. properly timed in a closed book environment).

In addition to the examiner's technical answer, enhanced with key answer tips and tutorial notes in this exam kit, online you can find an answer debrief by a top tutor that:

- works through the question in full

- points out how to approach the question

- how to ensure that the easy marks are obtained as quickly as possible, and

- emphasises how to tackle exam questions and exam technique.

These questions are indicated with the "clock" icon in the index.

 Online question assistance

Have you ever looked at a question and not know where to start, or got stuck part way through?

For selected questions, we have produced "Online question assistance" offering different levels of guidance, such as:

- ensuring that you understand the question requirements fully, highlighting key terms and the meaning of the verbs used

- how to read the question proactively, with knowledge of the requirements, to identify the topic areas covered

- assessing the detail content of the question body, pointing out key information and explaining why it is important

- help in devising a plan of attack

With this assistance, you should then be able to attempt your answer confident that you know what is expected of you.

These questions are indicated with the "signpost" icon in the index.

Online question enhancements and answer debriefs will be available from Spring 2010 on Kaplan EN-gage at:

www.EN-gage.co.uk

ANALYSIS OF PAST PAPERS

The table below summarises the key topics that have been tested in the new syllabus examinations to date.

Note that the references are to the original numbering in the paper itself.

	Pilot	Dec 07	Jun 08	Dec 08	Jun 09	Dec 09	Jun 10
Essential Elements Of The Legal System							
The English legal system		Q1	Q1		Q1	Q1	Q1
Sources of English law	Q1			Q1			
Human rights							
The Law Of Obligations							
Formation of contracts	Q8	Q2, 8	Q2	Q8	Q2		
Terms of contract	Q2				Q3	Q2	Q2
Breach of contract			Q8	Q2	Q8	Q3	Q8
Torts	Q3	Q3	Q3	Q3	Q4	Q8	Q3
Professional negligence						Q4	
Employment Law							
Employment contract			Q7			Q7	Q7
Dismissal and redundancy	Q7	Q6		Q7	Q7		
The Formation and Constitution Of Business Organisations							
Agency law							
Partnerships			Q9	Q10			Q9
Organisations and legal personality			Q4				
Company formation	Q4				Q4		Q4
Constitution of a company		Q4		Q9		Q5	
Capital And The Financing Of Companies							
Share capital	Q9		Q5	Q4			
Borrowing and loan capital							Q5
Capital maintenance and dividend law		Q5			Q5		
Management, Administration And Regulation Of Companies							
Company directors and other company officers		Q7, 10	Q6	Q6	Q6, 9		
Company meeting and resolutions	Q5			Q5			
Legal Implications Of Companies In Difficulty Or In Crisis							
Insolvency and administration		Q9				Q6	
Governance And Ethical Issues Relating To Business							
Corporate governance	Q6					Q9	Q6, 10
Fraudulent behaviour	Q10		Q10		Q10	Q10	

KAPLAN PUBLISHING

EXAM TECHNIQUE

- Use the allocated **15 minutes reading and planning time** at the beginning of the exam:
  - read the questions and examination requirements carefully, and
  - begin planning your answers.

  See the Paper Specific Information for advice on how to use this time for this paper.

- **Divide the time** you spend on questions in proportion to the marks on offer:
  - there are 1.8 minutes available per mark in the examination
  - within that, try to allow time at the end of each question to review your answer and address any obvious issues

  Whatever happens, always keep your eye on the clock and **do not over run on any part of any question!**

- Spend the last **five minutes** of the examination:
  - reading through your answers, and
  - **making any additions or corrections**.

- If you **get completely stuck** with a question:
  - leave space in your answer book, and
  - **return to it later.**

- Stick to the question and **tailor your answer** to what you are asked.
  - pay particular attention to the verbs in the question.

- If you do not understand what a question is asking, **state your assumptions**.

  Even if you do not answer in precisely the way the examiner hoped, you should be given some credit, if your assumptions are reasonable.

- You should do everything you can to make things easy for the marker.

  The marker will find it easier to identify the points you have made if your **answers are legible**.

- **Written questions**:

  Your answer should have:
  - a clear structure
  - a brief introduction, a main section and a conclusion.

  Be concise.

  It is better to write a little about a lot of different points than a great deal about one or two points.

PAPER SPECIFIC INFORMATION

THE EXAM

FORMAT OF THE EXAM

Number of marks

10 compulsory questions which will all be written questions:

Question 1:	English legal system	10
Question 2:	Contract law	10
Question 3:	Contract law/law of torts	10
Question 4:	Company law	10
Question 5:	Company law	10
Question 6:	Company law	10
Question 7:	Employment law	10
Question 8:	Contract law	10
Question 9:	Any area of the syllabus	10
Question 10:	Any area of the syllabus	10
		100

Total time allowed: 3 hours plus 15 minutes reading and planning time.

PASS MARK

The pass mark for all ACCA Qualification examination papers is 50%.

READING AND PLANNING TIME

Remember that all three hour paper based examinations have an additional 15 minutes reading and planning time.

ACCA GUIDANCE

ACCA guidance on the use of this time is as follows:

This additional time is allowed at the beginning of the examination to allow candidates to read the questions and to begin planning their answers before they start to write in their answer books.

This time should be used to ensure that all the information and, in particular, the exam requirements are properly read and understood.

During this time, candidates may only annotate their question paper. They may not write anything in their answer booklets until told to do so by the invigilator.

KAPLAN GUIDANCE

As all questions are compulsory, there are no decisions to be made about choice of questions, other than in which order you would like to tackle them.

Therefore, in relation to F4, we recommend that you take the following approach with your reading and planning time:

- **Skim through the whole paper**, assessing the level of difficulty of each question.

- **Write down** on the question paper next to the mark allocation **the amount of time you should spend on each part.** Do this for each part of every question.

- **Decide the order** in which you think you will attempt each question:

    This is a personal choice and you have time on the revision phase to try out different approaches, for example, if you sit mock exams.

    A common approach is to tackle the question you think is the easiest and you are most comfortable with first.

    Psychologists believe that you usually perform at your best on the second and third question you attempt, once you have settled into the exam.

    It is usual however that student tackle their least favourite topic and/or the most difficult question in their opinion last.

    Whatever your approach, you must make sure that you leave enough time to attempt all questions fully and be very strict with yourself in timing each question.

- **For each question** in turn, read the requirements and then the detail of the question carefully.

  Always read the requirement first as this enables you to **focus on the detail of the question with the specific task in mind**.

  Plan your beginning, middle and end and the key areas to be addressed and your use of titles and sub-titles to enhance your answer.

  Spot the easy marks to be gained in a question for example giving simple definitions. Make sure that you do incorporate these into your answer.

  Don't go overboard in terms of planning time on any one question – you need a good measure of the whole paper and a plan for all of the questions at the end of the 15 minutes.

  By covering all questions you can often help yourself as you may find that facts in one question may remind you of things you should put into your answer relating to a different question.

- With your plan of attack in mind, **start answering your chosen question** with your plan to hand, as soon as you are allowed to start.

 Always keep your eye on the clock and do not over run on any part of any question!

DETAILED SYLLABUS

The detailed syllabus and study guide written by the ACCA can be found at:

www.accaglobal.com/students/

KAPLAN'S RECOMMENDED REVISION APPROACH

QUESTION PRACTICE IS THE KEY TO SUCCESS

Success in professional examinations relies upon you acquiring a firm grasp of the required knowledge at the tuition phase. In order to be able to do the questions, knowledge is essential.

However, the difference between success and failure often hinges on your exam technique on the day and making the most of the revision phase of your studies.

The **Kaplan complete text** is the starting point, designed to provide the underpinning knowledge to tackle all questions. However, in the revision phase, pouring over text books is not the answer.

Kaplan Online fixed tests help you consolidate your knowledge and understanding and are a useful tool to check whether you can remember key topic areas.

Kaplan pocket notes are designed to help you quickly revise a topic area, however you then need to practice questions. There is a need to progress to full exam standard questions as soon as possible, and to tie your exam technique and technical knowledge together.

The importance of question practice cannot be over-emphasised.

The recommended approach below is designed by expert tutors in the field, in conjunction with their knowledge of the examiner and their recent real exams.

The approach taken for the fundamental papers is to revise by topic area. However, with the professional stage papers, a multi topic approach is required to answer the scenario based questions.

You need to practice as many questions as possible in the time you have left.

OUR AIM

Our aim is to get you to the stage where you can attempt exam standard questions confidently, to time, in a closed book environment, with no supplementary help (i.e. to simulate the real examination experience).

Practising your exam technique on real past examination questions, in timed conditions, is also vitally important for you to assess your progress and identify areas of weakness that may need more attention in the final run up to the examination.

In order to achieve this we recognise that initially you may feel the need to practice some questions with open book help and exceed the required time.

The approach below shows you which questions you should use to build up to coping with exam standard question practice, and references to the sources of information available should you need to revisit a topic area in more detail.

Remember that in the real examination, all you have to do is:

- attempt all questions required by the exam

- only spend the allotted time on each question, and

- get them at least 50% right!

Try and practice this approach on every question you attempt from now to the real exam.

EXAMINER COMMENTS

We have included the examiners comments to the specific new syllabus examination questions in this kit for you to see the main pitfalls that students fall into with regard to technical content.

However, too many times in the general section of the report, the examiner comments that students had failed due to:

- "misallocation of time"

- "running out of time" and

- showing signs of "spending too much time on an earlier questions and clearly rushing the answer to a subsequent question".

Good exam technique is vital.

THE KAPLAN PAPER F4 REVISION PLAN

Stage 1: Assess areas of strengths and weaknesses

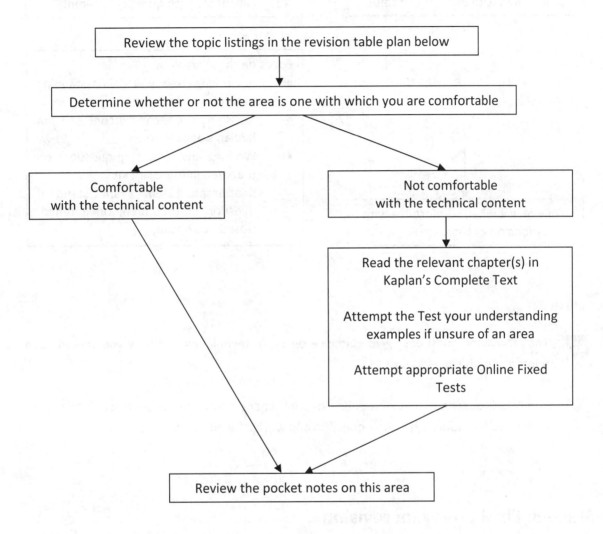

Stage 2: Practice questions

Follow the order of revision of topics as recommended in the revision table plan below and attempt the questions in the order suggested.

Try to avoid referring to text books and notes and the model answer until you have completed your attempt.

Try to answer the question in the allotted time.

Review your attempt with the model answer and assess how much of the answer you achieved in the allocated exam time.

Fill in the self-assessment box below and decide on your best course of action.

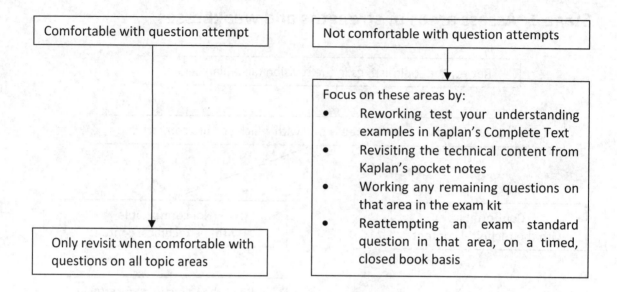

Note that :

 The "footsteps questions" give guidance on exam techniques and how you should have approached the question.

 The "clock questions" have an online debrief where a tutor talks you through the exam technique and approach to that question and works the question in full.

Stage 3: Final pre-exam revision

We recommend that you **attempt at least one three hour mock examination** containing a set of previously unseen exam standard questions.

It is important that you get a feel for the breadth of coverage of a real exam without advanced knowledge of the topic areas covered – just as you will expect to see on the real exam day.

Ideally this mock should be sat in timed, closed book, real exam conditions and could be:

- a mock examination offered by your tuition provider, and/or

- the pilot paper in the back of this exam kit, and/or

- the last real examination paper (available shortly afterwards on Kaplan EN-gage with "enhanced walk through answers" and a full "tutor debrief").

THE DETAILED REVISION PLAN

Topic	Complete Text Chapter	Pocket note Chapter	Questions to attempt	Tutor guidance	Date attempted	Self assessment

English legal system	1	1	1
			3
			4
			5
			6
				There will always be one question on this area, however, there are many potential areas that could be examined.
				You should be able to explain the following:
				  – differences between criminal and civil law;
				  – the court structures for criminal and civil law;
				  – sources of law;
				  – judicial precedent;
				  – purpose of delegated legislation;
				  – interpretation of statute
				  – the role of the Human Rights Act 1998 within the English legal system.		

Contract law	2	2	10
			11
			13
			14
			15
			17
			18
			23
			24
			25
				This is a detailed area of law on which there are always two questions in the exam. One will be a knowledge question and the other will be a scenario question.
				You should be able to:
				  – define offer and acceptance;
				  – give examples of invitation to treat;
				  – explain how an offer can be withdrawn;		

		– explain the postal rule; – define consideration; – explain the three types of consideration (executed, executory and past); – explain the part-payment problem; – differentiate between the intention to create legal relations for domestic and commercial agreements; – explain how terms can be express or implied; – explain and differentiate between conditions, warranties and innominate terms; – define and explain an exclusion clause and the common law rules and statutory rules on this area; – differentiate between actual and anticipatory breach of contract; – explain damages as a remedy; – explain equitable remedies for breach of contract.
		20 21 27
	3	
The law of torts	3	One question on this area always appears in the exam. You should be able to: – explain what a tort is; – define negligence – explain the three elements of

		negligence; – explain the 'neighbour' principle and the concept of special relationship; – explain professional negligence; – explain the tort of passing off.		
Employment law	4	Again, one question on this area of law will feature on the exam. You should be able to: – distinguish between an employee and self-employed; – explain express and implied terms in an employment relationship; – explain wrongful dismissal and the remedy; – explain unfair dismissal and the remedies; – explain redundancy and how redundancy pay is calculated;	33 35 36 38	4
Agency	5	This may be examined as part of wider question on partnerships or directors. You should be able to: – explain a principal and agent relationship; – explain the ways in how an agency relationship arises; – explain the three types of authority;	39 40	5
Partnerships	6	This topic tends to come up once every two to three sittings. You should be able to:	42 48	6

			– explain the different types of partners and their liabilities; – explain the different types of partnerships; – explain the authority of partners; – explain how a partnership can be dissolved.
Corporations and separate personality	7	7	43 44 46 50 52 53	This is a detailed area which comes up consistently in the exam. It is a particularly important chapter as it introduces the topic of company law. You should be able to: – explain the veil of incorporation and circumstances where it can be lifted; – discuss the consequences of incorporating a company; – explain the different types of business organisation; – distinguish between the different types of companies; – define a promoter and explain a pre-incorporation contract; – explain the company formation procedure including the documents which must be filed with the Registrar at Companies House; – explain the rules relating to the name of a company; – explain the purpose and effect of the articles of association.

Capital and financing	8	8	8	An important area of company law on which there is always one question in the exam. You should be able to: – distinguish between share and loan capital; – define a share; – explain share capital terminology; – explain the purpose of capital maintenance; – explain the procedure of capital reduction; – explain the rules on dividends; – define a debenture; – distinguish between fixed and floating charges; – place charges in priority.
				54 56 57 58 61 62
Directors	9	9	9	Again, another area of company law which features consistently in the exam. You should be able to: – define a director; – explain the various types of directors; – explain how directors can be appointed, removed or disqualified; – explain the duties of directors; – explain the authority of directors.
				63 64 66 69 70 72
Company administration	10	10	10	This area comes up periodically in the exam. You should be able to: – explain the rules relating to the
				65 75 76

			requirement of a company secretary; – explain the main duties of a company secretary and their authority; – explain the purpose and rules relating to an auditor; – explain and distinguish between an AGM, a GM and a class meeting; – explain special, ordinary and written resolutions.
Insolvency	11	11	77 79	An area that has not been examined in a great level of detail yet. You should be able to: – explain the procedures involved in the two types of voluntary liquidations; – explain the grounds for a compulsory liquidation; – explain the purpose and effect of administration; – list the order of application of assets
Corporate governance	12	12	82 6 (Pilot Paper)	An area that is not considered to be a key area but is on the pilot paper. Most likely to be tested on a question with directors. You should be able to: – define corporate governance; – explain the historic development of corporate governance;

Fraudulent behaviour	13	13	– explain briefly the main purpose of the Combined Code.
		84 85 88	There always tends to be a question on this area in the exam. You should be able to:
			– explain what is meant by insider dealing and the offences under the Criminal Justice Act 1993;
			– define an insider, inside information and dealing;
			– the consequences if found guilty of insider dealing
			– define money laundering and the offences under the Proceeds of Crime Act 2002;
			– the consequences of found guilty of money laundering;
			– explain and distinguish between fraudulent and wrongful trading and the consequences.

Note that not all of the questions in the exam kit are referred to in the programme above.

Section 1

QUESTIONS

ESSENTIAL ELEMENTS OF THE LEGAL SYSTEM

1   POWERS OF THE COURTS
(DECEMBER 2004)

(a)   Explain the powers of the courts in interpreting legislation, paying particular regard
to the rules they use in so doing.   **(7 marks)**

(b)   How has the Human Rights Act 1998 affected this process?   **(3 marks)**

(Total: 10 marks)

2   BINDING PRECEDENT
(JUNE 2004)

Explain the doctrine of binding precedent in English law, paying particular regard to:

- the hierarchy of the courts;   **(5 marks)**
- the relative advantages and disadvantages of the doctrine.   **(5 marks)**

(Total: 10 marks)

3   ENGLISH LEGAL SYSTEM
(DECEMBER 2002)

(a)   Briefly describe the main civil courts in the English legal system.   **(6 marks)**

(b)   Explain the three track system for allocating cases between courts.   **(4 marks)**

(Total: 10 marks)

4   DELEGATED LEGISLATION
(JUNE 2006)

In relation to the English legal system, explain:

(a)   the meaning, scope and effectiveness of delegated legislation;   **(7 marks)**

(b)   the powers of the courts to control such delegated legislation.   **(3 marks)**

(Total: 10 marks)

5   DOCTRINE OF PRECEDENT
(JUNE 2009)

 Timed question with Online tutor debrief

Explain and distinguish between the following terms in relation to the doctrine of precedent in the English legal system:

(a)   ratio decidendi and obiter dictum;   **(4 marks)**

(b)   binding precedent and persuasive precedent.   **(6 marks)**

(Total: 10 marks)

 Calculate your allowed time, allocate the time to the separate parts...............

6   TYPES OF LAW
(DECEMBER 2007)

(a)   In relation to the English legal system distinguish between the following:

    (i)   Criminal law;

    (ii)   Civil law.   **(5 marks)**

(b)   Explain the jurisdiction of the courts dealing with criminal and civil law.   **(5 marks)**

(Total: 10 marks)

7   SOURCES OF LAW
(DECEMBER 2008)

In relation to the English legal system, explain the main sources of contemporary law.

(10 marks)

THE LAW OF OBLIGATIONS

8   TERMINATION OF A CONTRACTUAL OFFER
(JUNE 1999)

Explain the ways in which a contractual offer can come to an end.   **(10 marks)**

9 TERMS AND REPRESENTATION
(JUNE 2009)

 Timed question with Online tutor debrief

In relation to the law of contract, distinguish between and explain the effect of:

(a)   a term and a mere representation;   **(3 marks)**

(b)   express and implied terms, paying particular regard to the circumstances under which terms may be implied in contracts.   **(7 marks)**

(Total: 10 marks)

 Calculate your allowed time, allocate the time to the separate parts...............

10 CONSIDERATION
(JUNE 2009)

 Timed question with Online tutor debrief

(a)   In relation to the law of contract, define and explain consideration.   **(3 marks)**

(b)   Explain the following statements regarding consideration:

   (i)   consideration must be sufficient but does not have to be adequate;   **(3 marks)**

   (ii)   past consideration is not good consideration.   **(4 marks)**

(Total: 10 marks)

 Calculate your allowed time, allocate the time to the separate parts...............

11 INVITATION TO TREAT
(JUNE 2008)

In relation to contract law explain the meaning and effect of:

(a)   an offer;   **(4 marks)**

(b)   an invitation to treat;   **(6 marks)**

(Total: 10 marks)

12 TERMS USED IN THE LAW OF CONTRACT
(JUNE 1998)

Briefly explain the meaning of the following terms in the law of contract:

(a)   an invitation to treat, compared with an offer for sale;   **(4 marks)**

(b)   revocation of an offer;   **(3 marks)**

(c)   the postal rule for acceptance of an offer.   **(3 marks)**

(Total: 10 marks)

13 EXCLUSION CLAUSES
(JUNE 2002)

(a)   Explain the meaning of exclusion clauses, also known as exemption clauses, in contract law.   **(2 marks)**

(b)   How are such clauses controlled:

    (i)   at common law;   **(4 marks)**

    (ii)   by statute?   **(4 marks)**

(Total: 10 marks)

14 CONDITIONS, WARRANTIES AND INNOMINATE TERMS
(DECEMBER 2003)

In relation to the contents of a contract explain the following:

(a)   conditions;   **(4 marks)**

(b)   warranties;   **(3 marks)**

(c)   innominate terms.   **(3 marks)**

(Total: 10 marks)

15 EXPRESS AND IMPLIED TERMS
(DECEMBER 2002)

In relation to the law of contract:

(a)   distinguish between express and implied terms;   **(4 marks)**

(b)   explain the circumstances under which terms may be implied in contracts. **(6 marks)**

(Total: 10 marks)

16 DAMAGES
(JUNE 2004)

In the law of contract, describe the rules relating to:

(a)   remoteness of damage;   **(5 marks)**

(b)   the measure of damages.   **(5 marks)**

(Total: 10 marks)

17 DAMAGES AND MITIGATING LOSSES
(JUNE 2003)

Explain in relation to remedies for breach of contract:

(a)   the difference between liquidated damages and penalty clauses;   **(5 marks)**

(b)   the duty to mitigate losses.   **(5 marks)**

(Total: 10 marks)

18 ANTICIPATORY BREACH
(DECEMBER 2008)

In relation to the law of contract, explain what is meant by breach of contract, paying attention to anticipatory breach.

(10 marks)

19 DOCTRINE OF PRIVITY
(DECEMBER 2007)

In relation to the law of contract explain the meaning and effect of:

(a)   the doctrine of privity;   **(6 marks)**

(b)   the intention to create legal relations.   **(4 marks)**

(Total: 10 marks)

20 REMOTENESS OF DAMAGE
(DECEMBER 2007)

In relation to the law of tort explain the concept of 'remoteness of damage'.   **(10 marks)**

21 STANDARD OF CARE
(JUNE 2008)

In relation to the tort of negligence explain the standard of care owed by one person to another.   **(10 marks)**

22 NEGLIGENCE
(DECEMBER 2008)

In relation to defences in the tort of negligence, explain the meaning of:

(a)   contributory negligence;   **(5 marks)**

(b)   *volenti non fit injuria* (consent).   **(5 marks)**

(Total: 10 marks)

23 BALL LTD
(ADAPTED FROM DECEMBER 2002)

In January 20X2, Alex, a business consultant, won a lucrative contract with Ball Ltd to provide them with a highly specialised computer system. The terms of the contract required the system to be fully operational by 30 May subject to a penalty of £1,000 for every day's delay. Alex entered into a subcontract with Chris to provide the software for the new system. Chris was to carry out his task out by 23 May and was to receive £5,000 for his work.

At the end of March, Chris told Alex that he would not complete the software in time unless Alex agreed to increase his payment by a further £1,000. Alex agreed to pay the increased sum in order to ensure that the job was done on time.

In the event, Chris completed his task by 16 May and the system was successfully installed before Alex's contractual deadline with Ball Ltd. However, Alex has now refused to make any additional payment beyond the original contractual price.

Required:

Advise Chris whether he has any rights in law to enforce Alex's promise to pay him an extra £1,000. **(10 marks)**

24 ALAN AND CATH
(ADAPTED FROM DECEMBER 2004)

Two years ago Alan separated from his wife Cath. As part of a written agreement between them, Alan agreed to pay Cath £1,000 per month in order to maintain her and their daughter Dawn. The money also had to be used to pay off the mortgage on the house that Alan and Cath jointly owned. Alan promised that when the mortgage was paid off he would transfer his share of the property to Cath. Now, however, although the mortgage has been paid off, Alan refuses to transfer his title in the house to Cath.

Required:

Analyse the above situation from the point of view of contract law and advise Alan whether Cath can require him to transfer his part of the house to her. **(10 marks)**

25 ARTI
(JUNE 2009)

 Timed question with Online tutor debrief

In January 2008 Arti entered in a contractual agreement with Bee Ltd to write a study manual for an international accountancy body's award. The manual was to cover the period from September 2008 till June 2009, and it was a term of the contract that the text be supplied by 31 June 2008 so that it could be printed in time for September. By 30 May, Arti had not yet started on the text and indeed he had written to Bee Ltd stating that he was too busy to write the text.

Bee Ltd was extremely perturbed by the news, especially as it had acquired the contract to supply all of the accountancy body's study manuals and had already incurred extensive preliminary expenses in relation to the publication of the new manual.

Required:

In the context of the law of contract, advise Bee Ltd whether they can take any action against Arti.

(10 marks)

 Calculate your allowed time..

26 ADAM
(ADAPTED FROM JUNE 2003)

Adam, who operates an accountancy practice, charges £1,000 per year for producing business accounts for tax purposes. Unfortunately he has had some difficulty in recovering his fees from a couple of clients as follows:

(1) Dawn, a not very successful musician, told Adam that she could only pay half of the money she owed him as she needed to use the other half to finance her new record. Adam agreed to accept the half-payment. Dawn's record subsequently became a major hit and she made £100,000 profit from it.

(2) Eric, a self-employed decorator, without any contact with Adam simply sent a cheque for half of his fees stating that he could not pay any more and that the cheque was in full settlement of his outstanding debt.

Adam himself is now in financial difficulty and needs cash to pay his own tax bill.

Required:

Advise Adam whether he can recover any of the outstanding money from the above clients.

(10 marks)

 Online question assistance

27 THE CROMWELL ARMS

Oliver was selling his inn, the Cromwell Arms, and Charles was considering buying it. Charles wrote to Oliver's accountant, Richard, and requested information about the annual turnover of the inn. The accountant wrote to Charles informing him that the inn's annual sales were 'in the region of £200,000', adding that the information was given without any responsibility on his part.

Charles purchased the inn and subsequently found that although several years previously turnover had once approached £200,000, generally it was about £150,000 a year.

Advise Charles in the tort of negligence   **(10 marks)**

28 BILD LTD
(JUNE 2008)

Astride entered into a contract with Bild Ltd to construct a wall around the garden of a house she had just purchased. The wall was to be three metres high to block out a view of a rubbish tip. The wall was due to be finished in May and Astride entered into another contract with Chris to landscape the garden starting on 1 June.

Bild Ltd finished the wall on 25 May. However when Astride came to examine it for the first time she found that it was only 2·50 metres high and that the rubbish tip was still visible from the top of her garden.

On 1 June, Chris informed Astride that he was too busy to landscape her garden and that she would have to get someone else to do it. The only person available, however, will charge Astride £500 more than Chris had agreed for doing the work.

Required:

Analyse the scenario from the perspective of the law of contract, advising Astride:

(a)   Whether she can require Bild Ltd to reconstruct the garden wall in order to make it the agreed height, and if not, what alternative action is available to her.   **(5 marks)**

(b)   Whether she can require Chris to undertake the work on the garden, and if not, what alternative action is available to her.   **(5 marks)**

(Total: 10 marks)

29   ALI
(DECEMBER 2007)

Ali is an antique dealer and one Saturday in November 2007 he put a vase in the window of his shop with a sign which stated 'exceptional piece of 19th century pottery – on offer for £500'.

Ben happened to notice the vase as he walked past the shop and thought he would like to have it. Unfortunately, as he was late for an important meeting, he could not go into the shop to buy it, but as soon as his meeting was finished he wrote to Ali agreeing to buy the vase for the stated price of £500. The letter was posted at 11:30 am.

Later on the same day, Chet visited Ali's shop and said he would like the vase but was only willing to pay £400 for it. Ali replied that he would accept £450 for the vase, but Chet insisted that he was only willing to pay £400 and left the shop. However, on his journey home Chet realised that £450 was actually a very good price for the vase and he immediately wrote to Ali agreeing to buy it for that price. His letter was posted at 12:30 pm.

Just before closing time at 5 pm. Di came into Ali's shop and she also offered £400 for the vase. This time Ali agreed to sell the vase at that price and Di promised to return the following Monday with the money.

On the Monday morning Ali received both of the letters from Ben and Chet before Di could arrive to pay and collect the vase.

Required:

From the point of view of the law of contract advise Ali as to his legal relations with Ben, Chet and Di.

(10 marks)

30   ALVIN
(DECEMBER 2008)

Alvin runs a business selling expensive cars. Last Monday he mistakenly placed a notice on one car indicating that it was for sale for £5,000 when in fact its real price was £25,000. Bert later noticed the sign and, recognising what a bargain it was, immediately indicated to Alvin that he accepted the offer and would take the car for the indicated amount. Alvin, however, told Bert that there had been a mistake and that the true price of the car was £25,000. Bert insisted that he was entitled to get the car at the lower price, and when Alvin would not give it to him at that price Bert said that he would sue Alvin.

After Bert had left, Alvin changed the price on the car to £25,000 and subsequently Cat came in and said she would like to buy the car, but that she would have to arrange finance.

On Tuesday Del came by and offered Alvin the full £25,000 cash there and then and Alvin sold it to him.

Required:

Advise Alvin, Bert, Cat and Del as to their rights and liabilities in the law of contract.

(10 marks)

31 SELLER LTD

Seller Ltd had used the services of Transport Ltd for a number of years. On this occasion, the managing director of Seller Ltd telephoned the offices of Transport Ltd and arranged for the transportation of some expensive machinery to a customer. Transport Ltd confirmed the order by sending a notice to this effect. Unfortunately, due to driver error, the vehicle carrying Seller Ltd's equipment crashed and the equipment was badly damaged. Transport Ltd has advised Seller Ltd that it intends to rely on the following clause:

Transport Ltd will not accept any liability for loss or damage caused to customer's property during transportation no matter how the loss or damage was caused. Customers are advised to take their own insurance'.

Transport Ltd has pointed out that the clause appears in a notice prominently displayed outside the entrance to the company's offices, and is reproduced on the back of all invoices, receipts and confirmation of order notices issued by the company.

Required:

Advise Seller Ltd whether Transport Ltd will be able to use the clause to avoid liability for damaged goods.

(10 marks)

EMPLOYMENT LAW

32 EMPLOYMENT CONTRACTS
(JUNE 2008)

In relation to employment law:

(a) Explain why it is important to distinguish between contracts of service and contracts for services. **(4 marks)**

(b) State how the courts decide whether someone is an employee or is self-employed.
(6 marks)

(Total: 10 marks)

33 DISMISSAL
(DECEMBER 2007)

In relation to employment law explain:

(a) the meaning of 'constructive dismissal'; **(5 marks)**

(b) the remedies available in relation to a successful claim for unfair dismissal. **(5 marks)**

(Total: 10 marks)

34   GROUNDS FOR DISMISSAL
(JUNE 2003)

In relation to the dismissal of employees, explain:

(a)   the grounds upon which dismissal may be fair   **(5 marks)**

(b)   the grounds upon which dismissal will be automatically unfair.   **(5 marks)**

(Total: 10 marks)

35   REDUNDANCY
(JUNE 2009)

 Timed question with Online tutor debrief

In relation to employment law, explain the meaning of redundancy and the rules that govern it.

(10 marks)

 Calculate your allowed time...

36   REMEDIES
(JUNE 2005)

Explain the remedies available in relation to a successful claim for:

(a)   redundancy;   **(3 marks)**

(b)   unfair dismissal;   **(5 marks)**

(c)   wrongful dismissal.   **(2 marks)**

(Total: 10 marks)

37   FINE LTD
(ADAPTED FROM DECEMBER 2004)

Fine Ltd specialises in providing software to the financial services industry. It has two offices, one in Edinburgh and the other, its main office, in London. In January 20X3 Gus was employed as a software designer attached to the Edinburgh office. However, by May 20X4, Gus was informed that he was to be transferred to the head office in London, which is more than 350 miles from his usual workplace.

Gus refused to accept the transfer on the basis that he had been employed to work in Edinburgh not London. Consequently, on 1 June 20X4 he wrote to Fine Ltd terminating his contract with them.

Required:

Analyse the scenario from the point of view of employment law and in particular advise Gus as to:

(a)   his rights on the termination of his contract of employment with Fine Ltd;   **(5 marks)**

(b)   the likelihood of a successful claim for unfair dismissal.   **(5 marks)**

(Total: 10 marks)

38   UNFAIR DISMISSAL
(DECEMBER 2008)

In relation to employment law, explain:

(a)   the grounds upon which dismissal may be fair;   **(5 marks)**

(b)   the meaning and effect of constructive dismissal.   **(5 marks)**

(Total: 10 marks)

 Online question assistance

THE FORMATION AND CONSTITUTION OF BUSINESS ORGANISATIONS

39   AGENT'S AUTHORITY
(DECEMBER 2001)

Explain the meaning of the following terms with regard to the law of agency:

(a)   express authority;   **(3 marks)**

(b)   implied authority;   **(3 marks)**

(c)   ostensible/apparent authority.   **(4 marks)**

(Total: 10 marks)

40   AGENCY RELATIONSHIP
(DECEMBER 2003)

Explain how an agency relationship can be established in the following ways:

(a)   by agreement;   **(2 marks)**

(b)   by ratification;   **(2 marks)**

(c)   by necessity;   **(3 marks)**

(d)   by estoppel.   **(3 marks)**

(Total: 10 marks)

41   TERMINATION OF PARTNERSHIP
(DECEMBER 2002)

Detail the grounds upon which a partnership can be terminated.   **(10 marks)**

42 PARTNERSHIPS AND LIABILITY
(DECEMBER 2003)

Explain the liability of the members of partnerships formed under the following Acts:

(a)   Partnership Act 1890;   **(3 marks)**

(b)   Limited Partnerships Act 1907;   **(3 marks)**

(c)   Limited Liability Partnerships Act 2000.   **(4 marks)**

(Total: 10 marks)

43 DOCTRINE OF SEPARATE PERSONALITY
(JUNE 2008)

In the context of company law explain:

(a)   the doctrine of separate personality and its consequences   **(6 marks)**

(b)   the circumstances under which separate personality will be ignored   **(4 marks)**

(Total: 10 marks)

44 TYPES OF COMPANY
(JUNE 2002)

Distinguish between:

*   Unlimited companies;   **(3 marks)**
*   Companies limited by guarantee;   **(3 marks)**
*   Companies limited by shares.   **(4 marks)**

(Total: 10 marks)

45 INCORPORATION AS A PRIVATE COMPANY
(JUNE 1995)

Explain briefly the likely advantages and disadvantages of incorporating a business as a private company.   **(10 marks)**

46 PLC DOCUMENTS
(DECEMBER 1999)

What documents and procedures are involved in a public limited company being registered and starting to trade?   **(10 marks)**

47 PROMOTER AND PRE-INCORPORATION CONTRACT
(DECEMBER 2002)

Explain in relation to the formation of a company what is meant by the terms:

(a)   promoter;   **(5 marks)**

(b)   pre-incorporation contract.   **(5 marks)**

(Total: 10 marks)

48 CLARE, DAN AND EVE
(JUNE 2008)

Clare, Dan and Eve formed a partnership 10 years ago, although Clare was a sleeping partner and never had anything to do with running the business. Last year Dan retired from the partnership. Eve has subsequently entered into two large contracts. The first one was with a longstanding customer Greg, who had dealt with the partnership for some five years. The second contract was with a new customer Hugh. Both believed that Dan was still a partner in the business. Both contracts have gone badly wrong leaving the partnership owing £50,000 to both Greg and Hugh. Unfortunately the business assets will only cover the first £50,000 of the debt.

Required:

Explain the potential liabilities of Clare, Dan, and Eve for the partnership debts. **(10 marks)**

49 HAM, SAM AND TAM
(DECEMBER 2008)

Ham, Sam and Tam formed a partnership to run a petrol station. The partnership agreement expressly stated that the partnership business was to be limited exclusively to the sale of petrol.

In January 2008 Sam received £10,000 from the partnership's bank drawn on its overdraft facility. He told the bank that the money was to finance a short-term partnership debt but in fact he used the money to pay for a round the world cruise. In February Tam entered into a £15,000 contract on behalf of the partnership to buy some used cars, which he hoped to sell from the garage forecourt. In March the partnership's bank refused to honour its cheque for the payment of its monthly petrol account, on the basis that there were no funds in its account and it had reached its overdraft facility.

Required:

Advise Ham, Sam and Tam as to their various rights and liabilities in relation to partnership law.

(10 marks)

50 COMPANY NAMES
(JUNE 2009)

In relation to company law, explain:

(a)   the limitations on the use of company names;   **(4 marks)**

(b)   the tort of 'passing off';   **(4 marks)**

(c)   the role of the company names adjudicators under the Companies Act 2006. **(2 marks)**

(10 marks)

51 ELEANOR
(ADAPTED FROM DECEMBER 1996)

Eleanor is thinking of forming a private limited company to develop and market a new papermaking process she has invented.

Eleanor consults you for advice on a couple of matters about which she is unsure and asks you the following questions:

(a)   What are the statutory registers which a company is required to keep?   **(5 marks)**

(b)   What is meant by the company's 'Registered Office'? How may its address be changed?   **(5 marks)**

Required:

Advise Eleanor.   **(Total: 10 marks)**

52 DON
(ADAPTED FROM JUNE 2005)

Don was instrumental in forming Eden plc, which was registered and received its trading certificate in December 2006. It has subsequently come to the attention of the board of directors that the following events had taken place prior to the incorporation of the company:

(i)   Don had sold the premises in which Eden plc was to conduct its business to the company without declaring his interest in the contract;

(ii)   Don entered into a contract in the company's name to buy computer equipment, which the board of directors do not wish to honour.

Required:

Analyse the situation from the perspective of the law relating to company promoters and in particular advise the parties involved in the transactions detailed.

(10 marks)

53 FORM OF BUSINESS

Andy, Nicola, Ian and Claire have just won £25,000 each on the lottery. They are highly skilled workers in the IT industry and believe that they could carry on their own business successfully.

Required:

Consider the advantages and disadvantages of the registered company as against the partnership as a form of business organisation and advise them as to which form best suits their situation.

(10 marks)

CAPITAL AND THE FINANCING OF COMPANIES

54 TYPES OF SHARES
(JUNE 2008)

In relation to company law explain the meaning of the following:

(a)	ordinary shares	**(3 marks)**
(b)	preference shares	**(3 marks)**
(c)	debentures	**(4 marks)**
		(Total: 10 marks)

55 SHARE ISSUES
(DECEMBER 2008)

In relation to a company's shares, explain the following:

(a)	the statement of capital and initial shareholdings;	**(4 marks)**
(b)	authorised minimum issued capital in a public company;	**(2 marks)**
(c)	paid-up capital;	**(2 marks)**
(d)	the difference between nominal value and market value.	**(2 marks)**
		(Total: 10 marks)

56 DEBENTURES, FIXED AND FLOATING CHARGES
(JUNE 2001)

In relation to companies' loan capital explain the following terms:

(a)	debenture;	**(3 marks)**
(b)	fixed charge;	**(3 marks)**
(c)	floating charge.	**(4 marks)**
		(Total: 10 marks)

57 CRUMS LTD
(ADAPTED FROM DECEMBER 2006)

At the start of 2006 Crums Ltd was faced with the need to raise a large amount of capital, which it was decided to raise through the mechanism of issuing a number of secured loans. In order to raise the capital Crums Ltd entered into the following transactions:

(i) it borrowed £50,000 from Don secured by a floating charge. The loan was given and the charge created on 1 February. The charge was registered on 15 February;

(ii) it borrowed £50,000 from Else, also secured by a floating charge. This charge was created on the morning of 1 April and it was registered on 15 April;

(iii) it borrowed £100,000 from Flash Bank plc. This loan was secured by a fixed charge. It was created in the afternoon of 1 April and was registered on 20 April;

(iv) it borrowed a further £50,000 from Gus. This loan was secured by a floating charge created on 3 April and registered on 12 April;

(v)   it borrowed £100,000 from High Bank plc. This loan was secured by a fixed charge. It was created on 5 April and was registered on 15 April.

Unfortunately the money borrowed was not sufficient to sustain Crums Ltd and in January 2007 proceedings were instituted to wind it up compulsorily. It is extremely unlikely that there will be sufficient assets to pay the debts owed to all of the secured creditors.

Required:

Place the above debts in order of security and payment and explain why they are placed in that order.   **(10 marks)**

58   DIVIDENDS
(JUNE 2005)

In relation to the rules governing the payment of company dividends explain:

(a)   how dividends may be properly funded;   **(4 marks)**

(b)   the rules which apply to public limited companies;   **(3 marks)**

(c)   the consequences of any dividend being paid in breach of those rules.   **(3 marks)**

(Total: 10 marks)

59   CAPITAL
(JUNE 2009)

 Timed question with Online tutor debrief

In relation to company law, explain:

(a)   the doctrine of capital maintenance;   **(4 marks)**

(b)   the circumstances under which both a private and a public company can reduce its capital and the procedure to be followed.   **(6 marks)**

(10 marks)

 Calculate your allowed time, allocate the time to the separate parts...............

60   CLASS RIGHTS
(DECEMBER 2002)

In company law:

(a)   explain the meaning of class rights in relation to company shares providing examples of such rights;   **(6 marks)**

(b)   state how such rights can be altered.   **(4 marks)**

(Total: 10 marks)

61   JUDDER LTD
(ADAPTED FROM DECEMBER 2002)

Hank is a director in Judder Ltd, which has an authorised and issued capital of 100,000 shares at a nominal value of £1. It has not traded profitably and has consistently lost capital for a number of years. Although the company has shown a profit on its current year's trading, its accounts still show a deficit of £50,000 between assets and liabilities. The board of directors thinks it would be beneficial if the company were to write off its previous losses and to that end are looking to reduce its share capital by £50,000.

Required:

Advise Hank as to the procedure involved in reducing Judder Ltd's share capital.

(10 marks)

62   FIN
(ADAPTED FROM JUNE 2004)

Two years ago Fin inherited £40,000 and decided to invest the money in company shares. Fin subscribed for 20,000 partly paid up shares in Gulp Ltd. He was only required to pay 50 pence per £1 share when he took the shares and has made no further payment on them to the company. Unfortunately, Gulp Ltd has gone into insolvent liquidation owing a substantial sum of money to its creditors.

At the same time, he heard that Heave Ltd was badly in need of additional capital and that the directors had decided that the only way to raise the needed money was to offer fully paid up £1 shares to new members at a discount price of 50 pence per share. Fin thought the offer was too good to miss and he subscribed for 20,000 new shares. However, the additional capital raised in this way did not save the company and Heave Ltd has also gone into insolvent liquidation, owing a considerable sum of money to its unsecured creditors.

Apart from the above shares, Fin has absolutely no other wealth.

Required:

Analyse the above scenario from the perspective of company law and in particular advise Fin as to the following matters:

(a)   his potential liability in relation to the debts of Gulp Ltd;   **(5 marks)**

(b)   his potential liability for the debts of Heave Ltd.   **(5 marks)**

(Total: 10 marks)

MANAGEMENT, ADMINISTRATION AND REGULATION OF COMPANIES

63   DIRECTORS DUTIES
(DECEMBER 2008)

In relation to the Companies Act, 2006, explain the duty of directors to promote the success of the company, and to whom such a duty is owed.   **(10 marks)**

64 TYPES OF DIRECTORS
(JUNE 2008)

In relation to company law explain the meaning of the following:

(a) executive directors;   **(3 marks)**

(b) non-executive directors;   **(3 marks)**

(c) shadow directors.   **(4 marks)**

                                                                                (Total: 10 marks)

65 COMPANY SECRETARIES
(JUNE 2005)

Explain the rules relating to the appointment, duties and powers of a company secretary in a public limited company.   **(10 marks)**

66 APPOINTING AND REMOVING DIRECTORS
(DECEMBER 2003)

In company law explain:

(a) how a director of a company may be appointed;   **(3 marks)**

(b) how a director may be removed from his position.   **(7 marks)**

                                                                                (Total: 10 marks)

67 DISQUALIFICATION
(JUNE 2009)

 Timed question with Online tutor debrief

Explain the grounds upon which a person may be disqualified under the Company Directors Disqualification Act 1986.

                                                                                (10 marks)

 Calculate your allowed time...

68 ROLE OF COMPANY AUDITORS
(JUNE 2003)

Explain the role of company auditors paying particular regard to their appointment, removal, rights and duties.   **(10 marks)**

69 AUTHORITY OF DIRECTORS
(DECEMBER 2005)

In relation to company directors explain how the following types of authority may arise and explain the extent of the authority arising under each category:

(a)	express authority;	**(3 marks)**
(b)	implied authority;	**(3 marks)**
(c)	apparent/ostensible authority.	**(4 marks)**

(Total: 10 marks)

70 FRAN, GILL AND HARRY
(ADAPTED FROM 2001 PILOT PAPER)

In 20X5 Fran, Gill and Harry formed a private limited company to pursue the business of computer software design. They each took 100 shares in the company and each of them became a director in the new company. The articles of association of the company were drawn up to state that Fran, a qualified lawyer, was to act as the company's solicitor for a period of five years, at a salary of £2,000 per year.

In 20X8 Gill and Harry found out that Fran had been working with a rival software company and has passed on some secret research results to that rival.

Required:

Advise Gill and Harry as to the legality of the following proposals and how they may be achieved:

(a)	they wish to remove Fran from the board of directors;	**(5 marks)**
(b)	they have told Fran that they no longer wish her to be the company solicitor and have refused to pay her for the work she has done previously. Fran, however, claims that she has a contract in the articles of association and that they cannot remove her before the five-year period is completed.	**(5 marks)**

(Total: 10 marks)

71 GLAD LTD
(DECEMBER 2008)

Fred is a member of Glad Ltd, a small publishing company, holding 100 of its 500 shares; the other 400 shares are held by four other members.

It has recently become apparent that Fred has set up a rival business to Glad Ltd and the other members have decided that he should be expelled from the company.

To that end they propose to alter the articles of association to include a new power to 'require any member to transfer their shares for fair value to the other members upon the passing of a resolution so to do'.

Required:

Advise the parties concerned whether or not the proposed change to the articles is legally enforceable and whether or not it can be used to force Fred to sell his shares.

(10 marks)

72 KING LTD
(ADAPTED FROM DECEMBER 2002)

King Ltd is a property development company. Although there are five members of its board of directors, the actual day-to-day running of the business is left to one of them, Lex, who simply reports back to the board on the business he has transacted. Lex refers to himself as the Managing Director of King Ltd, although he has never been officially appointed as such.

Six months ago, Lex entered into a contract on King Ltd's behalf with Nat to produce plans for the redevelopment of a particular site that it hoped to acquire. However, King Ltd did not acquire the site and due to its current precarious financial position, the board of directors have refused to pay Nat, claiming that Lex did not have the necessary authority to enter into the contract with him.

Required:

Analyse the situation with regard to the authority of Lex to make contracts on behalf of King Ltd and, in particular, advise the board of directors whether the company is liable for the contract.

(10 marks)

 Online question assistance

73 CLEAN LTD
(JUNE 2009)

 Timed question with Online tutor debrief

Clean Ltd was established some five years ago to manufacture industrial solvents and cleaning solutions, and Des was appointed managing director.

The company's main contract was with Dank plc a large industrial conglomerate.

In the course of its research activity, Clean Ltd's scientists developed a new super glue. Des was very keen to pursue the manufacture of the glue but the board of directors overruled him and decided that the company should stick to its core business.

The managing director of Dank plc is a friend of Des's and has told him that Dank plc will not be renewing its contract with Clean Ltd as he is not happy with its performance. He also told Des that he would be happy to continue to deal with him, if only he was not linked to Clean Ltd.

Following that discussion Des resigned from his position as managing director of Clean Ltd and set up his own company, Flush Ltd which later entered into a contract with Dank plc to replace Clean Ltd. Flush Ltd also manufactures the new glue discovered by Clean Ltd's scientists, which has proved to be very profitable.

Required:

In the context of company law, advise the board of Clean Ltd as to whether they can take any action against Des or Flush Ltd.

(10 marks)

 Calculate your allowed time..

74   CALLING AND VOTING
(DECEMBER 2001)

Explain the following within the context of company general meetings:

(a)   who has the power to call meetings; and   **(6 marks)**

(b)   how are votes taken?   **(4 marks)**

                                                                          (Total: 10 marks)

75   RESOLUTIONS
(DECEMBER 2008)

In relation to private companies, explain the meaning of, and the procedure for passing, the following:

(a)   an ordinary and a special resolution;   **(5 marks)**

(b)   a written resolution.   **(5 marks)**

                                                                          (Total: 10 marks)

76   TYPES OF MEETING
(ADAPTED FROM DECEMBER 2005)

In relation to company law explain and distinguish between the following:

(a)   annual general meeting;   **(5 marks)**

(b)   general meeting   **(3 marks)**

(c)   class meeting   **(2 marks)**

                                                                          (Total: 10 marks)

LEGAL IMPLICATIONS RELATING TO COMPANIES IN DIFFICULTY OR IN CRISIS

77   WINDING UP
(JUNE 2004)

In relation to company law explain:

(a)   the meaning of winding up;   **(3 marks)**

(b)   the procedures involved in:

   (i)   a members' voluntary winding up;   **(3 marks)**

   (ii)   a creditors' voluntary winding up.   **(4 marks)**

                                                                          (Total: 10 marks)

78   GROUNDS FOR WINDING UP
(DECEMBER 2004)

State and explain the grounds under which a company may be wound up under section 122 of the Insolvency Act 1986.   **(10 marks)**

79   ADMINISTRATION

What is 'administration'? In what circumstances may administration occur?   **(10 marks)**

GOVERNANCE AND ETHICAL ISSUES RELATING TO BUSINESS

80   TELA & CO
(ADAPTED FROM ACCA 2.6 JUNE 2006)

You are the audit manager of Tela & Co, a medium-sized firm of accountants. Your firm has just been asked for assistance from Jumper & Co, a firm of accountants in an adjacent town. Jumper & Co has a number of clients where the Combined Code on Corporate Governance is not being followed. One example of this, from SGCC plc, is shown below. As your firm has experience of dealing with corporate governance issues, Jumper & Co have asked for your advice regarding the changes necessary in SGCC plc to achieve appropriate compliance with corporate governance codes.

Extract from financial statements regarding corporate governance:

'Mr Sheppard is the Chief Executive Officer and board chairman of SGCC plc. He appoints and maintains a board of five executive and two non-executive directors. While the board sets performance targets for the senior managers in the company, no formal targets or review of board policies is carried out. Board salaries are therefore set and paid by Mr Sheppard based on his assessment of all the board members, including himself, and not their actual performance.

Internal controls in the company are monitored by the senior accountant, although detailed review is assumed to be carried out by the external auditors; SGCC plc does not have an internal audit department.

Annual financial statements are produced, providing detailed information on past performance.'

Required:

Explain why SGCC plc does not meet the Combined Code (of the Committee on Corporate Governance).

(10 marks)

81   STANDARDS

Discuss whether the Higgs Review (now appended to the Combined Code) will in the long run result in higher corporate governance standards.

(10 marks)

82   COMBINED CODE

Describe and analyse the content and structure of the Combined Code on Corporate Governance.

(10 marks)

83 FRAUDULENT TRADING
(JUNE 2005 GLOBAL)

Fraudulent trading is covered by both criminal and civil law.

Required:

Explain the difference between the two types of law and detail how each deals with fraudulent trading.

(10 marks)

84 WRONGFUL TRADING
(JUNE 2001)

Explain the meaning and effect of 'wrongful trading' under s.214 of the Insolvency Act 1986.

(10 marks)

85 HUGE PLC
(JUNE 2009)

 Timed question with Online tutor debrief

Greg is a member of the board of directors of Huge plc. He also controls a private limited company Imp Ltd through which he operates a management consultancy business. He also owns all the shares in Jet Ltd through which he conducts an investment business.

When Greg learns that Huge plc is going to make a take-over bid for Kop plc he arranges for Jet Ltd to buy a large number of shares in Kop plc on the London Stock Exchange on which it makes a large profit when it sells them after the takeover bid is announced. He then arranges for Jet Ltd to transfer the profit to Imp Ltd as the charge for supposed consultancy work. The money is then transferred to Greg through the declaration of dividends by Imp Ltd.

Required:

Analyse the above conduct from the perspective of criminal law paying particular attention to the issues of:

(a)   insider dealing; and   **(5 marks)**

(b)   money laundering.   **(5 marks)**

(10 marks)

 Calculate your allowed time, allocate the time to the separate parts...............

86 MONEY LAUNDERING
(DECEMBER 2005)

(a)   Explain the term 'money laundering' and how such activity is conducted;   **(5 marks)**

(b)   Explain how the Proceeds of Crime Act 2002 seeks to control money laundering.

(5 marks)

(Total: 10 marks)

87 KEN
(ADAPTED FROM DECEMBER 2006)

Ken is involved in illegal activity, from which he makes a considerable amount of money. In order to conceal his gain from the illegal activity, he bought a bookshop intending to pass off his illegally gained money as profits from the legitimate bookshop business. Ken employs Los to act as the manager of the bookshop and Mel as his accountant to produce false business accounts for the bookshop business.

Required:

Analyse the above scenario from the perspective of the law relating to money laundering. In particular, explain which criminal offences may have been committed by the various parties.

(10 marks)

88 SID AND VIC
(JUNE 2008)

Sid is a director of two listed public companies in which he has substantial shareholdings: Trend Plc and Umber Plc.

The annual reports of Trend Plc and Umber Plc have just been drawn up although not yet disclosed. They show that Trend Plc has made a surprisingly big loss and that Umber Plc has made an equally surprising big loss and that Umber Plc has made an equally surprising big profit. On the basis of this information Sid sold his shares in Trend Plc and bought shares in Umber Plc. He also advised his brother to buy shares in Umber Plc.

Vic who is also a shareholder in both companies sold a significant number of shares in Umber Plc only the day before its annual report is published.

Required:

(a)   Analyse the above scenario from the perspective of the law relating to insider dealing;

(8 marks)

(b)   In particular advise Vic as to his position.   **(2 marks)**

(Total: 10 marks)

Section 2

ANSWERS

ESSENTIAL ELEMENTS OF THE LEGAL SYSTEM

1   POWERS OF THE COURTS *Walk in the footsteps of a top tutor*

Key answer tips

This question requires candidates to consider the powers of judges to interpret legislation. Part (a) requires a general understanding of the manner in which judges approach legislative provisions together with some consideration of the three basic rules of interpretation. Part (b) requires a consideration of the effect of the Human Rights Act 1998 on this process. The highlighted words are key phrases that markers are looking for.

(a)   In order to apply any piece of legislation, judges have to determine its meaning. In other words they are required to interpret the statute before them in order to give it meaning. The difficulty, however, is that the words in statutes do not speak for themselves and interpretation is an active process, and at least potentially a subjective one depending on the situation of the person who is doing the interpreting. Judges, therefore, have considerable power in deciding the actual meaning of statutes, especially when they are able to deploy a number of competing, not to say contradictory, mechanisms for deciding the meaning of the statute before them.

There are three primary rules of interpretation:

The literal rule

Under this rule, the judge is required to consider what the legislation actually says rather than considering what it might mean. In order to achieve this end, the judge should give words in legislation their literal meaning, that is, their plain, ordinary, everyday meaning, even if the effect of this is to produce what might be considered an otherwise unjust or undesirable outcome (*Fisher v Bell* (1961)) in which the court chose to follow the contract law literal interpretation of the meaning of offer in the Act in question and declined to consider the usual non-legal literal interpretation of the word 'offer').

The golden rule

This rule is applied in circumstances where the application of the literal rule is likely to result in what appears to the court to be an obviously absurd result. It should be emphasised, however, that the court is not at liberty to ignore, or replace, legislative provisions simply on the basis that it considers them absurd; it must find genuine difficulties before it declines to use the literal rule in favour of the golden one. As examples, there may be two apparently contradictory meanings to a particular word used in the statute, or the provision may simply be ambiguous in its effect. In such situations, the golden rule operates to ensure that preference is given to the meaning that does not result in the provision being an absurdity. Thus in *Adler v George* (1964), the defendant was found guilty, under the Official Secrets Act 1920, with obstruction 'in the vicinity' of a prohibited area, although she had actually carried out the obstruction 'inside' the area.

The mischief rule

Where there is ambiguity in the legislation this rule permits the court to go behind the actual wording of a statute in order to consider the problem that the statute is supposed to remedy.

In its traditional expression it is limited by being restricted to using previous common law rules in order to decide the operation of contemporary legislation. Thus in Heydon's case (1584) it was stated that in making use of the mischief rule the court should consider the following four things:

(i)   what was the common law before the passing of the statute;

(ii)   what was the mischief in the law which the common law did not adequately deal with;

(iii)   what remedy for that mischief had Parliament intended to provide; and

(iv)   what was the reason for Parliament adopting that remedy?

Use of the mischief rule may be seen in *Corkery v Carpenter* (1950), in which a man was found guilty of being drunk in charge of a carriage although he was in fact only in charge of a bicycle.

It is sometimes suggested that the foregoing rules form a hierarchical order from the literal, through the golden to the mischief rule. On reflection, however, it is evident that the particular judge interpreting the statute has the power to deploy whichever rules he thinks fit to use, or alternatively whichever rule suits his own viewpoint of how the law should be interpreted and allows him to impose that view.

(b)   The Human Rights Act 1998, which incorporated the European Convention on Human Rights into United Kingdom law, has had profound implications for the operation of the English legal system.

Section 2 of the Act requires courts to take into account any previous decision of the European Court of Human Rights (ECtHR). This provision impacts on the operation of the doctrine of precedent within the English legal system, as it effectively sanctions the overruling of any previous English authority that was in conflict with a decision of the ECtHR. More importantly for this question, however, s.3, requires all legislation to be read so far as possible to give effect to the rights provided under the Convention. This power has the potential to invalidate previously accepted interpretations of statutes, which were made, by necessity, without recourse to the Convention (*R v A* (2001) is a case in point; see also *Mendoza v Ghaidan* (2003)).

Under the doctrine of parliamentary sovereignty, the legislature could pass such laws at it saw fit, even to the extent of removing the rights of its citizens. The new Act reflects a move towards the entrenchment of rights recognised under the Convention, but given the sensitivity of the relationship between Parliament and the judiciary, it has been thought expedient to minimise the change in the constitutional relationship of Parliament and the judiciary. To that effect, the Act expressly states that the courts cannot invalidate any primary legislation, essentially Acts of Parliament, which are found to be incompatible with the Convention. The higher courts can only make a declaration of such incompatibility, and leave it to the legislature to remedy the situation through new legislation (s.4). The Act, however, does provide for the provision of remedial legislation through a fast track procedure, which gives a Minister of the Crown the power to alter such primary legislation by way of statutory instrument. The courts have used this power to declare legislation incompatible in several cases to date, such as *R v Mental Health Review Tribunal, North & East London Region* (2001), *Wilson v First County Trust* (2000), *Bellinger v Bellinger* (2003).

2   BINDING PRECEDENT

Key answer tips

This question requires candidates to discuss the application of the doctrine of precedent within the English legal system.   You should also explain the main mechanisms through which judges can alter or avoid precedents, these being overruling and distinguishing.

The doctrine of binding precedent, or *stare decisis,* lies at the heart of the English legal system. The doctrine refers to the fact that, within the hierarchical structure of the English courts, a decision of a higher court will be binding on a court lower than it in that hierarchy. When judges try cases they will check to see if a similar situation has come before a court previously. If the precedent was set by a court of equal or higher status to the court deciding the new case then the judge in the present case should normally follow the rule of law established in the earlier case.

The Hierarchy of the Courts

The House of Lords stands at the summit of the English court structure and its decisions are binding on all courts below it in the hierarchy. As regards its own previous decisions, up until 1966 the House of Lords regarded itself as bound by its previous decisions. In a Practice Statement of that year, however, Lord Gardiner indicated that the House of Lords would in future regard itself as free to depart from its previous decisions where it appeared right to do so. There have been a number of cases in which the House of Lords has overruled or amended its own earlier decisions (e.g. *Conway v Rimmer* (1968); *Herrington v British Rail Board* (1972); *Miliangos v George Frank (Textiles) Ltd* (1976); *R v Shivpuri* (1986)) but this is not a discretion that the House of Lords exercises lightly. It has to be recognised that in the wider context the House of Lords is no longer the supreme court and its decisions are subject to decisions of the European Court of Justice in terms of European Union law, and, with the implementation of the Human Rights Act 1998, the decisions of the European Court of Justice in matters relating to human rights.

The Court of Appeal. In civil cases the Court of Appeal is generally bound by previous decisions of the House of Lords and its own previous decisions. There are, however, a number of exceptions to this general rule. The exceptions arise where:

(i)   there is a conflict between two previous decisions of the Court of Appeal;

(ii)   a previous decision of the Court of Appeal has been overruled by the House of Lords. The Court of Appeal can ignore a previous decision of its own which is inconsistent with European Union law or with a later decision of the European Court; or

(iii) the previous decision was given *per incuriam,* i.e. in ignorance of some authority that would have led to a different conclusion *(Young v Bristol Aeroplane Co Ltd* (1944)).

Courts in the criminal division, however, are not bound to follow their own previous decisions which they subsequently consider to have been based on either a misunderstanding or a misapplication of the law.

The Divisional Courts of the High Court are bound by the doctrine of stare decisis in the normal way and must follow decisions of the House of Lords and the Court of Appeal. They are also normally bound by their own previous decisions, although in civil cases they may make use of the exceptions open to the Court of Appeal in Young v Bristol Aeroplane Co Ltd, and in criminal appeal cases the Queen's Bench Divisional Court may refuse to follow its own earlier decisions where it feels the earlier decision to have been wrongly made.

The High Court is bound by the decisions of superior courts. Decisions by individual High Court judges are binding on courts inferior in the hierarchy, but such decisions are not binding on other High Court judges although they are of strong persuasive authority and tend to be followed in practice.

Crown Courts cannot create precedent and their decisions can never amount to more than persuasive authority. County courts and Magistrates' courts do not create precedents.

It is important to establish that it is not the actual decision in a case that sets the precedent; that is set by the rule of law on which the decision is founded. This rule, which is an abstraction from the facts of the case, is known as the ratio decidendi of the case.

Any statement of law that is not an essential part of the ratio decidendi is, strictly speaking, superfluous; and any such statement is referred to as obiter dictum, i.e. said by the way. Although obiter dicta statements do not form part of the binding precedent, they are persuasive authority and can be taken into consideration in later cases.

Advantages of Case Law

There are numerous perceived advantages of the doctrine of stare decisis, such as:

(i)   **Efficiency.** This refers to the fact that it saves the time of the judiciary, lawyers and their clients for the reason that cases do not have to be re-argued. In respect of potential litigants, it saves them money in court expenses because they can apply to their solicitor/barrister for guidance as to how their particular case is likely to be decided in the light of previous cases on the same or similar points.

(ii)   **Consistency.** It is important that cases with like facts are decided in a like way, in order that the rationale for a decision may be justified and to maintain confidence in the objectivity of the legal system.

(iii) **Certainty.** Once the legal rule has been established in one case, individuals can act with regard to that rule relatively secure in the knowledge that it will not be changed by some later court.

(iv) **Flexibility.** This refers to the fact that the various mechanisms by means of which the judges can manipulate the common law provide them with an opportunity to develop law in particular areas without waiting for Parliament to enact legislation.

The main mechanisms through which judges alter or avoid precedents are:

(i) overruling, which is the procedure whereby a court higher up in the hierarchy sets aside a legal ruling established in a previous case; and

(ii) distinguishing, which is when a later court regards the facts of the case before it as significantly different from the facts of a cited precedent. Consequently it will not be bound to follow that precedent. Judges use the device of distinguishing where, for some reason, they are unwilling to follow a particular precedent.

Disadvantages of Case Law

(i) **Uncertainty** This refers to the fact that the degree of certainty provided by the doctrine of stare decisis is undermined by the absolute number of cases that have been reported and can be cited as authorities. This uncertainty is increased by the ability of the judiciary to select which authority to follow through use of the mechanism of distinguishing cases on their facts.

(ii) **Fixity** This refers to the possibility that the law in relation to any particular area may become set on the basis of an unjust precedent with the consequence that previous injustices are perpetuated. An example of this is the long delay in the recognition of the possibility of rape within marriage, which has only been recognised relatively recently.

(iii) **Unconstitutionality** This is a fundamental question that refers to the fact that the judiciary may be overstepping their theoretical constitutional role by actually making law rather than restricting themselves to the role of simply applying it.

3 ENGLISH LEGAL SYSTEM

Key answer tips

This question requires candidates to describe the civil court structure in part (a) and the three track system for allocating cases in part (b). The civil court structure is quite extensive and therefore candidates should be brief in their explanation of each court to obtain a reasonable mark.

(a) The civil court structure in ascending order of authority is as follows:

Magistrates' courts

Magistrates' courts have a significant, if limited, civil jurisdiction. They hear family proceedings under the Domestic Proceedings and Magistrates' Courts Act (DPMCA) 1978 and the Children Act (CA) 1989. In such cases the court is termed a 'family proceedings court'. The magistrates' court deals with adoption proceedings, applications for residence and contact orders (CA 1989) and maintenance relating to spouses and children. Under the DPMCA 1978, the court also has the power to make personal protection orders and exclusion orders in cases of matrimonial violence.

More generally, magistrates' courts have powers of recovery in relation to council tax arrears and charges for water, gas and electricity. Importantly, the magistrates' courts have no jurisdiction over claims in contract or tort.

County courts

The network of county courts was introduced in 1846 to provide for local adjudication of relatively small-scale litigation. The county court jurisdiction extends to probate, property cases, tort, contract, bankruptcy and insolvency.

Of particular importance with regard to the County Court is the provision of a small claims procedure operated under its auspices. This procedure essentially allows for an arbitration hearing to be conducted by a District Judge in most cases involving claims of no more than £5,000. This small claims procedure is designed to be quicker, less formal and less expensive than a County Court hearing.

The High Court of Justice

The High Court has three administrative divisions: the Queen's Bench Division, the Court of Chancery and the Family Division.

The Queen's Bench Division

This is the main common law court and is the division with the largest workload. It has some criminal jurisdiction and appellate jurisdiction, but its main jurisdiction is civil concerning contract and tort cases. Within the Queen's Bench are located the specialist Commercial and Admiralty Courts. The former, as its title suggests, deals with commercial disputes whilst the latter has jurisdiction in relation to maritime matters.

The Queen's Bench Divisional Court

This court, as distinct from the Queen's Bench Division, exercises appellate jurisdiction on a point of law by way of case stated from magistrates' courts, tribunals and the Crown Court. It also exercises the power of judicial review of the decisions made by governmental and public authorities, inferior courts and tribunals.

The Chancery Division

The jurisdiction of the Chancery Division includes matters relating to the sale or partition of land and the raising of charges on land, mortgages, trusts, the administration of the estates of the dead, contentious probate business such as the validity and interpretation of wills, copyright law, company law, partnership law and revenue law, and insolvency.

Like the Queen's Bench Division, Chancery contains specialist courts; these are the Patents Court and the Companies Court.

Chancery Divisional Court

Comprising one or two Chancery judges, this appellate court hears appeals from the Commissioners of Inland Revenue on income tax cases, and from county courts on certain matters like bankruptcy.

The Family Division

The Family Division of the High Court deals with all matrimonial matters, both at first instance and on appeal, matters relating to minors, legitimacy, adoption and proceedings under the Domestic Violence and Matrimonial Proceedings Act 1976 and s.30 of the Human Fertilisation and Embryology Act 1990.

The Family Divisional Court

The Family Divisional Court, consisting of two High Court judges, hears appeals from decisions of magistrates' courts and county courts in family matters.

The Employment Appeal Tribunal is presided over by similar panels, hearing appeals from Industrial Tribunals. These courts are not part of the High Court but are termed 'superior courts of record'.

The Court of Appeal (Civil Division)

The Court of Appeal was established by the Judicature Act 1873. The court hears appeals from the three divisions of the High Court, the divisional courts, the county courts, the Employment Appeal Tribunal, the Lands Tribunal and the Transport Tribunal. The most senior judge is the Master of the Rolls. Usually, three judges will sit to hear an appeal although for very important cases five may sit.

The Supreme Court (previously the House of Lords)

The Supreme Court was established under the Constitutional Reform Act 2005 to achieve a complete separation between the United Kingdom's senior judges and the upper house of Parliament, emphasising the independence of the Law Lords. The first case was heard in the Supreme Court in October 2009.

Acting in its judicial capacity, as opposed to its legislative one, the Supreme Court is the final Court of Appeal in civil as well as criminal law. Most appeals reaching the Supreme Court come from the Court of Appeal, but there is also a 'leapfrog' procedure by which an appeal may go to the Lords direct from the High Court if the High Court judge certificates the case as being suitable for the Lords to hear and the Supreme Court gives leave to appeal. For most cases, five Lords will sit to hear the appeal but seven are sometimes convened to hear very important cases.

The European Court of Justice

The function of the European Court of Justice, which sits in Luxembourg, is to 'ensure that in the interpretation and application of this Treaty [the EEC Treaty 1957] the law is observed' (Art 200, formerly, 164). The court is the ultimate authority on European Union law. By virtue of the European Communities Act 1972, European law has been enacted into English law so the decisions of the court have direct authority in the English jurisdiction.

The European Court of Human Rights

The European Court of Human Rights, which sits in Strasbourg, is the final court of appeal in relation to matters concerning the 1950 European Convention on Human Rights which the United Kingdom has now made part of its domestic law through the enactment of the Human Rights Act 1998.

(b)   **Court allocation**

The civil system works on the basis of the court, on receipt of a claim, allocating the case to one of three 'tracks' for a hearing, being; (i) small claims; (ii) fast track; and (iii) multi-track (Civil Procedure Rules (CPR) Part 26).

The small claims track (CPR Part 27)

The small claims track is for cases involving a claim of no more than £5,000, except for personal injury claims and claims relating to housing disrepair where the limit is £1,000.

The procedure is informal with limited costs and limited grounds for appeal (misconduct of the district judge or an error of law made by the court).

Parties can consent to use the small claims track even if the value of their claim exceeds the normal value for that track, but subject to the court's approval.

The fast track (CPR Part 28)

The purpose of the fast track is to provide a streamlined procedure for the handling of moderately-valued cases, i.e. those with a value of more than £5,000 but less than £15,000.

The multi-track (CPR Part 29)

The multi-track is intended to provide a flexible regime for the handling of the higher-value, more complex claims, i.e. those with a value of over £15,000.

The Civil Procedure Rules operate the same process irrespective of whether the case forum is the High Court or the County Court. Broadly, County Courts hear small claims and fast track cases, while the more challenging multi-track cases are heard in the High Court.

4   DELEGATED LEGISLATION

Key answer tips

You should explain the purpose of delegated legislation and give examples of the types of delegated legislation. You should also discuss the advantages and disadvantages of delegated legislation, the main advantage being it saves Parliamentary time.

(a)   Within the United Kingdom, Parliament has the sole power to make law by creating legislation. Parliament, however, can pass on, or delegate, its law- making power to some other body or individual. Delegated legislation is of particular importance in the contemporary legal context. Instead of general and definitive Acts of Parliament, which attempt to lay down detailed provisions, the modern form of legislation tends to be of the enabling type, which simply states the general purpose and aims of the Act. Such Acts merely lay down a broad framework, whilst delegating to ministers of state the power to produce detailed provisions designed to achieve those general aims. Thus, delegated legislation is law made by some person or body to whom Parliament has delegated its general law-making power. The output of delegated legislation in any year greatly exceeds the output of Acts of Parliament and, therefore, at least statistically it could be argued that delegated legislation is actually more significant than primary Acts of Parliament.

There are various types of delegated legislation:

(i)   *Orders in Council* permit the government, through the Privy Council, to make law. The Privy Council is nominally a non party-political body of eminent parliamentarians, but in effect it is simply a means through which the government, in the form of a committee of Ministers, can introduce legislation without the need to go through the full parliamentary process.

(ii) *Statutory Instruments* are the means through which government ministers introduce particular regulations under powers delegated to them by Parliament in enabling legislation.

(iii) *Bye-laws* are the means through which local authorities and other public bodies can make legally binding rules and may be made under such enabling legislation as the Local Government Act (1972).

(iv) *Court Rule Committees* are empowered to make the rules which govern procedure in the particular courts over which they have delegated authority, under such Acts as the Supreme Court Act 1981, the County Courts Act 1984 and the Magistrates' Courts Act 1980.

(v) *Professional regulations* governing particular occupations may be given the force of law under provisions delegating legislative authority to certain professional bodies. An example is the power given to the Law Society, under the Solicitors' Act 1974, to control the conduct of practising solicitors.

The use of delegated legislation has the following advantages:

(i) *Time-saving.* Delegated legislation can be introduced quickly where necessary in particular cases and permits rules to be changed in response to emergencies or unforeseen problems. The use of delegated legislation also saves Parliamentary time generally. It is generally considered better for Parliament to spend its time in a thorough consideration of the principles of enabling legislation, leaving the appropriate minister, or body, to establish the working detail under their authority.

(ii) *Access to particular expertise.* Given the highly specialised and extremely technical nature of many of the regulations that are introduced through delegated legislation, the majority of members of Parliament simply do not have sufficient expertise to consider such provisions effectively. It is necessary therefore, that those authorised to introduce delegated legislation should have access to the external expertise required to make appropriate regulations. In regard to bye-laws, local knowledge should give rise to more appropriate rules than general Acts of Parliament.

(iii) *Flexibility.* The use of delegated legislation permits ministers to respond on an *ad hoc* basis to particular problems as and when they arise.

There are, however, some disadvantages in the prevalence of delegated legislation:

(i) *Accountability.* A key issue involved in the use of delegated legislation concerns the question of accountability. Parliament is presumed to be the source of statute law, but with respect to delegated legislation government ministers, and the civil servants, who work under them to produce the detailed provisions, are the real source of the legislation. As a consequence, it is sometimes suggested that the delegated legislation procedure gives more power than might be thought appropriate to such un-elected individuals.

(ii) *Bulk.* Given the sheer mass of such legislation, both Members of Parliament, and the general public, face difficulty in keeping abreast of delegated legislation.

(b)   The potential shortcomings in the use of delegated legislation considered above are, at least to a degree, mitigated by the fact that the courts have the ability to oversee and challenge such laws as are made in the form of delegated legislation.

Judicial control of delegated legislation.

A validly enacted piece of delegated legislation has the same legal force and effect as the Act of Parliament under which it is enacted; but equally it only has effect to the extent that its enabling Act authorises it. Consequently, it is possible for delegated legislation to be challenged, through the procedure of judicial review, on the basis that the person or body to whom Parliament as delegated its authority has acted in a way that exceeds the limited powers delegated to them or has failed to follow the appropriate procedure set down in the enabling legislation. Any provision in this way is said to be *ultra vires* and is void.

Additional powers have been given to the courts under the Human Rights Act 1998 (HRA) with respect to delegated legislation. Section 4 of the HRA expressly states that the courts cannot declare primary legislation invalid as being contrary to the rights protected by the Act and limits them to issuing a declaration of incompatibility in such circumstances (*Wilson* v *First County Trust* (2000)). It is then for Parliament to act on such a declaration to remedy any shortcoming in the law if it so wishes. However, such limitation does not apply to secondary legislation, which the courts can now declare invalid on the grounds of not being compatible with the HRA.

5   DOCTRINE OF PRECEDENT

Key answer tips

In this question candidates are required to explain the differences between key principles relating to the doctrine of precedent. Although not specifically asked for, candidates should give an explanation of the doctrine of precedent as an introduction to their answer.

(a)   The doctrine of binding precedent, or stare decisis, lies at the heart of the English legal system. The doctrine refers to the fact that, within the hierarchical structure of the English courts, a decision of a higher court will be binding on a court lower than it in that hierarchy. In general terms, this means that when judges try cases, they will check to see if a similar situation has come before a court previously. If the precedent was set by a court of equal or higher status to the court deciding the new case, then the judge in the present case should follow the rule of law established in the earlier case. Where the precedent is from a lower court in the hierarchy, the judge in the new case may not follow but will certainly consider it. Not everything in a case report sets a precedent. The contents of a report can be divided into two categories:

(i)   **Ratio decidendi**

It is important to establish that it is not the actual decision in a case that sets the precedent; that is set by the rule of law on which the decision is founded. This rule, which is an abstraction from the facts of the case, is known as the ratio decidendi of the case. The ratio decidendi of a case may be understood as the statement of the law applied in deciding the legal problem raised by the concrete facts of the case.

(ii)   **Obiter dictum**

Any statement of law that is not an essential part of the ratio decidendi is, strictly speaking, superfluous; and any such statement is referred to as obiter dictum (obiter dicta in the plural), that is, said by the way. Although obiter dicta statements do not form part of the binding precedent, they are persuasive authority and can be taken into consideration in later cases, if the judge in the later case considers it appropriate to do so. The division of cases into these two distinct parts is a theoretical procedure. Unfortunately, judges do not actually separate their judgments into the two clearly defined categories and it is up to the person reading the case to determine what the ratio is. In some cases, this is no easy matter, and it may be made even more difficult in appellate cases where each of the judges may deliver their own lengthy judgments with no clear single ratio.

(b)   **Binding precedent**

If a precedent was set by a court of equal or higher status to the court deciding the new case then the judge in the present case should normally follow the rule of law established in the earlier case.

The Hierarchy of the Courts

The House of Lords stands at the summit of the English court structure and its decisions are binding on all courts below it in the hierarchy. As regards its own previous decisions, up until 1966 the House of Lords regarded itself as bound by its previous decisions. In a Practice Statement ([1966] 3 All ER 77) of that year, however, Lord Gardiner indicated that the House of Lords would in future regard itself as free to depart from its previous decisions where it appeared right to do so. There have been a number of cases in which the House of Lords has overruled or amended its own earlier decisions.(e.g. Conway v Rimmer (1968); Herrington v British Rail Board (1972); Miliangos v George Frank (Textiles) Ltd (1976); R v Shivpuri (1986)) but this is not a discretion that the House of Lords exercises lightly. It has to be recognised that in the wider context the House of Lords is no longer the supreme court and its decisions are subject to decisions of the European Court of Justice in terms of European Community law, and, with the implementation of the Human Rights Act 1998, the decisions of the European Court of Justice in matters relating to human rights. In civil cases the Court of Appeal is generally bound by previous decisions of the House of Lords and its own previous decisions. There are, however, a number of exceptions to this general rule. The exceptions arise where:

(i)   there is a conflict between two previous decisions of the Court of Appeal.

(ii)   a previous decision of the Court of Appeal has been overruled by the House of Lords. The Court of Appeal can ignore aprevious decision of its own which is inconsistent with European Community law or with a later decision of the EuropeanCourt.

(iii)   he previous decision was given per incuriam, i.e. in ignorance of some authority that would have led to a different conclusion (Young v Bristol Aeroplane Co Ltd (1944)).

Courts in the criminal division, however, are not bound to follow their own previous decisions which they subsequently consider to have been based on either a misunderstanding or a misapplication of the law. The Divisional Courts of the High Court are bound by the doctrine of stare decisis in the normal way and must follow decisions of the House of Lords and the Court of Appeal. They are also normally bound by their own previous decisions, although in civil cases it may make use of the exceptions open to the Court of Appeal in Young v Bristol Aeroplane Co Ltd, and in criminal appeal cases the Queen's Bench Divisional Court may refuse to follow its own earlier decisions where it feels the earlierdecision to have been wrongly made. The High Court is bound by the decisions of superior courts. Decisions by individual High Court Judges are binding on courts inferior in the hierarchy, but such decisions are not binding on other High Court Judges although they are of strong persuasive authority and tend to be followed in practice.Crown Courts cannot create precedent and their decisions can never amount to more than persuasive authority. County courts and Magistrates' courts do not create precedents.

Tutorial Note: The House of Lords was replaced by the Supreme Court in October 2009.

Persuasive precedent

From the foregoing it can be seen that courts higher in the hierarchy are not bound to follow the reasoning of courts at a lower level in that hierarchy. However, the higher courts will consider, and indeed may adopt, the reasoning of the lower court. As a consequence of the fact that the higher court is at liberty not to follow the reasoning in the lower court such decisions are said to be of persuasive rather than binding authority. It should also be borne in mind that English courts are in no way boundto follow the reasoning of courts in different jurisdictions, and it should be remembered that for this purpose Scotland qualifiesas having its own legal system. However, where a court from another jurisdiction has considered a point of law thatsubsequently arises in an English case, the English courts will review the reasoning of the foreign courts and may follow their reasoning if they find it sufficiently persuasive.

Examiner's Report

This question required candidates to consider the doctrine of precedent and in particular to explain particular terms operative within that doctrine. On the whole it was done fairly well. However the greatest shortcoming was in relation to the lack of information about the hierarchy of the courts within the English legal system and the implications this has for the doctrine of precedent.

ACCA marking scheme		
		Marks
(a)	A thorough, to complete answer, explaining the meaning of the two terms.	3–4
	A less than complete answer, probably unbalanced, focusing only one of the terms, or lacking in detail.	0–2
(b)	Thorough treatment of the topic. Clearly explaining the meaning of the two types of precedent.	4–6
	Less thorough answer, but showing a reasonable understanding of the topic of precedent.	2–3
	Weak answer, perhaps showing some knowledge but little understanding of the topic generally.	0–1

6 TYPES OF LAW

Key answer tips

This question is divided in two parts. Part (a) requires a consideration of the difference between criminal and civil law. Part (b) requires an explanation of the various courts which deal with these categories of law. In part (a) firstly the types of law should be discussed and then the differences should be highlighted. In part (b) the court structure for each type of law should be considered separately. It should be noted that each part of the question is only five marks and therefore a brief explanation is required.

(a) (i) Criminal law relates to conduct which the State considers with disapproval and which it seeks to control. Criminal law involves the *enforcement* of particular forms of behaviour, and the State, as the representative of society, acts positively to ensure compliance. Thus, criminal cases are brought by the State in the name of the Crown and cases are reported in the form of *Regina* v ... (*Regina* is simply Latin for 'queen' and case references are usually abbreviated to *R* v ...). In criminal law the prosecutor prosecutes a defendant (or 'the accused') and is required to prove that the defendant is guilty *beyond reasonable doubt*.

(ii) Civil law on the other hand, is a form of private law and involves the relationships between individual citizens. It is the legal mechanism through which individuals can assert claims against others and have those rights adjudicated and enforced. The purpose of civil law is to settle disputes between individuals and to provide remedies; it is not concerned with punishment as such. The role of the State in relation to civil law is to establish the general framework of legal rules and to provide the legal institutions to operate those rights, but the activation of the civil law is strictly a matter for the individuals concerned. Contract, tort and property law are generally aspects of civil law. Civil cases are referred to by the names of the parties involved in the dispute, for example, *Smith* v *Jones*. In civil law, a claimant sues (or 'brings a claim against') a defendant and the degree of proof is *on the balance of probabilities*.

In distinguishing between criminal and civil actions, it has to be remembered that the same event may give rise to both. For example, where the driver of a car injures someone through their reckless driving, they will be liable to be prosecuted under the Road Traffic legislation, but at the same time, they will also be responsible to the injured party in the civil law relating to the tort of negligence.

(b) The essential criminal trial courts are the *magistrates' courts* and *Crown Courts*. In serious offences, known as *indictable offences*, the defendant is tried by a jury in a Crown Court; for *summary offences*, he is tried by magistrates; and for 'either way' offences, the defendant can be tried by magistrates if they agree, but he may elect for jury trial.

When defendants under 18 are tried by magistrates, the procedure will take place in special *Youth Courts*. There will generally be three justices to hear the case, of whom at least one must be a man and one a woman. These justices will have had special training to deal with such cases. There are also special provisions relating to punishments for this age group.

Criminal appeals from the magistrates go to the Crown Court or to the Queen's Bench Division (QBD) Divisional Court 'by way of case stated' on a point of law or on the ground that the magistrates went beyond their proper powers.

From the Crown Court, appeals against conviction and sentence lie to the Court of Appeal (Criminal Division) with the possibility of an appeal to the House of Lords on a point of law of general public importance.

Magistrates' courts have a significant civil jurisdiction, especially under the Children Act 1989 as 'family proceedings courts'.

There are about 220 county courts in England and Wales. They are presided over by District Judges and circuit judges. County courts hear small claims, that is, those whose value is £5,000 or under, and fast track cases.

In the High Court the Queens Bench Division deals with contract and tort, etc; its Divisional Court deals with judicial review and criminal appeals from magistrates' courts and Crown Courts. Chancery deals with cases involving land, mortgages, bankruptcy and probate, etc; its Divisional Court hears taxation appeals. The Family Division hears matrimonial and child related matters and its Divisional Court hears appeals from magistrates' courts and county courts on these issues.

The Court of Appeal (Civil Division) usually has three judges whose decision is by majority. For many purposes, it is the de facto final appeal court but on important points of law of general public importance, a final appeal may be made to the House of Lords.

Examiner's Report

This question produced few sound answers with the main difficulty being with the second part of the question.In part (a) there was often an attempt to consider certain relevant factors such as criminal proceedings are brought by the state and civil proceedings by the individual and the aim of criminal proceedings is to punish by fines or imprisonment while civil proceedings aim to compensate by way of damages. Also there was some mention of the different standards of proof. A small number noted the different methods of citation and the fact that different courts are involved. The outcome was that many candidates produced a reasonable response. Some candidates thought that the death penalty was still carried out in England.

Part (b) was generally not well done and certainly not as well as part (a). Firstly, many candidates attempted to answer in terms of the hierarchy of authority in the context of judicial precedent rather than jurisdiction. Secondly, even where an answer concentrated on jurisdiction there was often considerable confusion indicating a serious lack of knowledge. Perhaps the simplest way of proceeding would have been to state that criminal matters go to the magistrates' courts with the more serious ones like murder and robbery going to the Crown Court. Similarly in civil matters the relevant courts are the county courts while the complex and those involving large sums go to one of the three Divisions of the High Court. Indeed candidates showed more knowledge of civil jurisdiction than criminal such as the role of magistrates in family matters and an account of the Divisions of the High Court.

ACCA marking scheme		
		Marks
(a)	Ranging from some but little knowledge down to no understanding at all of the differences	0-2
	A thorough to comprehensive explanation of the difference between the two types of law.	3-5
(b)	Little or no knowledge of either court system or, at the higher end of this grade, some knowledge of one of the	0-1
	Some explanation of the courts in both systems.	2-3
	Full explanation of both court systems.	4-5

7 SOURCES OF LAW

Key answer tips

This question requires candidates to consider the various sources of United Kingdom law. The word 'contemporary' did confuse students in the exam, but even if you ignored this word you would still be able to obtain a pass on this question by talking about both legislation and case law being the primary sources of law.

Legislation

This is law produced through the Parliamentary system. This is the most important source of law today for two reasons. Firstly, in terms of quantity, Parliament produces far more legal rules than any other source. Secondly, and perhaps even more importantly, the doctrine of parliamentary sovereignty within the United Kingdom means that Parliament is the ultimate source of law and, at least in theory, it can make whatever laws it wishes. It is an effect of this doctrine that the courts cannot challenge, either the authority of Parliament, or the laws it makes in the exercise of that authority. Although the Human Rights Act 1998, which introduces the European Convention on Human Rights into the United Kingdom, does not directly challenge parliamentary sovereignty, it remains to be seen what effect it has on the long term relationship between judges and Parliament.

Parliament consists of three distinct elements: the House of Commons, the House of Lords and the Monarch, but the real source of power is the House of Commons which has the authority of being the democratically elected institution. Before any legislative proposal, known at that stage as a bill, can become an Act of Parliament it must proceed through, and be approved by, both Houses of Parliament and must receive the Royal Assent.

Since the Parliament Acts of 1911 and 1949, the blocking power of the House of Lords has been restricted to a maximum of one year. However, as bills must complete their process within the life of a particular parliamentary session, a failure to reach agreement in both Houses within that period can lead to the total loss of the bill. It is for that reason that the current government removed a clause on lowering the age of homosexual consent to 16 from the general Act in which it was contained.

Legislation can be categorised in a number of ways. Public Acts relate to matters affecting the general public, whereas Private Acts relate to particular individuals or institutions. Alternatively, Acts of Parliament can be distinguished on the basis of their function. Some create new laws, but others are aimed at rationalising or amending existing legislative provisions. Consolidating legislation is designed to bring together provisions previously contained in a number of different Acts, without actually altering them. The Companies Act of 2006 was an example of a consolidation Act. Codifying legislation, on the other hand, seeks not just to bring existing statutory provisions under one Act but also looks to give statutory expression to common law rules. The Partnership Act 1890 and the Sale of Goods Act 1893, now 1979, are good examples of this.

Delegated legislation is a particularly important aspect of the legislative process. It is law made by some person or body, usually a government minister or local authority, to whom Parliament has delegated its general law-making power. A validly enacted piece of delegated legislation has the same legal force and effect as the Act of Parliament under which it is enacted. Delegated legislation can take the form of: Orders in Council; Statutory Instruments; Bye-Laws; or Professional regulations. In numerical terms the production of individual pieces of delegated legislation greatly outnumbers the production of general public Acts of Parliament.

Case Law

This is law created by judges in the course of deciding cases. The doctrine of *stare decisis* or binding precedent refers to the fact that courts are bound by previous decisions of courts equal or above them in the court hierarchy. It is the reason for a decision, the *ratio decidendi*, that binds. Everything else is obiter dictum and need not be followed.

The House of Lords can now overrule its own previous rules, but the Court of Appeal cannot. Judges, however, do have the ability to avoid precedents they do not wish to follow through the procedure of distinguishing the cases on their facts, and, of course, they have a very large number of cases and precedents to choose from.

One of the major advantages of the system of precedent is that it provides for certainty and the saving of the time and money of all the parties concerned. This is achieved by the fact that it should be possible to predict how a case will be decided if it falls within a clear precedent without actually having to take the case to court. The system of judges making law through their decisions also allows them scope for introducing flexibility into the legal system as they extend or distinguish existing precedents. This flexibility, however, by necessity undermines the very certainty that is supposed to be one of the main benefits of the system of precedent. Finally, the role of the judges within the UK constitution is to interpret, and not to create, law, and perhaps this latter point explains why most judges are very wary of openly admitting that they actually do make law.

The European Union

Since joining the European Community, now the European Union, the United Kingdom and its citizens have become subject to European Community (EC) law. In areas where it is applicable, European law supersedes any existing United Kingdom law to the contrary (see *Factortame Ltd v Secretary of State for Transport* (1989)).

The sources of EC law are: internal treaties and protocols; international agreements; secondary legislation; and decisions of the European Court of Justice.

Custom

Although there is always the possibility of a specific local custom, which has been in existence since 'time immemorial', acting as a source of law, in practice the limitations which operate in relation to custom render it an extremely unlikely source of contemporary law.

With regard to the operation of the Law Commission it should be noted that its role is to make recommendations relating to changes in legal provision, but it has no power itself to make such alterations

---

Examiner's Report

This question required the candidates to consider the various sources of contemporary United Kingdom law. The better answers displayed a competent understanding of what was required. There was firstly, a reference tolegislation being formulated by Parliament, along with the process involved. Many answers continued with arather detailed coverage of delegated legislation- examples, advantages and disadvantages. On precedent thegood answers explained the nature of judicial precedent including the legal rule on which a judicial decision isbased – ratio decidendi comparing that with other statements of law which do not form the basis of the decision-obiter dicta. However most coverage concerned the hierarchy of authority as a factor in determining theimportance of a precedent. On the debit side a number of responses concentrated either on legislation more usually delegated legislation onprecedent, which limited the possible marks available. A noticeable number of answers considered the historicalsources – common law and equity but managed some marks if this involved an account of case law. It is maybe that some candidates, especially the overseas ones, were not familiar with the word 'contemporary'. The third contemporary source of law is of course EU Law but only a few candidates made a reasonable attempt to explain its role and many who mentioned it showed some confusion with the European Convention on Human Rights.

ACCA Marking Scheme	
	Marks
Shows little understanding of the subject matter of the question.	0-1
Some understanding but lacking in detail. Perhaps unbalanced answer, focusing on only one aspect of the question and ignoring the others.	2-4
Thorough treatment of two of the sources, or a less complete treatment of the three.	5-7
Thorough treatment of the three major sources with perhaps reference to other sources such as custom or perhaps the role of the Law Commission, although the latter is certainly not necessary.	8-10

THE LAW OF OBLIGATIONS

8   **TERMINATION OF A CONTRACTUAL OFFER**

Key answer tips

You should discuss the three main ways in which offers may end, citing cases and examples where appropriate. Note that the question is about the termination of contractual offers, and not the termination of contracts.

It is a fundamental part of contract law that it is the acceptance of an offer by an offeree which gives rise to a binding contractual relationship. It is therefore necessary that, for there to be any possibility of a contract, there must be an offer, capable of acceptance. The effect of the lack of an offer is clearly seen in situations where no offer has ever been made, such as cases involving invitations to treat. However, it is possible for an offer to come to an end, and after such an event it would be equally impossible for anyone to purport to accept the former offer. It is, therefore, important to be aware of the various circumstances in which offers can come to an end.

Rejection of offers

Express rejection of an offer has the effect of terminating the offer and the offeree cannot subsequently accept the original offer. Thus for example, if someone were offered a car for £1,000 and said they did not want to buy it at that price, then they cannot subsequently change their mind and try to accept the original offer and enforce a sale of the car at that price.

A counter-offer, where the offeree tries to change the terms of the offer, acts as an implied rejection of the original offer and has the same effect as an express rejection (*Hyde v Wrench* (1840)). It is important, however, not to confuse a counter-offer with a request for information. Such a request does not end the offer, which can still be accepted after the new information has been obtained (*Stevenson v McLean* (1880)).

Revocation of offer

The second way in which an offer can come to an end is as a consequence of the offer being revoked. Revocation is merely the technical term for cancellation, and takes place when the offeror withdraws their offer. Once the offer is withdrawn it is no longer open to the offeree to accept it.

There are a number of points that have to be made with respect to the revocation of offers.

Firstly, an offer may be revoked at any time before acceptance *(Routledge v Grant* (1828)). The corollary of this point is that once the offer is accepted it cannot be withdrawn.

Secondly, revocation is not effective until it is actually received by the offeree. This means that the offeror must make sure that the offeree is made aware of the withdrawal of the offer, otherwise it might still be open to the offeree to accept the offer. This applies equally when the offeror uses the post to withdraw the offer, as the postal rule does not apply in relation to the withdrawal of offers (*Byrne v Tienhoven* (1880)).

Thirdly, however, communication of revocation may be made through a reliable third party. Thus where the offeree finds out about the withdrawal of the offer from a reliable third party the revocation is effective and the offeree can no longer seek to accept the original offer (*Dickinson v Dodds* (1876)).

Even where the offeror promises to keep an offer open for a certain time they may still withdraw the offer before that period is up. Such a promise is only binding where there is a separate contract, known as an option contract and complete with distinct consideration, to that effect.

The situation with regards to withdrawal of offers is somewhat different in relation to unilateral contracts, which are contracts in which one party promises something in return for some action on the part of another party; e.g. reward cases. Although the offeree is not obliged to undertake the action requested by the offeror, it would be unfair if the promisor were entitled to revoke their offer just before the offeree was about to complete their part of the contract. In such cases revocation is not permissible once the offeree has started performing the task requested (*Errington v Errington* (1952)).

Lapsing of offers

Offers will lapse i.e. come to an end automatically and no longer be capable of acceptance, in a number of instances.

Firstly, both the parties may agree or the offeror may set a time limit within which acceptance has to take place. In such situations if the offeree has not accepted the offer within the stated period then the offer lapses and can no longer be accepted.

Secondly, where the parties have not set an express time limit on accepting the offer, it will, nonetheless, lapse after the passage of a reasonable time. What amounts to a reasonable time depends on the circumstances of each particular case.

Finally, the death of the offeree automatically brings the offer to a close, and the death of the offeror normally has the same effect.

9   TERMS AND REPRESENTATION

Key answer tips

This question requires candidates to consider the law relating to terms in contracts. It specifically requires the candidates to distinguish between terms and mere representations and then to establish the difference between express and implied terms in contracts. In part (a) candidates should ensure they do not talk about the various types of terms. In part (b) it should be explained that a term ,although not expressly agreed on, can form part of a contract if it is implied by statute or custom.

(a)   As the parties to a contract will be bound to perform any promise they have contracted to undertake, it is important to distinguish between such statements that will be considered part of the contract, i.e. terms, and those other pre-contractual statements which are not considered to be part of the contract, i.e. mere representations. The reason for distinguishing between them is that there are different legal remedies available if either statement turns out to be incorrect.

A representation is a statement that induces a contract but does not become a term of the contract. In practice it is sometimes difficult to distinguish between the two, but in attempting to do so the courts will focus on when the statement was made in relation to the eventual contract, the importance of the statement in relation to the contract and whether or not the party making the statement had specialist knowledge on which the other party relied (*Oscar Chess* v *Williams* (1957) and *Dick Bentley* v *Arnold Smith Motors* (1965)).

(b)   Express terms are statements actually made by one of the parties with the intention that they become part of the contract and thus binding and enforceable through court action if necessary. It is this intention that distinguishes the contractual term from the mere representation, which, although it may induce the contractual agreement, does not become a term of the contract. Failure to comply with the former gives rise to an action for breach of contract, whilst failure to comply with the latter only gives rise to an action for misrepresentation. Such express statements may be made by word of mouth or in writing as long as they are sufficiently clear for them to be enforceable. Thus in *Scammel* v *Ouston* (1941) Ouston had ordered a van from the claimant on the understanding that the balance of the purchase price was to be paid 'on hire purchase terms over two years'. When Scammel failed to deliver the van Ouston sued for breach of contract without success, the court holding that the supposed terms of the contract were too uncertain to be enforceable. There was no doubt that Ouston wanted the van on hire purchase but his difficulty was that Scammel operated a range of hire purchase terms and the precise conditions of his proposed hire purchase agreement were never sufficiently determined. Implied terms, however, are not actually stated or expressly included in the contract, but are introduced into the contract by implication. In other words the exact meaning and thus the terms of the contract are inferred from its context. Implied terms can be divided into three types.

Terms implied by statute

In this instance a particular piece of legislation states that certain terms have to be taken as constituting part of an agreement, even where the contractual agreement between the parties is itself silent as to that particular provision. For example, unders.5 of the Partnership Act 1890, every member of an ordinary partnership has the implied power to bind the partnership ina contract within its usual sphere of business. That particular implied power can be removed or reduced by the partnershipagreement and any such removal or reduction of authority would be effective as long as the other party was aware of it. Someimplied terms, however, are completely prescriptive and cannot be removed.

Terms implied by custom or usage

An agreement may be subject to terms that are customarily found in such contracts within a particular market, trade or locality. Once again this is the case even where it is not actually specified by the parties. For example, in Hutton v Warren (1836), it was held that customary usage permitted a farm tenant to claim an allowance for seed and labour on quitting histenancy. It should be noted, however, that custom cannot override the express terms of an agreement (Les Affreteurs Reunnis SA v Walford (1919)). Terms implied by the courts

Generally, it is a matter for the parties concerned to decide the terms of a contract, but on occasion the court will presume that the parties intended to include a term which is not expressly stated. They will do so where it is necessary to give business efficacy to the contract. Whether a term may be implied can be decided on the basis of the officious bystander test. Imagine two parties, A and B, negotiating a contract, when a third party, C, interrupts to suggest a particular provision. A and B reply that that particular term is understood. In just such a way, the court will decide that a term should be implied into a contract. In *The Moorcock (1889),* the appellants, owners of a wharf, contracted with the respondents to permit them to discharge their ship at the wharf. It was apparent to both parties that when the tide was out the ship would rest on the riverbed. When the tide was out, the ship sustained damage by settling on a ridge. It was held that there was an implied warranty in the contract that the place of anchorage should be safe for the ship. As a consequence, the ship owner was entitled to damages for breach of that term.

Alternatively the courts will imply certain terms into unspecific contracts where the parties have not reduced the general

agreement into specific details. Thus in contracts of employment the courts have asserted the existence of implied terms toimpose duties on both employers and employees, although such implied terms can be overridden by express contractual provision to the contrary.

Examiner's Report

This question required candidates to consider the law relating to terms in contracts. Part (a) specifically required the candidate to distinguish between terms and mere representations while part (b) required them to explain the difference between express and implied terms in contracts.

Part (a) tended to be answered fairly well and most candidates were able to distinguish between terms and misrepresentation, although some candidates spent too much time in developing extended answers on the various types of terms.

Part (b) was also fairly well answered and most candidates were aware of the various sources of implied terms and their effects. Perhaps not surprisingly less detail was provided about express terms.

	ACCA marking scheme	Marks
(a)	A good explanation of the distinction between terms and representations. No reference to misrepresentation is needed.	2–3
	Very little knowledge of the meaning of the concepts.	0–1
(b)	Thorough treatment of the topic. Clearly distinguishing between the two types of terms and explaining most, if not all of the ways in which terms may be implied into contracts.	5–7
	Less thorough answer, but showing a reasonable understanding of the topic.	2–4
	Weak answer, perhaps showing some knowledge but little understanding of the topic generally.	0–1

10   CONSIDERATION

Key answer tips

This question requires candidates to examine some of the principles relating to consideration. The key principle is that at the time a contract is made consideration must be provided by both parties. That consideration must have some monetary value but does not need to be equal in value.

(a)   English law does not enforce every promise that might be made under every circumstance. One way in which the courts limit the type of promise that they have to deal with is through the operation of the doctrine of consideration. English law does not enforce gratuitous promises, i.e. promises given for no return, unless of course such promises are given by way of formal deed. The requirement is that for a simple promise to be enforced in the courts as a binding contract, it is necessary that the person to whom the promise was made, i.e. the promisee, should have done something in return for the promise. That something done, or to be done, constitutes consideration. Consideration can be understood, therefore, as the price paid for a promise. The element of bargain implicit in the idea of consideration may be seen in Sir Frederick Pollock's definition of it, subsequently adopted by the House of Lords in *Dunlop v Selfridge* (1915), as: 'An act or forbearance of one party, or the promise thereof, is the price for which the promise of the other is bought, and the promise thus given for value is enforceable.'

An alternative and shorter definition of consideration is that it is 'some benefit to the promisor or detriment to the promisee'. It is important to note, however, that both elements stated in that definition are not required to be present to support a legally enforceable agreement. Although in practice there usually is a reciprocal exchange of benefit and detriment, it is nonetheless possible for a promisee to provide consideration for a promise without the action directly benefiting the promisor. For example, A can promise to pay B for doing something that benefits C. In such a situation A enjoys no direct benefit but can enforcethe agreement, whilst C who enjoys the benefit cannot directly enforce the agreement between A and B.

(b)   (i)   The statement that consideration must be sufficient but need not be adequate refers to the fact that it is for the partiesthemselves to determine the terms of their contract. In deciding the contractual validity of any agreement, the court willmerely look to ensure that there is some element that constitutes valid consideration. As long as it finds formalconsideration, the court will not intervene to require substantive equality in the value of the goods or promisesexchanged, as long as the agreement has been freely entered into. Thus in *Thomas v Thomas* (1842) the executors ofa man's will promised to let his widow live in his house in return for rent of £1 per year. It was held that £1 was sufficientconsideration to validate the contract, although it did not represent an adequate rent in economic terms. Equally, in *Chappell & Co* v *Nestle Co* (1959), it was held that a used chocolate wrapper was sufficient consideration to form acontract, even although it had no economic value whatsoever to Nestle. It has generally been accepted that performance of an existing duty does not provide valid consideration (*Glassbrook* v *Glamorgan CC* (1925) and *Stilk* v *Myrick* (1809)). However, the more recent authority of *Williams* v *Roffey Bros* (1990) has indicated a contrary possibility.

      (ii)   Past consideration does not actually count as valid consideration sufficient to make any agreement based on it a bindingcontract. Normally consideration is provided either at the time of the creation of a contract or at a later date. In the case of past consideration, however, the action is performed before the promise that it is supposed to be the consideration for. Such action is not sufficient to support a promise, as consideration cannot consist of any action already wholly performed before the promise was made (*Re McArdle* (1951)).

           There are exceptions to the rule that past consideration will not support a valid contract. For example, where the plaintiff performed the action at the request of the defendant *and payment was expected*, then any subsequent promise to pay will be enforceable (*Re Caseys Patents* (1892)). Also, under s.27 of the Bills of Exchange Act 1882, past consideration can create liability on a bill of exchange.

Examiner's Report

This question required candidates to examine some of the essential principles relating to the doctrine of consideration in relation to the law of contract.

Part (a) required an explanation consideration and on the whole it was done very well, with the majority of candidates either giving quotations from appropriate case or providing examples of consideration. Part (b) was divided into two separate elements. Part (i) focuses on the meaning of and difference between sufficiency and adequacy. By and large candidates were much clearer as regards the issue of adequacy and only a relative few were able to give a clear or detailed explanation of the requirement relating to sufficiency.

Part (ii), on past consideration was done fairly well and most candidates were able to cite *McArdle.* However, only a few went further to consider the exceptions to the general rule as set out in such cases as *Lampleigh.*

ACCA marking scheme	
	Marks
A thorough, to complete answer detailing what is meant by consideration and the two rules. It is likely that case authority will be provided, and they will be rewarded accordingly.	8–10
A limited understanding, or a lack of balance or clarity in regard to the various parts of the question.	5–7
Very unbalanced, only dealing with parts of the question or lacking in detail.	0–4

11   INVITATION TO TREAT

Key answer tips

This question is divided in two parts. Part (a) requires an explanation of an offer. Part (b) requires an explanation of invitation to treat. Candidates should give examples of an invitation to treat, citing case law to support their answer.

(a)   **Offer**

An offer sets out the terms upon which an individual is willing to enter into a binding contractual relationship with another person. It is a promise to be bound on particular terms, which is capable of acceptance. The essential factor to emphasise about an offer is that it may, through acceptance by the offeree, result in a legally enforceable contract. The person who makes the offer is the offeror; the person who receives the offer is the offeree.

Offers, once accepted, may be legally enforced but not all statements will amount to an offer. It is important, therefore, to be able to distinguish what the law will treat as an offer from other statements which will not form the basis of an enforceable contract. An offer must be capable of acceptance. It must therefore not be too vague (*Scammel* v *Ouston* (1941)). In *Carlill* v *Carbolic Smoke Ball Co* (1893) it was held that an offer could be made to the whole world and could be accepted and made binding through the conduct of the offeree.

In addition an offer should be distinguished, from the following:

- *A mere statement of intention* – Such a statement cannot form the basis of a contract even though the party to whom it was made acts on it (*Re Fickus* (1900)).

- *A mere supply of information* – As in *Harvey* v *Facey* (1893) where it was held that the defendant's telegram, in which he stated a minimum price he would accept for property, was simply a statement of information, and was not an offer capable of being accepted by the plaintiff.

(b) **Invitation to treat**

Invitations to treat are distinct from offers in that rather than being offers to others, they are in fact invitations to others to make offers. The person to whom the invitation to treat is made becomes the actual offeror, and the maker of the invitation becomes the offeree. An essential consequence of this distinction is that, in line with the not bound to accept any offers subsequently made to them.

The following are examples of common situations involving invitations to treat:

(i) *The display of goods in a shop window* – The classic case in this area is *Fisher v Bell* (1961) in which a shopkeeper was prosecuted for offering offensive weapons for sale, by having flick-knives on display in his window. It was held that the shopkeeper was not guilty as the display in the shop window was not an offer for sale but only an invitation to treat.

(ii) *The display of goods on the shelf of a self-service shop* - In this instance the exemplary case is *Pharmaceutical Society of Great Britain* v *Boots Cash Chemists* (1953). The defendants were charged with breaking a law which provided that certain drugs could only be sold under the supervision of a qualified pharmacist. They had placed the drugs on open display in their self-service store and, although a qualified person was stationed at the cash desk, it was alleged that the contract of sale had been formed when the customer removed the goods from the shelf. It was held that Boots were not guilty. The display of goods on the shelf was only an invitation to treat. In law, the customer offered to buy the goods at the cash desk where the pharmacist was stationed.

(iii) *A public advertisement* – Once again this does not amount to an offer. This can be seen from *Partridge* v *Crittenden* (1968) in which a person was charged with 'offering' a wild bird for sale contrary to the Protection of Birds Act 1954, after he had placed an advert relating to the sale of such birds in a magazine. It was held that he could not be guilty of offering the bird for sale as the advert amounted to no more than an invitation to treat.

(iv) *A share prospectus* – Contrary to common understanding such a document is not an offer. It is merely an invitation to treat, inviting people to make offers to subscribe for shares in a company.

12 TERMS USED IN THE LAW OF CONTRACT

Key answer tips

In this question candidates are required to explain key terms at the core of the law of contract. As in the previous question candidates should use case law to support their answer.

(a) **Invitation to treat**

In the course of the preliminary statements and actions which precede two parties entering into a valid and binding contract, many of the statements which are made will have no contractual significance. Only an offer is capable of maturing, through acceptance, into a legally binding contract. 'Invitations to treat', which are statements or actions which precede an offer, are not capable of being accepted.

Prima facie, the question of whether a pre-contractual statement is an offer or is merely an invitation to treat depends upon the intention of the party making the statement, but there are certain areas where this question can only be answered by reference to some wider policy. The following well-known examples illustrate some of the applicable principles:

- In *Fisher v Bell* (1961) it was held that a display of goods in a shop window, with price tickets attached, was an invitation to treat and not an offer for sale.

- In *Pharmaceutical Society of Great Britain v Boots Cash Chemists (Southern) Ltd* (1953) it was held that a display of goods on the shelves of a self-service shop was an invitation to treat and not an offer for sale.

- In *Partridge v Crittenden* (1968) an advertisement in a specialist magazine was held not to be an offer, with the consequence that the advertiser escaped conviction for 'offering for sale' certain wild birds, contrary to the provisions of the Protection of Birds Act 1954.

Invitations to tender are usually regarded as invitations to treat and not as offers. When a tender is actually made this is regarded as an offer, which the party inviting the tenders is free to accept or reject. For an example of a case where an invitation to tender may give rise to some contractual consequences, see *Blackpool & Fylde Aero Club v Blackpool Borough Council* (1990).

(b)   **Revocation of an offer**

In the course of concluding a valid contract, an offer is open to acceptance until it either lapses (e.g. after a stated or reasonable time) or until it is revoked by the offeror. The general rule is that an offeror is free to revoke an offer at any time until it is accepted, although the revocation needs to be communicated to the offeree: a revocation is only effective when it has been communicated. This does not mean that it has to be communicated by the offeror – see *Dickinson v Dodds* (1876) where communication of revocation by a third party was held to be sufficient.

Unlike in the case of postal acceptance (see below) a letter of revocation is effective only on delivery, not on posting: see *Byrne & Co v Van Tienhoven* (1880). One question which is not yet completely resolved is whether an offeror can revoke the offer once the offeree has commenced acceptance. Although the matter is not completely free of doubt, on the basis of the decision in *Errington v Errington* (1953) it seems that in the case of unilateral contracts – where an offer is accepted by conduct – once the offeree has commenced the act of acceptance the offer cannot be revoked.

(c)   **The postal rule for acceptance of an offer**

The essential issue to be considered here is the question of when a letter of acceptance is deemed to constitute an acceptance. At the moment the letter is posted? At the moment when it is delivered? At the point when it is actually read by the offeror? Logical arguments can be constructed for the adoption of any one of the three possibilities outlined above, but the solution adopted in the law of contract is that an acceptance is effective at the point when the letter of acceptance is posted: *Adams v Lindsell* (1818).

This rule only applies when the use of the postal service is reasonable in the circumstances – as it will be, for example, where an offer has been made by post and the offeror has indicated the use of the post for the purpose of making the acceptance.

The logic underlying the use of the above postal rule is that the main risks associated with its use lie with the offeror, should the letter of acceptance be lost or delayed in the post. It is the offeror who will, in most cases, have initiated or indicated the post as the medium for communication and accordingly it is appropriate that the offeror should bear the risks involved in its use. The principle does mean, however, that where an offeree has put a letter of acceptance in the post a subsequent, but speedier, message countermanding that acceptance will be ineffective.

13 EXCLUSION CLAUSES

Key answer tips

This is a fairly straightforward question requiring candidates to explain the purpose of exclusion clauses and how they are controlled at common law and by statute. Part (a) is only worth two marks so candidates should ensure their answer reflects this weighting and does not go into too much detail which is then repeated in part (b) of their answer.

(a) **Exemption or exclusion clauses**

In a sense, an exemption clause is no different from any other term, in that it sets out the rights and obligations of the parties to a contract. However, exemption clauses are intended to exempt, or limit, the liability of a party in breach of the agreement. The law relating to exclusion clauses is governed by the common law, the Unfair Contract Terms Act 1977, the Unfair Terms in Consumer Contract Regulations 1999 and the various Acts which imply certain terms into particular contracts.

(b) **Common law**

(i) Two distinct issues arise at common law. The first issue relates to incorporation. An exclusion clause cannot be effective unless it is actually a term of a contract. It is essential, therefore, to decide whether or not the exclusion clause has been incorporated into the contract. There are three ways in which such a term may be inserted into a contractual agreement:

(1) **Signature**: If a person signs a contractual document, then they are bound by its terms, even if they did not read it (*L'Estrange v Graucob* (1934)). The rule in *L'Estrange v Graucob* may be avoided where the party seeking to rely on the exclusion clause misled the other party into signing the contract (*Curtis v Chemical Cleaning & Dyeing Co* (1951)).

(2) **Notice**: Apart from the above, an exclusion clause will not be incorporated into a contract unless the party affected actually knew of it, or was given sufficient notice of it. In order for notice to be adequate, the document bearing the exclusion clause must be an integral part of the contract and given at the time the contract is made (*Chapleton v Barry UDC* (1940) and *Olley v Marlborough Court Ltd* (1949)). Whether the degree of notice given has been sufficient is a matter of fact, but in *Thornton v Shoe Lane Parking Ltd* (1971) it was stated that the greater the exemption, the greater the degree of notice required.

(3)   **Custom**: Where the parties have had previous dealings on the basis of an exclusion clause, that clause may be included in later contracts (*Spurling v Bradshaw* (1956)), but it has to be shown that the party affected had actual knowledge of the exclusion clause (*Hollier v Rambler Motors* (1972)).

The second issue relates to the matter of construction or interpretation. Thus, for example, the 'contra proferentum' rule was developed by the judges to restrict the effectiveness of exclusion clauses. It requires that any uncertainties or ambiguities in the exclusion clause be interpreted against the meaning claimed for it by the person seeking to rely on it. So in *Hollier v Rambler* it was stated that as the exclusion clause in question could be interpreted as applying only to non-negligent accidental damage, or alternatively to include damage caused by negligence, it should be restricted to the former, narrower, interpretation. As a consequence, the plaintiff was entitled to recover for damages caused to his car by the defendant's negligence.

(ii)   **Statutory protection**

The Unfair Contract Terms Act 1977 represents the statutory attempt to control exclusion clauses. In spite of its title, it is really aimed at unfair exemption clauses, rather than contract terms generally. In this regard the Unfair Terms in Consumer Contracts Regulations 1999 are wider.

The controls under the Act relate to two areas:

(1)   **Negligence**

There is an absolute prohibition on exemption clauses in relation to liability in negligence resulting in death or injury (ss.2 and 5). Exemption clauses relating to liability for other damage caused by negligence will only be enforced to the extent that they satisfy the 'requirement of reasonableness' (s.2). Thus in *Smith v Bush* (1989), the plaintiff bought a house on the basis of a valuation report carried out for her building society by the defendant. The surveyor had included a disclaimer of liability for negligence in his report to the building society and sought to rely on that fact when the plaintiff sued after the chimneys of the property collapsed. The House of Lords held that the disclaimer was an exemption clause and that it failed the requirement that such terms should be reasonable.

(2)   **Contract**

Any exclusion clause which seeks to avoid liability for breach of contract in a consumer transaction is only valid to the extent that it complies with the requirement of reasonableness (s.3). This test also applies where a clause seeks to permit a party to avoid performing the contract completely, or to permit performance less than reasonably expected.

The implied term relating to title under s.12 of the Sale of Goods Act 1979 cannot be excluded in any contract (s.6(1)). The other implied terms as to description, fitness, merchantable quality, and sample, cannot be excluded in a consumer contract (s.6(2)); and in a non-consumer transaction any restriction is subject to the requirement of reasonableness (s.6(3)).

The second schedule of the Act provides guidelines for the application of the reasonableness test with regard to non-consumer transactions, but it is likely that similar considerations will be taken into account by the courts in consumer transactions. Amongst these considerations are:

- the relative strength of the parties' bargaining power;
- whether any inducement was offered in return for the limitation on liability;
- whether the customer knew, or ought to have known, about the existence or extent of the exclusion having regard to custom or a course of previous dealings between the parties;
- whether the goods were manufactured or adapted to the special order of the customer.

An example of the court's approach may be seen in *George Mitchell (Chesterhall) Ltd v Finney Lock Seeds Ltd* (1983). In this case the respondents planted 63 acres with cabbage seed supplied by the appellants. The crop failed, due partly to the fact that the wrong type of seed had been supplied and partly to the fact that the seed supplied was of inferior quality. When the respondents claimed damages, the sellers relied on the protection of a clause in their standard conditions of sale limiting their liability to replacing the seeds supplied or refunding payment. It was held, however, that the respondents were entitled to compensation for the loss of the crop. The House of Lords decided that although the exemption clause was sufficiently clear and unambiguous to be effective at common law, it failed the test of reasonableness under the Unfair Contract Terms Act.

The Unfair Terms in Consumer Contracts Regulations 1999 replace the original regulations of 1994 which were enacted to implement the European Unfair Contract Terms Directive. They apply to all terms and strike down any that are found to be 'unfair' as being contrary to the establishment of good faith between the parties. Terms should be such as meet the consumer's reasonable expectation and should enable them to make an informed choice whether to form the contract or not (*Director General of Fair Trading v First National Bank* (2000)).

14 CONDITIONS, WARRANTIES AND INNOMINATE TERMS

Key answer tips

This question invites candidates to demonstrate their knowledge of the contents of contracts. In particular it requires an examination of the way in which contractual terms can be classified and invites candidates to consider the effect of this classification in relation to a breach of any such term.

Contractual terms are statements which form part of the contract. Parties to a contract will normally be bound to perform any promise that they have agreed to and failure to perform will lead to an action for breach of contract, although the precise nature of the remedy will depend upon the nature of the promise broken.

Some statements do not form part of a contract, even though they might have induced the other party to enter into the contract. These pre-contractual statements are called

representations. The consequence of such representations being false is an action for misrepresentation, not an action for breach of contract, and leads to different remedies. It is important, therefore, to decide precisely what promises are included in the contract. Once it is decided that a statement is a term, rather than merely a pre-contractual representation, it is further necessary to decide which type of term it is in order to determine what remedies are available for its breach.

Terms can be classified as one of three types.

(a) **Conditions**

A condition is a fundamental part of the agreement; it is something which goes to the root of the contract. Breach of a condition gives the injured party the right either to terminate the contract and refuse to perform their part of it, or to go through with the agreement and sue for damages. The classic case in relation to breach of condition is *Poussard* v *Spiers & Pond* (1876) in which the plaintiff had contracted with the defendants to sing in an opera they were producing. Due to illness she was unable to appear on the first night, or for some nights thereafter. When Mme. Poussard recovered, the defendants refused her services as they had hired a replacement for the whole run of the opera. It was held that her failure to appear on the opening night had been a breach of a condition, and the defendants were at liberty to treat the contract as discharged.

(b) **Warranties**

A warranty is a subsidiary obligation which is not vital to the overall agreement, and in relation to which failure to perform does not totally destroy the whole purpose of the contract. Breach of a warranty does not give the right to terminate the agreement. The injured party has to complete their part of the agreement, and can only sue for damages. As regards warranties, the classic case is *Bettini* v *Gye* (1876) in which the plaintiff had contracted with the defendants to complete a number of engagements. He had also agreed to be in London for rehearsals six days before his opening performance. Due to illness, however, he only arrived three days before the opening night, and the defendants refused his services. On this occasion it was held that there was only a breach of warranty. The defendants were entitled to damages, but could not treat the contract as discharged.

The distinction between the effects of a breach of condition as against the effects of a breach of warranty was enshrined in s.11 of the Sale of Goods Act 1893 (now SGA 1979). For some time it was thought that these were the only two types of term possible, the nature of the remedy available being prescribed by the particular type of term concerned. This simple classification has subsequently been rejected by the courts as too restrictive, and a third type of term has emerged: the innominate term.

(c) **Innominate terms**

In this case, the remedy is not prescribed in advance simply by whether the term breached is a condition or a warranty, but depends on the consequence of the breach.

If the breach deprives the innocent party of 'substantially the whole benefit of the contract', then the right to repudiate will be permitted, even if the term might otherwise appear to be a mere warranty.

If, however, the innocent party does not lose 'substantially the whole benefit of the contract' then they will not be permitted to repudiate but must settle for damages, even if the term might otherwise appear to be a condition. The way in which the courts approach such terms may be seen in *Cehave* v *Bremer (The Hansa Nord)*

(1976). In this case a contract for the sale of a cargo of citrus pulp pellets, to be used as animal feed, provided that they were to be delivered in good condition. On delivery, the buyers rejected the cargo as not complying with that provision, and claimed back the money they had paid to the sellers. Subsequently the same buyers obtained the pellets, when the cargo was sold off, and used them for their original purpose. It was held that since the breach had not been serious, the buyers had not been free to reject the cargo, and the sellers had acted lawfully in retaining the money paid.

15 EXPRESS AND IMPLIED TERMS

Key answer tips

This question requires candidate to explain the differences between express and implied terms in part (a). Part (b) requires an explanation of how terms can be implied on contracts which are by statute, by custom or by the courts.

(a)   **Express terms** are statements actually made by one of the parties with the intention that they become part of the contract and thus binding and enforceable through court action if necessary. It is this intention that distinguishes the contractual term from the mere representation, which, although it may induce the contractual agreement, does not become a term of the contract. Failure to comply with the former gives rise to an action for breach of contract, whilst failure to comply with the latter only gives rise to an action for misrepresentation.

Such express statements may be made by word of mouth or in writing as long as they are sufficiently clear for them to be enforceable. Thus in *Scammel v Ouston* (1941) Ouston had ordered a van from the claimant on the understanding that the balance of the purchase price was to be paid 'on hire purchase terms over two years'. When Scammel failed to deliver the van Ouston sued for breach of contract without success, the court holding that the supposed terms of the contract were too uncertain to be enforceable. There was no doubt that Ouston wanted the van on hire purchase but his difficulty was that Scammel operated a range of hire purchase terms and the precise conditions of his proposed hire purchase agreement were never sufficiently determined.

(b)   **Implied terms**, however, are not actually stated or expressly included in the contract, but are introduced into the contract by implication. In other words the exact meaning and thus the terms of the contact are inferred from its context. Implied terms can be divided into three types.

Terms implied by statute

In this instance legislation states that certain terms have to be taken as constituting part of an agreement, even where the contractual agreement between the parties is silent as to that particular provision. Some statutes provide that particular terms are to apply unless the contract in question specifically states otherwise. An example of this type of implied term in the area of company law is the model articles of association. The provisions of the model articles apply to a company unless they are specifically excluded. If they are not excluded, they apply even if the actual articles make no reference to the provision. Other implied terms are completely prescriptive and cannot be removed.

For example, under the Sale of Goods Act 1979 and the Supply of Goods and Services Act (SGSA) 1982, terms relating to the description, quality and fitness for purpose are all implied into sale of goods contracts and cannot be removed even with the consent of the parties to the contract.

Terms implied by custom or usage

An agreement may be subject to terms that are customarily found in such contracts within a particular market, trade or locality. Once again this is the case even where it is not actually specified by the parties. For example, in *Hutton* v *Warren* (1836), it was held that customary usage permitted a farm tenant to claim an allowance for seed and labour on quitting his tenancy. It should be noted, however, that custom cannot override the express terms of an agreement *(Les Affreteurs Reunis SA* v *Walford* (1919))*.

Terms implied by the courts

Generally it is a matter for the parties concerned to decide the terms of contract, but on occasion the court will presume that the parties intended to include a term which is not expressly stated. They will do so where it is necessary to give 'business efficacy' to the contract.

Whether a term may be implied can be decided on the basis of the 'officious bystander test'. Imagine two parties, A and B, negotiating a contract. A third party, C, interrupts to suggest a particular provision. A and B reply that that particular term is understood. In just such a way, the court will decide that a term should be implied into a contract. In *The Moorcock* (1889), the appellants, owners of a wharf, contracted with the respondents to permit them to discharge their ship at the wharf. It was apparent to both parties that when the tide was out the ship would rest on the riverbed. When the tide was out, the ship sustained damage by settling on a ridge. It was held that there was an implied warranty in the contract that the place of anchorage should be safe for the ship. As a consequence, the ship owner was entitled to damages for breach of that term.

Alternatively, the courts will imply certain terms into unspecific contracts where the parties have not reduced the general agreement into specific details. Thus in contracts of employment, the courts have asserted the existence of implied terms to impose duties on both employers and employees, although such implied terms can be overridden by express contractual provision to the contrary.

16 DAMAGES

Key answer tips

This question requires candidates to explain in part (a) the concept of remoteness of damage in the law of contract and in part (b) how such damages are measured. The case of Hadley v Baxendale (1854) is the leading case on this area and candidates should explain the principles that it established.

Damages is the common law remedy for breach of contract and, unlike discretionary equitable awards, is available as of right where a pecuniary loss has been sustained by the innocent party. In deciding what damages are to be paid, the courts deploy a number of rules and principles to guide their action. These various rules may be considered under two headings: the rules relating to remoteness of damage and rules relating to the measure of damages.

(a) **Remoteness of damage**

It would be unfair if the party in breach of contract were held to be liable for every consequence of their action no matter how far down the chain of causation it appeared. In order to limit potential liabilities, the courts have established clear rules about consequential liability in such a way as to deny the award of damages for consequences that are deemed to be too remote from the original breach. The rule relating to remoteness of damages was clearly stated for the first time in *Hadley v Baxendale* (1854) to the effect that damages will only be awarded in respect of losses which:

(i) arise naturally i.e. in the usual course of events; or which

(ii) both parties may reasonably be supposed to have contemplated as a probable result of its breach when the contract was made.

As a consequence of the first part of the rule in *Hadley v Baxendale,* the party in breach is deemed to expect the normal consequences of the breach, whether they actually expected them or not. It does not matter that they did not actually think of the consequences if those consequences were the natural outcome of their breach.

Under the second part of the rule, however, the party in breach can only be held liable for abnormal consequences where they have actual knowledge that the abnormal consequences might follow. In *Victoria Laundry Ltd v Newman Industries Ltd* (1949) it was decided that the plaintiff could claim damages in relation to the loss of normal profits due to the defendant's delay, as that loss was a natural consequence of the delay. A second claim for damages in relation to an especially lucrative contract failed, however, on the grounds that the loss was not a normal one but was a consequence of an abnormal contract about which the defendant knew nothing.

The decision in the *Victoria Laundry* case was confirmed by the House of Lords in *The Heron II* (1969), although the actual test for remoteness was reformulated in terms of whether the consequence should have been 'within the reasonable contemplation of the parties' at the time of the contract.

(b) **The measure of damages**

The courts use a number of rules and principles to determine the actual extent of monetary damages owed. The general rule is that damages in contract are intended to be compensatory rather than punitive. The aim is to put the injured party in the same position they would have been in had the contract been properly performed. As the object is not to punish the party in breach but to compensate the injured party for any financial loss sustained as a consequence of the other party's breach, so the amount of damages awarded can never be greater than the actual loss suffered. It should be noted that the exact amount of the loss may differ depending on whether the innocent party's 'reliance interest' or 'expectation interest' is used as the criterion against which damages are measured. In practice, it is usually the expectation loss that is compensated, except where this permits the innocent party to escape responsibility for any loss they would have made in the contract in the absence of breach (see *CCC Films (London) Ltd v Imperial Quadrant Films Ltd* (1985)).

Where the breach relates to a contract for the sale of goods, damages are usually assessed in line with the market rule. This means that if goods are not delivered under a contract, the buyer is entitled to go into the market and buy similar goods, and pay the market price prevailing at the time. They can then claim the difference in price between what they paid and the original contract price as damages. Conversely, if a buyer refuses to accept goods under a contract, the seller can sell the goods in the market', and accept the prevailing market price. Any difference between the price they receive and the contract price can be claimed in damages.

The injured party is under a duty to take all reasonable steps to mitigate their loss. So in the above examples, the buyer of goods which are not delivered has to buy the replacements as cheaply as possible; and the seller of goods which are not accepted has to try to get as good a price as they can when they sell them. In such a way they are expected to minimise the actual loss they sustain, as may be seen in *Payzu v Saunders* (1919).

The foregoing has dealt with losses that are relatively easily quantified in monetary terms, but matters are more complicated when it comes to assessing damages for non-pecuniary loss.

At one time, damages could not be recovered where the loss sustained through breach of contract was of a non-financial nature. The modern position is that such non-pecuniary damages can be recovered. Thus in *Jarvis v Swan Tours Ltd* (1973), it was held that the plaintiff was entitled to recover not just the substantial financial loss he suffered, but also for the loss of entertainment and enjoyment which amounted to an even greater sum.

The job of estimating damages may be made much simpler where the parties to an agreement make provisions for possible breach by stating in advance the amount of damages that will have to be paid in the event of any breach occurring. Damages under such a provision are known as 'liquidated damages'. They will be recognised by the court as long as they represent a genuine pre-estimate of losses, and are not intended to operate as a penalty against the party in breach. If the court considers the provision to be a penalty', it will not give it effect, but will award damages in the normal way *(Dunlop v New Garage & Motor Co* (1915)).

17 DAMAGES AND MITIGATING LOSSES

Key answer tips

This question requires candidates in part (a) to consider the use of liquidated damages when a breach of contract occurs and how this can be considered to be a penalty clause in which case the court will not give it effect. Part (b) requires an explanation of the duty to mitigate losses, the key point here being that an injured party should take all **reasonable** steps to minimise their loss.

(a) **Liquidated damages and penalty clauses**

It is possible, and common in business contracts, for the parties to an agreement to make provisions for a possible breach by stating in advance the amount of damages that will have to be paid in the event of any breach occurring. Damages under such a provision are known as liquidated damages. They will only be recognised by the court if they represent a genuine pre-estimate of loss, and are not intended to operate as a penalty against the party in breach. If the court considers the provision to be a penalty it will not give it effect, but will award damages in the normal way.

In *Dunlop* v *New Garage and Motor Co* (1915), the plaintiffs supplied the defendants with tyres under a contract designed to achieve resale price maintenance (i.e. ensure that the tyres were sold on to customers at a minimum resale price). The contract provided that the defendants had to pay Dunlop £5 for every tyre they sold in breach of the resale price agreement. When the garage sold tyres at less than the agreed minimum price, they resisted Dunlop's claim for £5 per tyre, on the grounds that it represented a penalty clause. On the facts of the situation the court decided that the provision was a genuine attempt to fix damages and was not a penalty. It was, therefore, enforceable.

In deciding the legality of such clauses the courts will consider the effect rather than the form of the clause, as is seen in *Cellulose Acetate Silk Co Ltd* v *Widnes Foundry Ltd* (1933). In that case, the contract expressly stated that damages for late payment would be paid by way of penalty at the rate of £20 per week. In fact, the sum of £20 pounds was in no way excessive and represented a reasonable estimate of the likely loss. On that basis, the House of Lords enforced the clause in spite of its actual wording.

(b) **The duty to mitigate losses**

This rule states that the injured party in the event of a breach of contract is under a duty to take all reasonable steps to minimise his or her loss. The operation of the rule means that the buyer of goods that are not delivered, as required under the terms of a contract, has to buy the replacements as cheaply as possible. Similarly, the seller of goods that the buyer refuses to accept, in breach of a contractual agreement, has to try to sell the goods to someone else and get as good a price as possible.

In *Payzu* v *Saunders* (1919), the parties entered into a contract for the sale of fabric, which was to be delivered and paid for in instalments. When the purchaser, Payzu, failed to pay for the first instalment on time, Saunders refused to make any further deliveries unless Payzu agreed to pay cash on delivery. The plaintiff refused to accept this and sued for breach of contract. The court decided that the delay in payment had not given the defendant the right to repudiate the contract. As a consequence, he had breached the contract by refusing further delivery. The buyer, however, should have mitigated his loss by accepting the offer of cash on delivery terms. His damages were accordingly restricted to what he would have lost under those terms, namely, interest over the repayment period.

In *Western Web Offset Printers Ltd* v *Independent Media Ltd* (1995), the parties had entered into a contract under which the plaintiff was to publish 48 issues of a weekly newspaper for the defendant. In the action which followed the defendant's repudiation of the contract, the only issue in question was the extent of the damages to be awarded. The plaintiff argued that damages should be decided on the basis of gross profits, merely subtracting direct expenses such as paper and ink, but not labour costs and other overheads: this would result in a total claim of some £177,000. The defendant argued that damages should be on the basis of net profits with labour and other overheads being taken into account: this would result in a claim of some £38,000. Although the trial judge awarded the lesser sum, the Court of Appeal decided that he had drawn an incorrect analogy from cases involving sale of goods. In this situation, it was not simply a matter of working out the difference in cost price from selling price in order to reach a nominal profit. The plaintiff had been unable to replace the work due to a recession in the economy and therefore had not been able to mitigate the loss. In the circumstances, the plaintiff was entitled to receive the full amount that would have been due in order to allow it to defray the expenses it would have had to pay during the period the contract should have lasted.

However, in relation to anticipatory breach of contract the injured party can wait until the actual time for performance before taking action against the party in breach. In such a situation, the injured party is entitled to make preparations for performance and to claim the agreed contract price, even though this apparently conflicts with the duty to mitigate losses (*(White and Carter (Councils)* v *McGregor* (1961*)*).

18   ANTICIPATORY BREACH

Key tips

This question requires candidates to show an understanding of what is meant by breach of contract paying particular attention to anticipatory breach. Candidates should explain the consequences of a breach of contract according to the status of the term – either condition, warranty or innominate term. A good answer will explain and differentiate between express/implied anticipatory breach.

Breach of contract occurs when one of the parties to the contract fails to perform their part of the agreement, either fully or partially i.e. they fail completely to perform what they have contracted to do, or they perform their obligation in a defective manner. As a consequence of this failure the court may award remedies against the party in breach of the contract, the most usual of which is damages.

Usually breach of contract only becomes apparent at, or after, the time set for the performance of the contract. Anticipatory breach, however, occurs before the due date of performance. It occurs where one of the parties shows a clear intention not to be bound by their agreement and indicates that they will not perform their contractual obligations on the actual due date of performance.

In the situation of anticipatory breach, the innocent party can sue for damages immediately they are made aware of the breach. However, they are not required to take immediate action. They can, if they so choose, wait until the actual time for performance before taking action. If they do elect to wait until the set time for performance, then they are entitled to make preparations for performance of their part of the contract; and claim the agreed contract price. In *White & Carter (Councils)* v *McGregor* (1961), McGregor contracted with the plaintiffs to have advertisements placed on litter bins which were supplied to local authorities. The defendant wrote to the plaintiffs asking them to cancel the contract. The plaintiffs refused to cancel, and produced, and displayed, the adverts as required under the contract. They then claimed payment. It was held that the plaintiffs were not obliged to accept the defendant's repudiation, but could perform the contract and claim the agreed price.

Anticipatory breach can take either of two specific forms: express anticipatory breach or implied anticipatory breach.

Express anticipatory breach occurs where one of the parties declares, before the due date of performance, that they have no intention of complying with the terms of the contractual agreement. An example of this may be seen in *Hochster v De La Tour* (1853). In April, De La Tour engaged Hochster to act as his courier on his European tour, starting on 1 June. On 11 May De La Tour wrote to Hochster stating that he would no longer be needing his services. The plaintiff started proceedings for breach of contract on 22 May, and the defendant claimed that there could be no cause of action until 1 June. It was held, however, that the plaintiff was entitled to start his action as soon as the anticipatory breach occurred, i.e. when De La Tour stated he would not need Hochster's services.

Implied anticipatory breach does not arise from any direct indication from either of the parties that they will not perform their contractual agreement, but results from the situation where one of the parties does something, which makes subsequent performance of their contractual undertaking impossible. An example of this may be seen in *Omnium D'Enterprises v Sutherland* (1919). In this case the defendant had agreed to let a ship to the plaintiff, but before the actual time for performance, he actually sold the ship to another party. It was held that the sale of the ship amounted to a clear repudiation of the contract and that the plaintiff could sue for breach of contract from that date, without having to wait until the actual date of performance of the contract.

Examiner's Report

This question required candidates to show understanding of what is meant by breach of contract payingparticular attention to anticipatory breach. On the whole the question was answered well. Many candidates were able to explain breach and the consequences according to the status of the term broken – either warranty, condition or innominate term, although some candidates did take this as an opportunity to answer a question on terms rather than breach. In this question it is pleasing to note that explanations were very often supported by accurate references to relevant case law. Anticipatory breach was dealt with equally well on the whole, with many candidates drawing the distinction between express/implied anticipatory breach. Once again the relevant case law was cited in support of the explanations. However, in spite of the question generally being well done there was considerable room for improvement, not just in terms of being better prepared to answer the question but also in terms of examination technique. Too many candidates spent an inordinate amount of time and effort in producing an introduction to their answer by explaining inconsiderable detail the essential elements of legally binding contracts, when in fact the question assumed the existence of the same. Such an approach not only wasted valuable time but also produced unfocused answers that gained fewer marks that they might otherwise have gained had they limited their time and effort to the essential matter of the question.

ACCA Marking Scheme	
	Marks
No real understanding of the meaning of the term	0-1
Some understanding of the breach, but confused or lacking in explanation as to meaning or effect.	2-4
A clear understanding of what is meant by breach but perhaps lacking in the detail expected of the very best answers.	5-7
A thorough explanation of the concept of breach providing cases or examples by way of explanation.	8-10

19   DOCTRINE OF PRIVITY

Key answer tips

This question required candidates t o explain the doctrine of privity in part (a) and explain the meaning of the intention to create legal relations in part (b). The general rule on the doctrine of privity is that only parties to a contract acquire rights and obligations under that contract and only those parties can sue or be sued on that contract. In relation to the intention to create legal relations candidates should state the presumption and cite case law to support their answer.

(a)   **Privity**

As a general rule contractual agreements can only affect those persons who have entered into the agreement expressed in the terms of the contract. Thus, it is normally the case that no third party can rely on, or enforce, any terms in a contractual agreement to which they are not themselves a party (*Dunlop* v *Selfridge* (1915)).

However, it is possible to formally transfer the benefit of a contract to a third party. This process, known as assignment, must be in writing. It should be noted that the burden of a contract cannot be assigned without the consent of the other party to the contract.

It is also possible for a person to create a contract specifically for the benefit of a third party. In such limited circumstances the promisee is considered as a trustee of the contractual promise for the benefit of the third party. In order to enforce the contract the third party must act through the promisee by making them a party to any action (*Les Affreteurs Reunis SA* v *Leopold Walford (London) Ltd* (1919)).

A third party may enforce a contract in the following circumstances:

- the beneficiary sues in some other capacity. Although not a party to the original agreement, individuals may, nonetheless, acquire the power to enforce the contract where they are legally appointed to administer the affairs of one of the original parties (*Beswick* v *Beswick* (1967)) where a widow, appointed administrator of her late husband's estate, was able to successfully sue her nephew for specific performance of a beneficial agreement in that capacity.

- the situation involves a collateral contract. This situation arises where one party promises something to another party if that other party enters into a contract with a third party: e.g. A promises to give B something if B enters into a contract with C. In such a situation B can insist on A complying with the original promise (Shanklin Pier v Detel Products Ltd (1951)).

- it is foreseeable that damage caused by any breach of contract will cause a loss to a third party (Linden Gardens Trust Ltd v Lenesta Sludge Disposals Ltd (1994)).

The other main common law exception to the privity rule is agency, where the whole point is for the agent to bring about contractual relations between their principal and a third party.

In the area of motoring insurance Statute law has intervened to permit third parties to claim directly against insurers, but much wider statutory intervention has been introduced by the Contracts (Rights of Third Parties) Act 1999.

(b)   **Intention to create legal relations**

A contract is defined as a binding agreement, however in order to limit the number of cases that might otherwise be brought, the courts will only enforce those agreements which the parties intended to have legal effect. Although expressed in terms of the parties' intentions, the test for the presence of such intention is an objective, rather than a subjective, one. Agreements can be divided into two categories, in which different presumptions apply.

(i)   **Domestic and social agreements**

In these agreements, there is a presumption that the parties do not intend to create legal relations (*Balfour* v *Balfour* (1919)). However, any such presumption against the intention to create legal relations in such relationships may be rebutted by the actual facts and circumstances of a particular case as may be seen in *Merritt* v *Merritt* (1970).

(ii)   **Commercial agreements**

In these situations, the strong presumption is that the parties intend to enter into a legally binding relationship in consequence of their dealings (*Edwards* v *Skyways* (1964)). However, as with other presumptions, this one is also open to rebuttal. In commercial situations, however, the presumption is so strong that it will usually take express wording to the contrary to avoid its operation as may be seen in *Rose and Frank Co* v *Crompton Bros* (1925).

Examiner's Report

This question was in two parts and required candidates to show knowledge of English contract law. Part (a) was concerned with the doctrine of privity of contract and the exceptions thereto, whilst part (b) related to the intention to create legal relations. On the whole the question was reasonably well.

In part (a) whilst many candidates could state the basic principle of privity and some could cite the case of *Dunlop v Selfridge* to explain it, their knowledge of the exceptions to the rule left much to be desired. A surprising number knew very little and indeed many confused privity with the unrelated concept of privacy.

In part (b) many candidates were able to give a full account of the relevant principles and provide case authorities in support of their explanations. Part (b) was answered better than part (a).

ACCA marking scheme	
	Marks
Little or no knowledge of either of the topics.	0-1
Some, but limited, understanding of both topics, or clear understanding of only one of the topics.	2-4
A clear understanding of both topics but perhaps lacking in detail. Alternatively an unbalanced answer showing good understanding of one part but less in the other.	5-7
A thorough understanding of both topics demonstrated by references to cases or examples	8-10

20   REMOTENESS OF DAMAGE

Key answer tips

Candidates must be clear that is question deals with the remoteness of damage in the law of tort **not** in the law of contract and therefore candidates must ensure their answer deals with the principles of the law of tort. Case law should be cited to support their answer.

Even where someone has been held to owe a duty of care to another person and to have breached that duty in such a way as to cause them to sustain loss or injury it does not follow as a matter of course that the person so responsible will be liable to provide recompense for all the loss sustained. Just as in contract law, the position in negligence is that the person ultimately liable in damages is only responsible to the extent that the loss sustained was considered not to be too remote. This was not always the case as may be seen in *Re Polemis and Furness, Withy and Co* (1921), in which it was held that the defendants were liable for the loss of a ship, even though the circumstances under which it was lost were unforeseen. It was held that as the fire, which destroyed the ship, was the direct result of a breach of duty, the defendant was liable for the full extent of the damage, in spite of the fact that the manner in which it took place was unforeseen. The Court of Appeal held that as damage would result from the act of negligence, the party responsible was liable for the whole extent of the damage, even though they could not have been aware of the extent of the damage that was actually caused.

However, the *Re Polemis* test has been replaced by a less draconian test involving an assessment of the remoteness of the damage actually sustained. The current test was established in *The Wagon Mound (No 1)* (1961). As the facts will demonstrate the way in which the current doctrine operates they will be set out in more detail than is usual. The defendants negligently allowed furnace oil to spill from a ship into Sydney harbour. The oil spread and came to lie beneath a wharf, which was owned by the plaintiffs. The plaintiffs had been carrying out welding operations and, on seeing the oil, they stopped welding in order to ascertain whether it was safe. They were assured that the oil would not catch fire, and so resumed welding. Cotton waste, which had fallen into the oil, caught fire. This in turn ignited the oil and a fire spread to the plaintiff's wharf. It was held that the defendants were in breach of duty. However, they were only liable for the damage caused to the wharf and slipway through the fouling of the oil. They were not liable for the damage caused by fire because damage by fire was at that time unforeseeable. This particular oil had a high ignition point and it could not be foreseen that it would ignite on water. The Privy Council refused to apply the rule in *Re Polemis* and its formulation of the rules of causation and remoteness has prevailed since then.

The test of reasonable foresight arising out of *The Wagon Mound* clearly takes into account such things as scientific knowledge at the time of the negligent act. The question to be asked in determining the extent of liability is, 'is the damage of such a kind as the reasonable man should have foreseen?'. This does not mean that the defendant should have foreseen precisely the sequence or nature of the events. Lord Denning in *Stewart* v *West African Air Terminals* (1964) said:

> 'It is not necessary that the precise concatenation of circumstances should be envisaged. If the consequence was one which was within the general range which any reasonable person might foresee (and was not of an entirely different kind which no one would anticipate), then it is within the rule that a person who has been guilty of negligence is liable for the consequences.'

This is illustrated in the case of *Hughes* v *Lord Advocate* (1963), where employees of the Post Office, who were working down a manhole, left it without a cover but with a tent over it and lamps around it. A child picked up a lamp and went into the tent. He tripped over the lamp, knocking it into the hole. An explosion occurred and the child was burned. The risk of the child being burned by the lamp was foreseeable. However, the vapourisation of the paraffin in the lamp and its ignition were not foreseeable. It was held that the defendants were liable for the injury to the plaintiff. It was foreseeable that the child might be burned and it was immaterial that neither the extent of his injury nor the precise chain of events leading to it was foreseeable.

The test of remoteness is not easy to apply. The cases themselves highlight the uncertainty of the courts. For example, in *Doughty* v *Turner Manufacturing Co Ltd* (1964), an asbestos cover was knocked into a bath of molten metal. This led to a chemical reaction, which was at that time unforeseeable. The molten metal erupted and burned the plaintiff, who was standing nearby. It was held that only burning by splashing was foreseeable and that burning by an unforeseen chemical reaction was not a variant on this. It could be argued that the proper question in this case should have been, 'was burning foreseeable?', as this was the question asked in *Hughes*.

Examiner's Report

This question quite clearly stated that it required candidates to explain the concept of 'remoteness of damage' in relation to *the law of tort*. As this was the first question to be asked in relation to this new area of law in the syllabus it was expected either that candidates would be a little uncertain or alternatively that they would have prepared for it extremely thoroughly. However, the vast majority of candidates simply ignored the reference to tort and answered the question on the basis of contract law and consequently got very few if indeed any marks, depending on whether they gave a sufficiently general explanation of remoteness that could be applied to tort. Even those candidates who did recognise that the question related to tort rather than contract still tended to produce overly general answers, treating the questions as an invitation to write all they knew about tort law. That being said of the very few answers that managed to achieve pass marks, some did provide sound answers.

ACCA marking scheme	
	Marks
Little or no knowledge of either of the topics.	0-1
Some, but limited, understanding of both topics, or clear understanding of only one of the topics.	2-4
A clear understanding of both topics but perhaps lacking in detail. Alternatively an unbalanced answer showing good understanding of one part but less in the other..	5-7
A thorough understanding of both topics demonstrated by references to cases or examples	8-10

21 STANDARD OF CARE

Key answer tips

This question requires candidates to explain how once it has been established that a duty of care exists, how can it be shown that duty has been breached i.e. the consideration of what would a reasonable man have done or not done.

Once a claimant has established that the defendant owes them a duty of care, they must then establish that the defendant has actually breached that duty. The test for establishing breach of duty is an objective one and was set out in *Blyth* v *Birmingham Waterworks Co* (1856). Thus a breach of duty occurs if the defendant:

… fails to do something which a reasonable man, guided upon those considerations which ordinarily regulate the conduct of human affairs, would do; or does something which a prudent and reasonable man would not do.

The fact that the defendant has acted less skilfully than the reasonable man would expect will usually result in breach being established. This is the case even where the defendant is inexperienced in his particular trade or activity. For example, a learner driver must drive in the manner of a driver of skill, experience and care (*Nettleship* v *Weston* (1971)). It is, however, clear from the case law that, depending on the age of the child, the standard of care expected from a child may be lower than that of an adult. Children should be judged on whether they have the 'foresight and prudence of a normal child of that age' (see *Mullin* v *Richards* (1998)). The degree or standard of care to be exercised by such a person will vary, as there are factors, such as the age of the claimant, which can increase the standard of care to be exercised by the defendant. The test is, therefore, flexible but the following factors will be taken into consideration in determining the issue:

The probability of injury

The degree of care must be balanced against the degree of risk involved if the defendant fails in his duty. It follows, therefore, that the greater the risk of injury or the more likely it is to occur, the more the defendant will have to do to fulfil his duty. Thus in *Glasgow Corporation* v *Taylor* (1992) the provision of a warning notice was not considered sufficient to absolve the corporation from liability of injury sustained by young children eating poisonous berries in its park (See also In *Bolton* v *Stone* (1951) where the likelihood of the injury occurring was small, as was the risk involved).

The seriousness of the risk

The degree of care to be exercised by the defendant may be increased if the claimant is very young, old or less able bodied in some way. The rule is that 'you must take your victim as you find him' (this is known as the egg-shell skull rule).

In *Haley* v *London Electricity Board* (1965) the defendants, in order to carry out repairs, had made a hole in the pavement. The precautions taken by the Electricity Board were sufficient to safeguard a sighted person, but Haley, who was blind, fell into the hole, striking his head on the pavement, and became deaf as a consequence. It was held that the Electricity Board was in breach of its duty of care to pedestrians. It had failed to ensure that the excavation was safe for all pedestrians, not just sighted persons. It was clearly not reasonably safe for blind persons, yet it was foreseeable that they may use this pavement.

There are other cases in this field which should be referred to, for example, *Gough* v *Thorne* (1966), concerning young children; *Daly* v *Liverpool Corp* (1939), concerning old people; and *Paris* v *Stepney BC* (1951), concerning disability (see below).

Cost and practicability

Any foreseeable risk has to be balanced against the measures necessary to eliminate it. If the cost of these measures far outweighs the risk, the defendant will probably not be in breach of duty for failing to carry out those measures. Thus in *Latimer* v *AEC Ltd* (1952) a factory belonging to AEC became flooded after an abnormally heavy rainstorm. The rain mixed with oily deposits on the floor, making the floor very slippery. Sawdust was spread on the floor, but it was insufficient to cover the whole area. Latimer, an employee, slipped on a part of the floor to which sawdust had not been applied. It was held that AEC Ltd was not in breach of its duty to the plaintiff. It had taken all reasonable precautions and had eliminated the risk as far as it practicably could without going so far as to close the factory. There was no evidence to suggest that the reasonably prudent employer would have closed down the factory and, as far as the court was concerned, the cost of doing that far outweighed the risk to the employees.

Social benefit

The degree of risk has to be balanced against the social utility and importance of the defendant's activity. For example in Watt v Hertfordshire CC (1954), injury sustained by the plaintiff, a fireman, whilst getting to an emergency situation, was not accepted as being the result of a breach of duty of care as in the circumstances time was not available to take the measures that would have removed the risk.

Common practice

Actions in line with common practice or custom, may be sufficient to meet the expected standard of care, except, of course, where the common practice is in itself negligent. Thus in Paris v Stepney BC (1951) not wearing safety glasses in a foundry was common practice but it was in itself essentially negligent and the defendant could rely on it as a defence.

Skilled persons

Individuals who hold themselves out as having particular skills are not judged against the standard of the reasonable person, but the reasonable person possessing the same professional skill as they purport to have. In Roe v Minister of Health (1954), a patient was paralysed after being given a spinal injection. This occurred because the fluid being injected had become contaminated with the storage liquid, which had seeped through minute cracks in the phials. It was held that there was no breach of duty, since the doctor who administered the injection had no way of detecting the contamination at that time.

Examiner's Report

This question required candidates to explain the standard of care owed by one person to another in relation to the tort of negligence. This was the least poplar question in the paper and also the one with the poorest performance.

The majority of candidates did not answer the question asked and produced general explanation of the law of tort or the duty of care, rather than the specific issue of standard of care. It is clear that many candidates have not yet come to terms with this relatively new aspect of the F4 syllabus and much work remains to be done. The repeated refrain of this report is that candidates must study the whole syllabus and be properly prepared to deal with any issue that might arise. As in question 1, candidates must be warned against not studying particular aspects of the syllabus in sufficient detail to deal with questions in those areas. It is apparent, however, that this is not the case in relation to tort law, where knowledge is clearly extremely limited. This may be the result of the newness of the subject area and the fact that there is not a background of previous questions and answers in the area; however the study manuals all deal thoroughly with the topic.

ACCA marking scheme	
	Marks
Little if any knowledge of the topic	0-2
Some, but little, knowledge of the topic	3-4
Lacking in detail in some or all aspects of the topic. Unbalanced answer that only focuses on some of particular issues	5-7
Full understanding and explanation of the topic. It is likely that cases will be cited as authority although examples will be accepted as an alternative.	8-10

22 NEGLIGENCE

Key answer tips

This question required candidates to explain the concepts of contributory negligence an consent. A good answer would focus on the reduction of damages and the defences to negligence respectively. Also candidates must ensure that they do not just write everything they know about the tort of negligence and recognise that there are different elements to the law of torts just like there are with the law of contract.

A tort is a wrongful act against an individual which gives rise to a non-contractual civil claim. The claim is usually for damages, although other remedies are available. Liability in tort is usually based on the principle of fault, although there are exceptions. Negligence is recognised as the most important of the torts, its aim being to provide compensation for those injured through the fault of some other person. However, an individual is not automatically liable for every negligent act that he or she commits and in order to sustain an action in negligence it must be shown that the party at fault owed a duty of care to the person injured as a result of their actions. Consequently, the onus is on the claimant to establish that the respondent owed them a duty of care. Even then there are defences available for the defendant in a tort action.

(a)   Although not strictly a defence for negligence, the application of the concept of contributory negligence can be used to reduce the amount of damages awarded in a particular case. It arises where the party making the claim is found to have contributed, through their own fault, to the injury they sustained. The onus is on the defendant to show that the claimant was at fault and contributed to their own injury. An early example of the principle may be seen in *Jones v Livox Quarries* (1952) in which a claimant was found to have contributed to their own injury by showing a lack of care for their own safety by riding on the back of a dumper truck. Another example may be found in *Sayers v Harlow* (1958) in which the damages awarded to a woman, who was injured escaping from a public toilet in which she had been trapped due to a defective lock, were reduced as her injuries had been exacerbated by the manner in which she tried to make her escape by climbing out of it.

If contributory negligence is demonstrated, then by virtue of the Law Reform (Contributory Negligence) Act 1945, the level of damages awarded will be reduced in line with and will depend upon the extent to which the claimant's fault contributed to the injury sustained (in *Jayes v IMI (Kynoch)* (1985) the award suffered a 100% reduction).

(b)   *Volenti non fit injuria* is a Latin tag which essentially translates as 'no injury can be done to a person who willingly accepts the risk'. Of course very serious injury can in fact be done to such a person; the point is that, as a result of their consent they lose their right to sue for damages for any injury suffered. Whilst contributory negligence operates to reduce the level of damages awarded, consent acts as a complete defence and no damages will be awarded if it is shown to apply.

Consent can be given expressly where the claimant expressly agrees to the risk of injury or it may be implied from the claimant's conduct. An example of express consent may be seen in relation to medical treatment. In such situations the patient may be required to sign a consent form which removes the right to complain about what would otherwise amount to the tort of battery. Of course the patient does not consent to the surgeon carrying out any procedure negligently and on the occasion of such negligence an action for damages would still arise.

The principle of implied consent arose in *ICI v Shatwell* (1964) in which two brothers employed in a quarry ignored their employer's rules relating to safety, by testing detonators without using the shelter provided. As a result, the claimant was injured and sued the employer for breach of statutory duty as a result of his brother's actions. The court held that both brothers had impliedly consented to the risks by their actions and had participated quite willingly. Consequently the employer was not responsible to the injured brother.

As may be seen the defence relies upon the claimant's consent to the risks, which should be distinguished from mere knowledge of it. Thus in *Dunn v Hamilton* (1939) a passenger accepted a lift in a car driven by a person she knew to be drunk. When she was injured as a result of the driver's careless driving it was held that she had not actually consented to the risk of being injured, even although she knew there was such a risk. Section 149 of the Road Traffic Act 1988 removed the possibility of consent being used as a defence against car passengers.

Examiner's Report

This question required candidates to explain the concepts of contributory negligence and consent. Answers required focussed on the reduction to damages and the defences to negligence respectively. As in previoussittings, questions on this area proved extremely difficult for candidates to answer.

Answers varied in standard although on the whole, this question was answered very unsatisfactorily. It was apparent that candidates were not comfortable with this area of law. They tended to either write hardly anything at all, or wrote everything they knew on the area starting with the neighbour principle, regularly citing *Donoghue v Stevenson* and going on to write in detail about the consequences of negligent advice. *Hedley Byrne v Heller* featured very frequently in answers. There was also discussion of remoteness of damage and the quantum of damages, which would be awarded in cases of personal injury. There were some focussed answers which correctly analysed the principles in the question and some sound examples of case law were produced. However, answers such as these were very few in number. Candidates need to realise that there are different elements to the law of tort, just like there are with the law of contract. Acomplete knowledge regurgitation of every bit of law on the area will not suffice and will not be awarded decent. marks. More practice is needed in this area. That said the area is still relatively new and answers were slightly improved from those at the last sitting.

Although some candidates may have been out off by the Latin tag in part (b), a number of weaker candidates managed to work out from the English explanation of consent what it related to.

ACCA Marking Scheme	
	Marks
Very unbalanced answer, lacking in detailed understanding	0-2
Some but limited knowledge of both elements or only dealing with one of them.	3-4
Reasonable explanation of both concepts but perhaps lacking in detail or cases authority.	5-7
Thorough explanation of the meaning and effect of both elements of the question. Cases or examples wil be expected to gain full marks.	8-10

23   BALL LTD

Key answer tips

This scenario question requires candidates to apply the law relating to sufficient consideration to this particular scenario and to conclude whether Chris is entitled to the extra money from Alex. The case of Williams v Roffey Bros laid down important principles which though they should be applied in this scenario, candidates should be able to distinguish between this case and the facts in this question.

Alex has a contract with Ball Ltd for the provision of the computer system. It is important to note that the contract contained a penalty clause which provided that Alex would have had to pay Ball Ltd £1,000 per day if he had failed to deliver it in time. Chris is not contractually bound to Ball Ltd, but he is contracted to Alex. The terms of his contract required him to complete his work by 23 May. In return, he would receive £5,000. However, before the completion of the contract, Alex promised him a further £1,000, although he is now refusing to pay more than the original agreed sum of £5,000. The question is whether Chris can enforce Alex's promise to pay him an additional £1,000.

In order to require Alex to make payment at the new level, Chris must show that he provided **sufficient consideration** for his promise. The question, therefore, is whether the performance of existing contractual duties can ever provide consideration for a new promise. Previously it generally was accepted that performance of an existing duty does not provide valid consideration, but *Williams* v *Roffey Bros* (1991) has indicated a contrary possibility. As stated, the long-established rule was that the mere performance of a contractual duty already owed to the promisor could not be consideration for a new promise. Thus in *Stilk* v *Myrick* (1809), when two members of a ship's crew deserted, the captain promised the remaining members of the crew that they would share the deserter's wages if they completed the voyage. However, when the ship eventually got to London, the owners refused to make the promised payment. In an action for the money promised, the court held that the captain's promise could not be legally enforced as the sailors had only done what they were already obliged to do by their contracts of employment.

Where, however, the promisee did more than he was already contractually bound to do then the performance of an additional task may constitute valid consideration for a new promise. The facts in *Hartley* v *Ponsonby* (1857) were somewhat similar to those in *Stilk* v *Myrick* in that it also related to a promise of extra payment to the remaining members of a ship's crew after some others had deserted. In this case, however, it was decided that the crew were entitled to the additional money because they had done more than they previously had agreed to do. The reason, or at least the justification, for the decision was because the number of deserters had been so great as to make the return of the ship unusually hazardous.

In any event, the continued relevance and application of *Stilk* v *Myrick* in commercial cases has been placed in doubt in recent years by the Court of Appeal in *Williams* v *Roffey Bros* (1991). The facts of this case were as follows. Roffey Bros had entered into a contract to refurbish a block of flats and subcontracted with Williams to carry out carpentry work for a fixed price of £20,000. It became apparent that Williams was in such financial difficulties that he might not be able to complete his work on time, with the consequence that Roffey Bros would be subject to a penalty clause in the main contract. As a result, Roffey Bros offered to pay Williams an additional £575 for each flat he completed. On that basis Williams carried on working, but when it seemed that Roffey Bros were not going to pay him, he stopped work and sued for the additional payment in relation to the eight flats he had completed after the promise of the additional payment. The Court of Appeal held that Roffey Bros had enjoyed practical benefits as a consequence of their promise to increase Williams's payment: the work would be completed on time; they would not have to pay any penalty; and they would not suffer the bother and expense of getting someone else to complete the work. These benefits were sufficient, in the circumstances, to provide consideration for the promise of extra money and Williams was held to be entitled to recover the extra money owed to him. Although the Court of Appeal did not overrule *Stilk* v *Myrick* it is clear that its sphere of relevance will be curtailed by the application of *Williams* v *Roffey Bros*.

As a result **it would now seem that the performance of an existing contractual duty can amount to consideration for a new promise** in:

(i)   circumstances where there is no question of fraud or duress, and

(ii)   where practical benefits accrue to the promisor.

These legal principles can be applied to the case in question. Chris had a contract with Alex to produce software but insisted that Alex increase his money before he would complete the contract. Chris might try to argue that his situation falls within the ambit of *Williams v Roffey Bros*, and that therefore he can enforce the promise. He would point out that Alex did enjoy practical benefits in that the software was produced on time, thus saving Alex from suffering a substantial loss. It is clear, however, that this situation is significantly different. Whereas in *Williams v Roffey Bros* the plaintiff did not exert any undue pressure on the defendants to induce them to make their promise of additional money, in this situation Chris has clearly exerted a form of economic duress on Alex to force him to increase the contract price. Alex was left with no real choice but to agree to Chris's terms or else he would have suffered the substantial loss. Such unfair pressure would take the case outside of *Williams v Roffey Bros*, and the old rule as stated in *Stilk v Myrick* would apply, and Chris would be unable to enforce the promise for the additional £1,000.

24   ALAN AND CATH

Key answer tips

This question relates to the issue of whether the parties to an agreement can enforce its terms through court action. By definition, a contract is a binding agreement, but the important thing for this question is that not all agreements are contracts. In order to limit the number of cases that might otherwise be brought, the courts will only enforce those agreements which the parties intended to have legal effect. Although expressed in terms of the parties' intentions, the test for the presence of such intention is an objective, rather than a subjective, one. For the purposes of this question with regard to intention to create legal relations, agreements can be divided into two categories to which different presumptions apply.

Domestic and social agreements

In domestic and social agreements, there is a presumption that the parties do not intend to create legal relations.

In *Balfour v Balfour* (1919), a husband returned to Ceylon to take up his employment and he promised his wife, who could not return with him due to health problems, that he would pay her £30 per month as maintenance. When the marriage later ended in divorce, the wife sued for the promised maintenance. It was held that the parties had not intended the original promise to be binding and therefore it was not legally enforceable.

Another situation where it held that there was no intention to create legal relations can be seen in *Jones v Padavatton* (1969), in which a mother was not held liable to maintain an agreement to pay her daughter a promised allowance.

It should be emphasised, however, that the presumption against the intention to create legal relations in such relationships is only that; a presumption. As with all presumptions, it may be rebutted by the actual facts and circumstances of a particular case as may be seen in the case of *Merritt v Merritt* (1970). After a husband had left the matrimonial home, he met his wife and promised to pay her £40 per month, from which she undertook to pay the outstanding mortgage on their house. The husband, at the wife's insistence, signed a note agreeing to transfer the house into the wife's sole name when the mortgage was paid off.

The wife paid off the mortgage but the husband refused to transfer the house. It was held that the agreement was enforceable as in the circumstances the parties had clearly intended to enter into a legally enforceable agreement.

Commercial agreements

In commercial situations, the strong presumption is that the parties intend to enter into a legally binding relationship in consequence of their dealings.

In *Edwards v Skyways* (1964), employers undertook to make an ex gratia payment to an employee whom they had made redundant. It was held that in such a situation the use of the term 'ex gratia' was not sufficient to rebut the presumption that the establishment of legal relations had been intended. The former employee, therefore, was entitled to the payment promised.

As with other presumptions, this one is open to rebuttal. In commercial situations, however, the presumption is so strong that it will usually take express wording to the contrary to avoid its operation. An example can be found in *Rose and Frank Co v Crompton Bros* (1925) in which it was held that an express clause stating that no legal relations were to be created by a business transaction was effective.

Applying the above law to the facts in the problem scenario provides the following conclusion:

Cath and Alan

This situation is similar to that in *Merritt v Merritt* and it is likely that that case would be followed and Cath would be able to enforce the agreement for Alan to pass the title of the house into her sole ownership. The usual presumption against husband and wife intending to form legally binding agreements (*Balfour v Balfour*) would be rebutted not just by the fact that they were separating, but by the fact that the agreement was reduced to a written document.

25   ARTI

Key answer tips

This scenario deals with an express anticipatory breach and the consequences arising. After explaining the meaning of express anticipatory breach candidates must then go on to explain the remedies available to Bee Ltd, the one applicable being damages. A good answer will expand on how the damages would be calculatesd

The essential issues to be disentangled from the problem scenario relate to breach of contract and the remedies available for such breach. There seems to be no doubt that there is a contractual agreement between Arti and Bee Ltd. Normally breach of a contract occurs where one of the parties to the agreement fails to comply, either completely or satisfactorily, with their obligations under it.However,such a definition does not appear to apply in this case as the time has not yet come when Arti has to produce the text. He has merely indicated that he has no intention of doing so. This is an example of the operation of the doctrine of anticipatory breach.This arises precisely where one party, prior to the actual due date of performance, demonstrates an intention not to perform theircontractual obligations. The intention not to fulfil the contract can be either express or implied.

Express anticipatory breach occurs where a party actually states that they will not perform their contractual obligations (*Hochster* v *De La Tour* (1853)). Implied anticipatory breach occurs where a party carries out some act which makes performance impossible *Omnium Enterprises* v *Sutherland* (1919)). When anticipatory breach takes place the innocent party can sue for damages immediately on receipt of the notification of the other party's intention to repudiate the contract, without waiting for the actual contractual date of performance as in *Hochster* v *De La Tour*. Alternatively, they can wait until the actual time for performance before taking action. In the latter instance, they are entitled to make preparations for performance, and claim the agreed contract price (*White and Carter (Councils)* v *McGregor* (1961)).

It would appear that Arti's action is clearly an instance of express anticipatory breach and that Bee Ltd has the right either to accept the repudiation immediately or affirm the contract and take action against Arti at the time for performance (*Vitol SA* v *Norelf Ltd* (1996)). In any event Arti is bound to complete his contractual promise or suffer the consequences of his breach of contract.

Remedies for breach of contract

(i)   Specific performance

It will sometimes suit a party to break their contractual obligations, even if they have to pay damages. In such circumstances the court can make an order for specific performance to require the party in breach to complete their part of the contract. However, as specific performance is not available in respect of contracts of employment or personal service Arti cannot be legally required to write the book for Bee Ltd (*Ryan* v *Mutual Tontine Westminster Chambers Association (1893)*). This means that the only remedy against Arti lies in the award of damages.

(ii)   Damages

A breach of contract will result in the innocent party being able to sue for damages. Bee Ltd, therefore, can sue Bob for damages, but the important issue relates to the extent of such damages. The estimation of what damages are to be paid by a party in breach of contract can be divided into two parts: remoteness and measure.

Remoteness of damage

The rule in *Hadley* v *Baxendale* (1845) states that damages will only be awarded in respect of losses which arise naturally, or which both parties may reasonably be supposed to have contemplated when the contract was made, as a probable result of its breach. The effect of the first part of the rule in *Hadley* v *Baxendale* is that the party in breach is deemed to expect the normal consequences of the breach, whether they actually expected them or not. Under the second part of the rule, however, the party in breach can only be held liable for abnormal consequences where they have actual knowledge that the abnormal consequences might follow (*Victoria Laundry Ltd* v *Newham Industries Ltd* (1949)).

Measure of damages

Damages in contract are intended to compensate an injured party for any financial loss sustained as a consequence of another party's breach. The object is not to punish the party in breach, so the amount of damages awarded can never be greater than the actual loss suffered. The aim is to put the injured party in the same position they would have been in had the contract been properly performed. In order to achieve this end the claimant is placed under a duty to mitigate losses. This means that the injured party has to take all reasonable steps to minimise their loss (*Payzu* v *Saunders* (1919)). Although such a duty did not appear to apply in relation to anticipatory breach as decided in *White and Carter (Councils)* v *McGregor* (1961) (above).

Applying these rules to the fact situation in the problem it is evident that as Arti has effected an anticipatory breach of his contract with Bee Ltd he will be liable to them for damages suffered as a consequence, if indeed they suffer damage as aresult of his breach. As Bee Ltd will be under a duty to mitigate their losses, they will have to commit their best endeavours to find someone else to produce the required text on time. If they can do so at no further cost then they would suffer no loss, but any additional costs in producing the text will have to be borne by Arti. However, if Bee Ltd is unable to produce the required text on time the situation becomes more complicated.

(i) As regards the profits from the contract to supply the accountancy body with all its text, the issue would be as to whetherthis was normal profit or amounted to an unexpected gain, as it was not part of Bee Ltd's normal market when thecontract was signed. If *Victoria Laundry Ltd* v *Newham Industries Ltd* were to be applied it is unlikely that Bee Ltd wouldbe able to claim that loss of profit from Arti. However, it is equally plausible that the contract was an ordinary commercialone and that Arti would have to recompense Bee Ltd for any losses suffered from its failure to complete contractualperformance.

(ii) As for the extensive preliminary expenses Arti would certainly be liable for them, as long as they were in the ordinary course of Bee Ltd's business and were not excessive (*Anglia Television* v *Reed* (1972)).

Examiner's Report

This question required candidates to analyse a problem scenario from the perspective of contract law and apply the appropriate legal rules, specifically relating to anticipatory breach of contract and the remedies subsequent to any such action.

On the whole the question was dealt with fairly well, with the majority of candidates recognising that the issue involved anticipatory breach and providing appropriate case authority to support their analysis. A number, however, spent a largely wasted time considering the distinction between conditions and warranties and citing the cases in that area. This would appear to be the follow on from question 3, which raised the issue of terms. A smaller group suggested that there was no real problem in any case as Arti might still produce the material, so they didn't write anything about the law relating to the problem scenario.

The remedies issue was done less well, with the majority failing to pursue it with the necessary detail and a surprising minority suggesting that specific performance could be awarded.

ACCA marking scheme	
	Marks
Clear analysis of the problem scenario – recognition of the contract law issues raised and a convincing application of the legal principles to the facts. Appropriate case authorities are likely to be cited.	8–10
Sound analysis of the problem – recognition of the major principles involved and a fair attempt at applying them. Perhaps sound in knowledge but lacking in analysis and application.	6–7
Unbalanced answer perhaps showing some appropriate knowledge but weak in analysis or application.	3–5
Very weak answer showing little analysis, appropriate knowledge or application.	0–2

26   ADAM

Key answer tips

This scenario question requires candidates to explain the law relating to the part payment problem and candidates should use cases such as Pinnels Case (1602) and Foakes v Beer (1884) in their answer to explain the conclusion that they have reached.

English law does not enforce gratuitous promises unless they are made by deed. Consideration has to be provided as the price of a promise. This is equally the case where a party promises to give up some existing rights that he has. Thus, at common law, if A owes B £10, but B agrees to accept £5 in full settlement of the debt, B's promise to give up existing rights must be supported by consideration on the part of A. This principle, that a payment of a lesser sum cannot be any satisfaction for the whole, was originally stated in *Pinnel's case* (1602), and reaffirmed in *Foakes v Beer* (1884). In the latter case Mrs Beer had obtained a judgement in debt against Dr Foakes for £2,091. She had agreed in writing to accept payment of this amount in instalments, but when payment was finished she claimed a further £360 as interest due on the judgement debt. It was held that Beer was entitled to the interest as her promise to accept the bare debt was not supported by any consideration from Foakes.

This principle has been reconfirmed in the more recent case of *Re Selectmove Ltd* (1994). In this case, the company owed the Inland Revenue outstanding taxes. After some negotiation, the company agreed to pay off the debt by instalments. The company started paying but, before completion, it received a demand from the Revenue that the total be paid off immediately. The company relied on the authority of *Williams v Roffey Bros* (1990), which had established that the performance of an existing duty could, under particular circumstances, amount to valid consideration for a new promise. On that basis it was argued that its payment of the tax debt was sufficient consideration for the promise of the Revenue to accept it in instalments. The Court of Appeal held, however, that situations relating to the payment of debt were distinguishable from those relating to the supply of goods and services, and that in the case of the former the court was bound to follow the clear authority of the House of Lords in *Foakes v Beer*.

However, the equitable doctrine of promissory estoppel sometimes can be relied on to prevent promissors from going back on their promises. The doctrine first appeared in *Hughes* v *Metropolitan Railway Co* (1877) and was revived by Lord Denning, albeit obiter dictum, in the *High Trees* case *(Central London Property Trust Ltd* v *High Trees House Ltd* (1947))*.

Estoppel arises from a promise made by a party to an existing contractual agreement. The promise must have been made with the intention that it be acted upon and must actually have been acted on *(W.J. Alan & Co* v *El Nasr Export & Import Co* (1972)).

It only varies rights or discharges rights within a contract. It does not apply to the formation of a contract, and therefore it does not avoid the need for consideration to establish a contract in the first instance *(Combe* v *Combe* (1951)).

It normally only suspends rights, so it is possible for the promisor, with reasonable notice, to retract the promise and revert to the original terms of the contract *(Tool Metal Manufacturing Co* v *Tungsten Electric Co* (1955)). Rights may be extinguished, however, in the case of a non-continuing obligation, or where the parties cannot resume their original positions *(D & C Builders* v *Rees* (1966)).

It is also essential that the promise relied upon must be given voluntarily. As an equitable remedy, the benefit of promissory estoppel will not be extended to those who have behaved in an inequitable manner *(D & C Builders* v *Rees* (1966)).

Applying the foregoing to the facts of the problem leads to the following results:

(1) Dawn's case would appear to be an example of promissory estoppel. The only real question is whether Adam could retract his promise and recover the full amount owing to him. On the basis of *Tool Metal Manufacturing Co* v *Tungsten Electric Co* and *D & C Builders* v *Rees*, it would appear that he could.

(2) Eric acted unilaterally and did nothing additional to compensate Adam for his part payment. Consequently Eric is covered by the general rule in *Pinnel's* case and remains liable to pay Adam the remaining half of his bill *(D & C Builders* v *Rees* and *Re Selectmove* Ltd).

27 THE CROMWELL ARMS

Key answer tips

This scenario question deals with the issue of professional negligence in the law of tort. Candidates should explain the causal link which must be established and use case law to support their answer.

Charles should pursue an action in tort against the accountant for negligence.

For an action for negligence to succeed the claimant must show:

- That a duty of care was owed to him in law

- That such a duty has been breached – i.e. negligence

- That damage has been suffered, and

- That such damage was principally caused by the defendant's negligence.

Hedley Byrne & Co v *Heller & Partners Ltd.* (1963) established that as professional people owe a duty of care to those whom they should reasonably recognize will rely on their professional opinion, a negligent mis-statement will in such circumstances be actionable. An action will succeed for negligent misstatement not only where a contractual relationship exists, but also when the professional person should reasonably foresee that another party will act on the basis of his professional statement.

JEB Fasteners Ltd v Marks, Bloom & Co. (1983)] demonstrated that the claimant must rely on the defendant's professional advice which must be the principal cause of his decision. In this case a company's auditors valued the company's stock negligently. The company was subsequently acquired. However, the reason for taking over the company was to secure the services of two directors and therefore the claimant could not show reliance on the negligent valuation.

It must be reasonable in the circumstances for the claimant to rely on the defendant's advice. Whether this is so will be determined from the facts of the case, taking account of the relevant expertise and bargaining positions of the parties.

The case of *Caparo Industries pic v Dickman [1990]* shows that the defendant must be in a position to foresee that the claimant will rely on his advice. It was held that company auditors do not owe a duty of care to individual members of a company as prospective purchasers of shares. Lord Oliver said that:

- the purpose of the advice must be made known to the person giving the advice, either specifically or by implication,

- the adviser must be aware that the advice will be acted upon,

- the adviser must know that the advice will be communicated to the claimant, and

- the advice must be acted upon to the detriment of the claimant.

The facts of this situation suggest that an action for negligence will succeed.

The accountant appears to have given advice in a professional capacity. One can expect him to be reasonably competent in his profession. He owes a duty of care to Charles.

There appears to have been negligence. Negligence is a matter of fact and the court will determine from the facts whether or not there has been negligence.

The accountant should have foreseen that Charles would rely on his advice and it was reasonable for Charles to do so. Although the accountant has disclaimed responsibility this cannot remove the existence of a duty *(Smith v Eric Bush,* where a negligently given survey opinion was subject to a disclaimer which was defeated). The Unfair Contract Terms Act 1977 subjects exclusion of liability clauses in a contract to a reasonableness test.

Charles must show that the damage he has suffered has resulted from the negligence and that he has not made decisions on the basis of other principal factors.

The damage must not be too remote, it must be a direct consequence and reasonably foreseeable. It should not be difficult to demonstrate that the economic loss – excessive purchase consideration on the acquisition of the inn – was foreseeable.

Liability will only be reduced if contributory negligence on Charles's part can be demonstrated. This appears unlikely.

Following the decision in *Smith v Eric Bush,* it would seem that the defendant will be liable for the losses which Charles has suffered.

28   BILD LTD

Key answer tips

This is a scenario question relating to breach of contract and remedies available for such a breach with two contracts in this scenario. Candidates should ensure they deal with each scenario in turn and make it clear which scenario they are dealing with.

As the scenario states, Astride entered into contracts with Bild Ltd and Chris, so there is no need to deal with the issue relating to the formation of contract, the problem clearly relates to breach of contract and the remedies available for such breach.

In relation to the first contract with Bild Ltd, the wall was not built to the agreed height and in relation to the second contract Chris has refused to carry out his contractual agreement.

Remedies for breach of contract

By implication of the common law, any breach of contract gives rise to the requirement that the contract-breaker should pay monetary compensation to the other party for the loss sustained in consequence of the breach. Such monetary compensation for breach of contract is damages. The estimation of what damages are to be paid by a party in breach of contract can be divided into two parts: remoteness and measure.

Remoteness of damage involves a consideration of causation, and the remoteness of cause from effect, but is not a relevant issue in either of these instances. What is at the heart of the matter is the *measure of damages*, which relates to the actual amount of loss sustained by the injured party. Damages in contract are intended to compensate the injured party for any financial loss sustained as a consequence of another party's breach. As the object is to compensate rather than to punish, the amount of damages awarded can never be greater than the actual loss suffered. The aim is to put the injured party in the same position they would have been in had the contract been properly performed.

Particular difficulties arise in relation to estimating the damages liable in construction contracts. Where builders either have not carried out work required, or have carried it out inadequately, they will be in breach of contract and liable for damages. The usual measure of such damages is the cost of carrying out the work or repairing the faulty work. However, this may not be the case where the costs of remedying the defects are disproportionate to the difference in value between what was supplied and what was ordered. Thus in *Ruxley Electronics and Construction Ltd v Forsyth* (1995) the parties had entered into a contract for the construction of a swimming pool. Although the contract stated that the pool was to be 7ft 6in deep at one end, the actual depth of the pool was only 6ft 9in. The total contract price was £70,000. Fixing the error would have required a full reconstruction and would have cost around £20,000. The House of Lords considered that, as the costs of reinstatement would have been out of all proportion to the benefit gained, the difference in value only should be awarded.

In certain circumstances, rather than merely award damages, the court can make an order for *specific performance* to require the party in breach to complete their part of the contract. However, an order for specific performance is not available in respect of contracts of employment or personal service (*Ryan v Mutual Tontine Westminster Chambers Association* (1893)).

It remains to apply the foregoing general statements of law to the facts of the problem as follows:

(a)   An order of specific performance will only be granted in cases where the common law remedy of damages is inadequate and it will not be granted where the court cannot supervise its enforcement as in cases of contracts of employment or personal service (*Ryan* v *Mutual Tontine Westminster Chambers Association* (1893)). It is therefore clear that Astride will not be able to force Bild Ltd to carry out the remedial work, and that her only remedy will be in relation to damages. As regards the extent of those damages it appears that Astride's case is different from *Ruxley Electronics and Construction Ltd* v *Forsyth*, and that, as a consequence, she will be awarded damages to the extent of the cost of raising the wall to the contractual height.

(b)   When as in this situation anticipatory breach takes place, the innocent party can sue for damages immediately on receipt of the notification of the other party's intention to repudiate the contract, without waiting for the actual contractual date of performance as in *Hochster* v *De La Tour* (1853). Alternatively, they can wait until the actual time for performance before taking action. In the latter instance, they are entitled to make preparations for performance, and claim the agreed contract price (*White and Carter (Councils)* v *McGregor* (1961)). It would appear that Chris's action is a clear instance of express anticipatory breach and that Astride has the right either to accept the repudiation immediately or affirm the contract and take action against him at the time for performance (*Vitol SA* v *Norelf Ltd* (1996)). In any event Chris is bound to complete his contractual promise or suffer the consequences of his breach of contract. Although Astride will not be able to get an order for specific performance against Chris, as the contract is one of personal service, she will be entitled to claim damages from Chris to the extent of the difference in his contractual price as against the price that Astride will have to pay someone else to get the work done: i.e. £500.

Examiner's Report

This question required candidates to discuss the various remedies for breach of contract available to Astride. The question divided into two parts, each carrying 5 marks, was fairly straightforward and once again the well prepared candidates scored reasonable marks. Overall, candidates acknowledged that there had been a breach of contract and displayed a good understanding of the various remedies available and the better answers recognised that the estimation of damages in relation to construction contracts was difficult. A sound understanding of relevant case law was displayed with many candidates referring to *Ruxley Electronics and Construction Ltd v Forsyth (1995)* and acknowledging that the cost of remedying defects has to be proportionate to the difference between the services ordered and those supplied.

There were also a range of alternative answers produced. Most noticeably, candidates discussed the difference between warranties and conditions within contracts and the various remedies. These answers were awarded reasonable marks if candidates developed the points considered. Where, blocking out the view of the rubbish tip was at the heart of the contract, candidates concluded that the remedy of specific performance was most appropriate. Whereas, if the blocking out of the rubbish tip was ancillary to the main purpose of the contract, i.e. the building of the wall was the main focus of the contract, then damages were more appropriate. The majority of candidates concluded in part (a) that an order of specific performance was perhaps not viable and opted for damages to compensate Astride.

Answers to part (b) tended to be a repeat of discussions in part (a). Only a small number of candidates acknowledged that there was an anticipatory breach of contract and therefore, Astride would be entitled to damages. The majority of candidates, did however recognise that the contract between Astride and Chris was one for personal service and therefore, Astride would be entitled to claim damages of £500, being the difference in cost between Chris's contract and the cost of an alternative supplier.

ACCA marking scheme	
	Marks
Some but little knowledge of the topic with little appropriate application.	0-2
Lacking in detail in some or all aspects or lacking in application.	3-4
Good treatment of the topic but perhaps not dealing with all the issues raised or lacking in some knowledge or application. Perhaps lacking balance	5-7
Full and thorough explanation of the law relating to remedies for breach of contract, with case authorities or examples. Good and accurate application of the law to the particular issues raised in the problem.	8-10

29 ALI

Key answer tips

This question requires candidates to analyse the problem scenario from the perspective of contract law paying particular regards to the rules relating to: invitation to treat, offers, counter offers, option contracts and the postal rule of acceptance. The scenario involves three distinct cases which should be dealt with applying the appropriate rules of contract law.

In spite of its wording the sign in the window does not constitute a legal offer, it is merely an invitation to treat. As such it is not an offer to sell but merely an invitation to others to make offers. The point of this is that the person extending the invitation is not bound to accept any offers made to them as may be seen in *Fisher* v *Bell* (1961) in which it was held that having switch-blade knives in the window of a shop was not the same as offering them for sale.

A counter-offer arises where the offeree tries to change the terms of an original offer. The counter-offer has the same effect as an express rejection of an offer (*Hyde* v *Wrench* (1840)) and as a result the offeree cannot subsequently accept the original offer.

Where acceptance is made through the postal service, it is complete as soon as the letter, properly addressed and stamped, is posted. The contract is concluded even if the letter subsequently fails to reach the offeror (*Adams v Linsell (1818)*)

A contract may be entered into through the exchange of executory consideration; i.e. a promise for a promise. Although the actual exchange of concrete consideration may not take place until a later time, the agreement is none the less binding from the time of the exchange of promises.

Ali and Ben

As stated above, the sign in the window was merely an invitation to treat and the postal rule only applies to offers and does not apply to invitations to treat. Consequently as Ben was in fact making an offer to Ali when he sent his letter, it was for Ali to accept or reject the offer on receipt of the letter, providing he had not already bound himself to any alternative contractual agreement.

Ali and Chet

The first real offer is made by Chet when he says that he would give Ali £400 for the vase. Ali responded by making a counteroffer to sell the vase for £450 to which Chet restated his original offer, this time in the form of a counter-offer to Ali's new offer. As a result Chet, by insisting on his offer of £400, cannot at a later time attempt to accept Ali's offer of £450.

At first look it might appear that Chet may have taken advantage of the postal rule; however, when it is realised that it was not open to him to make any acceptance as he had rejected Ali's offer, it is apparent that the postal rule is of no avail to Chet, so he has no contract with Ali. Once again Ali might have accepted the offer on receipt of the letter, providing he had not already bound himself to any alternative contractual agreement.

Ali and Di

In line with the preceding analysis Di made an offer to Ali, which he readily accepted. The parties entered into a binding contract by their mutual exchange of promises: Di to bring the £400 on the following Monday and Ali to give her the vase. As a result although Ali might prefer to accept Ben's offer, he is nonetheless contractually bound to deliver the vase to Di if and when she brings the agreed sum of £400 to him on Monday. Of course if Di does not provide the money by the agreed time Ali would be at liberty to sell the vase to either Ben or Chet, as he chose.

> **Examiner's Report**
>
> This question required candidates to analyse a problem scenario from the perspective of the law of contract and to apply that law appropriately. In particular it focuses on the creation of contractual relations and required an explanation of offers, invitations to treat, counter offers. The postal offer was involved not operational.
>
> The question tended to be done reasonably well with most candidates achieving a pass mark on the basis of their recognition of the law involved in the scenario and their application of that law.
>
> However, some of the problems inherent in the old exam structure were carried on in some answers. For example some candidates simply reproduced general contract essays, referring to issues that were not part of the problem scenario. Such irrelevant material gained no credit, indeed it tended to deflect from the candidates performance by indicating that they actually did not recognise what the key issues in the problem were.
>
> As for those who at least tried to focus on the issues, most recognised that the first one related to the difference between offers and invitations to treat. Disappointingly a number who explained the difference then went on to contradict themselves by stating that what they had seen as an invitation to treat could still be accepted through the postal rule. As regards the second element in the question almost all of those candidates who

knew any contract law were able to explain the meaning and effect of a counter-offer. Yet once again, many went on to contradict their explanation in their application. The final element, which involved a straight forward contractual agreement apparently, confused some candidates because it did *not* involve an option contract.

ACCA marking scheme	
	Marks
Little or no knowledge of the law.	0-1
Some, but limited, understanding of company of the law or completely lacking in application.	2-4
A clear understanding of the general law but perhaps lacking in detail or unbalanced only dealing with some issues.	5-7
A thorough analysis of the scenario focusing on the appropriate rules of law and applying them accurately. It is extremely likely that cases will be cited in support of the analysis and/or application.	8-10

30 ALVIN

Key answer tips

This is a very similar scenario to the previous question and is typical of the type of question the examiner frequently sets on the topic of offer and acceptance. Again candidates shoud ensure they split the question up and deal with each case individually and do not attempt to answer the question in one go.

Alvin and Bert

The price notice on the car did not constitute a legal offer, it was merely an invitation to treat. As such it is not an offer to sell but merely an invitation to others to make offers. The point of this is that the person extending the invitation is not bound to accept any offers made to them as may be seen in *Fisher v Bell* (1961) in which it was held that having switch-blade knives in the window of a shop was not the same as offering them for sale. Consequently Bert is not in a position to sue Alvin.

Alvin and Cat

An offeror may withdraw their offer at any time before it has been accepted and once revoked it is no longer open to the offeree to accept the original offer. Also a promise to keep an offer open is only binding where there is a separate contract to that effect. This is known as an option contract, and the offeree must provide additional consideration for the promise to keep the offer open. If not, then the offeror can simply withdraw the offer under the normal rules relating to revocation of offers.

As Cat did not provide any consideration to form an option contract, Alvin is not bound to wait for her to return and can sell the car to anyone else if he so chooses.

Alvin and Del

This is a perfectly ordinary contract. The fact that Alvin had previously contracted not to sell it, does not affect Del and he is entitled to take good title to the car.

Examiner's Report

Answers broke the question down into a statement of relevant law and then applying that law to the three customers – Bert, Cat and Del. Credit was given for a brief statement of the key essentials for a valid contract, and then the distinction between an offer and an invitation to treat. The vast majority of students rightly identified that Alvin's notice was in fact an invitation to treat, correctly citing or describing the case of *Fisher v Bell*. However, in applying the law to the scenario, many candidates jumped straight into dealing with each customer as though Alvin's notice was an offer and therefore Alvin was the offeror. Some of these students then went on to reach the correct conclusions – that Bert and Cat had no right to sue Alvin as no contract had been made.

Generally speaking, marks were gained by dealing with Bert since that is when candidates went into detail about Alvin's offer being an invitation to treat, to which Bert responded by making an offer, which Alvin was at liberty to accept or reject. Some students became confused at this stage by saying that Alvin could revoke his offer of £5,000 as long as it was before Bert's acceptance; whereas some candidates kept on track by treating the notice as an invitation to treat which was not capable of acceptance. Therefore Alvin was free to change the price on the notice.

Cat's scenario was more problematic for candidates. Many candidates did not specifically identify the issue concerning the option contract, which would have obliged Alvin to honour any promise he makes to keep the offer open if Cat had paid some consideration for him to do so. The reason for this is that a promise to keep an offer open is only binding where there is a separate contract to this effect. However many candidates did cover the issue of Cat's failure to give consideration so credit was given accordingly. Most students also correctly identified that Alvin did not, in any case, expressly accept Cat's offer. Some candidates raised the issue ofcounter-offer, but the question was not inviting a discussion of counter-offer.

Del's scenario was a simple case of legally enforceable contract being entered into, with Del being the offeror and Alvin being the offeree. For some reason, many candidates just simply restated the facts given in the question rather than actually concluding that a contract had been reached because the essentials for a contract were all present.

ACCA Marking Scheme	
	Marks
Very weak answers which might recognise what the question is about but show no ability to analyse or answer the problem as set out.	0-2
Recognition of the areas covered by the question, but lacking in detail.	3-4
Good analysis and case support, although perhaps limited in appreciation.	5-7
A thorough treatment of all of the rules relating to the formation of contracts together with a clear and correct application of those rules to the problem scenario. Cases will be expected to be provided at this level.	8-10

31   SELLER LTD

Key answer tips

This scenario question deals with validity of exclusion clauses. Candidates must make reference to the common law rules and the statutory rules in order to come to a concusion as to whether the exclusion clause in this scenario is valid or not. It should be noted that the Unfair Terms in Consumer Contracts Regulations 1999 is not applicable here as the statute only applies to a business and consumer relationship.

There are three ways in which exclusion clauses can be incorporated into contracts: by signature, by notice and by a course of dealing.

The terms may be incorporated into the contract by the signature of the other party on a document bearing the terms. The signatory is taken to know of the terms, even if he could not read them (*L'Estrange v Graucob (1934))*.

With regard to incorporation by notice, it must be shown that the person seeking to rely on the exclusion clause has taken reasonable steps to bring the existence of the clause to the attention of the other party at the time the contract was made. Thus in *Olley v Marlborough Court (1949)* a sign on a hotel room wall was not incorporated into the contract between hotel and client since it was not seen until after the contract was made.

The court will have regard to the nature of the liability which is being excluded when deciding whether a clause has been effectively incorporated. If the terms are particularly unusual or wide, a more prominent notice may be necessary.

Where the parties deal frequently in transactions of a similar nature and on the same terms, the courts are ready to hold that the exclusion clause has been incorporated into the last agreement by virtue of its being present in the previous dealing, even if the claimant never read it (*Spurling v Bradshaw (1996))*. The position is not as a straightforward where the previous dealings have not been on a consistent basis (*Hollier v Rambler Motors (1972))*.

In the case if Seller and Transport, the court will consider each of these tests. There is no evidence that Transport's exclusion clause has been incorporated by signature. With regard to incorporation by notice, it seems that visitors to Transport's premises will be made aware of the clause by virtue if the 'notice prominently displayed', however, as the order was places by telephone, it is unlikely that Transport can use this in its defence. Equally, the notice provided with the confirmation of order is provided too late to be incorporated into the contract, as the contract has already been concluded by this stage. Following *Olley v Marlborough Court*, this precludes incorporation of the clause by notice to other party.

The court will also consider the fact that there have been previous dealings between the parties and will need to determine whether unspecified dealings over 'a number of years' are enough to constitute a regular consistent course of dealing. In *Hollier v Rambler Motors* a course of dealing which amounted to 3 or 4 transactions over 5 years was held not to be sufficient. On the facts given it is not possible to conclude on this point.

Statute also imposes some very important restrictions on the use of exclusion clauses. The Unfair Contract Terms Act 1977, which applies to clauses covering business liability, divides these clauses into two types; those which are void (any clause exempting liability for death or personal injury) and those which are valid only as far as they are reasonable (any other loss).

The burden of proving reasonableness is on the party seeking to rely on the clause, in this case Transport Ltd. In assessing whether a term is unfair or unreasonable, the court will have regard to:

- the strength of the bargaining positions of the parties

- whether the buyer received an inducement to agree to the term

- whether the buyer knew or ought to have known of the existence and extent of the term

- the ability of the party to insure against the liability.

EMPLOYMENT LAW

32 EMPLOYMENT CONTRACTS

Key answer tips

This is a fairly straightforward question dealing with the distinction between a contract for service and a contract of service in part (a) and a discussion of the factors a court would take into account when deciding if someone is employed or self-employed. It is important in part (a) to explain also why the distinction is important but candidates should be careful not to repeat this is in their answer to part (b).

(a)   Employees are people working under a contract of service. Those who work under a contract for services are independent contractors. They are not employees, but are self-employed. If you have a problem with your motor car you may take it to a large garage and have one of its mechanics look at the car. That mechanic would be an employee of the garage and would work under a contract of service with his employers. Your contract would not be with the mechanic but with his employer, the garage. Alternatively you might take the car to a one man garage and get that person to look at the car. In that situation the mechanic is self-employed and you and he are entering into a contract for services.

It is essential to distinguish the two categories clearly, because important legal consequences follow from the placing of a person in one or other of the categories. For example, although employees are protected by various common law and statutory rights in relation to their employment, no such wide scale protection is offered to the self-employed. Also ultimate liability for breach of contract or liability in tort depends on the person's status as an employee or self-employed. In the example above in the first instance the mechanic's employers, the garage, are responsible for the consequence of his actions whilst acting in their employment; whereas in the second case, the mechanic alone is responsible for any liabilities that arise from his work. Given the importance of the distinction and the allocation of essential statutory rights that follow from it, it is perhaps somewhat surprising that no clear statutory definition of the distinction has been provided. Section 230 of the Employment Rights Act 1996, for example defines an employee as 'an individual who has entered into or works under a contract of employment' and states that a contract of employment 'means a contract of service'.

(b)   Such circularity and lack of clarity means that it has been left to the courts to develop tests for distinguishing the employee from the self-employed.

The first test to be applied by the courts was known as the control test. In using this test the key element is the degree of control exercised by one party over the other. The question to be determined is the degree to which the person who is using the other's services actually controls, not only what they do, but how they do it. An example of the use of the test can be seen in *Walker* v *Crystal Palace Football Club* (1910) in which it was held that a professional football player was an employee of his club, on the ground that he was subject to control in relation to his training, discipline and method of payment. Thus to revert to the example given in part (a) the first mechanic, the employee, can be told what to do and how to do it, whereas the second, the self-employed mechanic, takes all such decisions as those in his own right.

The control test looks back to and reflects previous master/servant relationships of employment, but its main shortcoming lay in its lack of any degree of subtlety. Highly skilled professionals, such as surgeons, by necessity have a high level of control over how they perform their day-to-day work, but the consequence of that, at least under the control test, was that they were deemed to be self-employed rather than employees, and patients who had suffered as a consequence of negligence would only be able to sue the doctor rather than the Health Authority which used their services. Such weakness in the control test led to the courts developing a more subtle test.

The integration test shifted the emphasis from the degree of control exercised of an individual to the extent to which the individual was integrated into the business of their putative employer. An example of the application of the integration test may be seen in *Whittaker* v *Minister of Pensions & National Insurance* (1967) in which the court found that the degree to which a circus trapeze artist was required to do other general tasks in relation to the operation of the circus in which she appeared, indicated that she was an employee rather than self-employed. As a consequence she was entitled to claim compensation for injuries sustained in the course of her employment. However, even the integration test was not without problems, as some employers attempted to give the impression of using a self-employed workforce whilst effectively still controlling what that workforce did.

The response on the parts of the courts was the development of the multiple, or economic reality, test. Rather than relying on one single factor, this test uses a more general assessment of the circumstances of any particular case in order to decide whether, or not, someone is an employee. In so deciding the courts will not be bound by how the parties themselves describe the relationship. Thus it is immaterial that the agreement between the parties states that someone is to be self-employed; if the indications are otherwise then the person will be recognised, and treated, as an employee (*Market Investigations* v *Minister of Social Security* (1969)).

The economic reality test was first established in *Ready Mixed Concrete (South East) Ltd* v *Minister of Pensions and National Insurance* (1968) in which it was held that there were three conditions supporting the existence of a contract of employment:

(i)   the employee agrees to provide his own work and skill in return for a wage,

(ii)   the employee agrees, either expressly or impliedly, that he will be subject to a degree of control, exercisable by the employer,

(iii)   the other provisions of the contract are consistent with its being a contract of employment.

In deciding whether or not there is a contract of employment the courts tend to focus on such issues as whether wages are paid regularly or by way of a single lump sum; whether the person receives holiday pay; and on who pays the due national insurance and income tax. However, there can be no definitive list of tests as the whole point of the multiple test is that it examines all aspects of the situation in order to reach a determination. For example in *Nethermore (St Neots)* v *Gardiner & Taverna* (1984), a group of home workers, i.e. people who carried out paid work in their own homes, were held to be employees on the grounds that they were subject to an irreducible minimum obligation to work for their employer.

Examiner's Report

This question asked candidates to explain the common law rules used to distinguish contracts of service from contracts for services and why it is important to distinguish between them. Part (a) relating to the distinction carried 4 marks and part (b) relating to the tests carried 6 marks.

This was clearly a topic that many candidates had prepared for well. On the whole this question was well done and in some instances done very well indeed, with the well prepared candidates provided good case authority to support their explanations. Of those who did not do well in their answers, the major shortcoming was a tendency to focus just on one of the test and not to consider the others.

ACCA marking scheme	
	Marks
Little or no analysis or knowledge of the subject in question	0-1
Recognition of the areas covered by the question, but lacking in detailed analysis.	2-4
Good analysis and case support, although perhaps limited in appreciation	5-7
A thorough treatment of all of the rules, perhaps placing them in their historical context but certainly providing case support and providing a good application of the law to the scenario	8-10

33   DISMISSAL

Key answer tips

This is a fairly straightforward question requiring candidates to explain constructive dismissal in part (a) and the remedies available for unfair dismissal in part (b). Candidates should ensure they deal with each part of the requirement in equal depth to achieve a well balanced answer.

(a)   Normally employees who resign deprive themselves of the right to make a claim for redundancy or other payments. However s.136 Employment Rights Act 1996 (ERA) covers situations where 'the employee terminates the contract with, or without, notice in circumstances which are such that he or she is entitled to terminate it without notice by reason of the employer's conduct'. This provision relates to what is known as 'constructive dismissal' which covers the situation where an employer has made the situation of the employee such that the employee has no other option than to resign. In other words the unreasonable actions of the employer force the employee to resign. In such a situation the employee is entitled to make a claim for unfair dismissal no matter the fact that they actually resigned. In *Simmonds* v *Dowty Seals Ltd* (1978) Simmonds had been employed to work on the night shift. When his employer attempted to force him to work on the day shift he resigned. It was held that he could treat himself as constructively dismissed because the employer's conduct had amounted to an attempt to unilaterally change an express term of his contract. An employee may also be able to claim constructive dismissal where the employer is in breach of an implied term in the contract of employment (*Gardner Ltd* v *Beresford* (1978)). In *Woods* v *WM Car Services (Peterborough)* (1982) it was further held that there is a general implied contractual duty that employers will not, without reasonable or proper cause, conduct themselves in a manner that is likely to destroy the relationship of trust and confidence between employer and employee and that such obligation is independent of and in addition to the express terms of the contract.

The action of the employer, however, must go to the root of the employment contract if it is to allow the employee to resign. In other words it must be a breach of some significance. In *Western Excavating Ltd* v *Sharp* (1978), Sharp was dismissed for taking time off from work without permission. On appeal to an internal disciplinary hearing, he was reinstated but was suspended for five days without pay. He agreed to accept this decision but asked his employer for an advance on his holiday pay as he was short of money: this was refused. He then asked for a loan of £40: that was also refused. Consequently Sharp decided to resign in order to get access to his holiday pay. Sharp instituted a claim for unfair dismissal on the basis that he had been forced to resign because of his employer's unreasonable conduct. The employment tribunal found in Sharp's favour on the grounds that his employer's conduct had been so unreasonable that Sharp could not be expected to continue working there. However, on appeal the Court of Appeal held that before a valid constructive dismissal can take place the employer's conduct must amount to a breach of contract, which is such that it entitles the employee to resign. In Sharp's case there was no such breach and therefore there was no constructive dismissal. However, in *British Aircraft Corporation* v *Austin* (1978) a failure to investigate a health and safety complaint was held to be conduct amounting to a breach of contract on the part of the employer which was sufficient to entitle the employee to treat the contract as terminated.

If the employee does not resign in the event of a breach by the employer the employee will be deemed to have accepted the breach and waived any rights. However, they do not need to resign immediately and may, legitimately, wait until they have found another job (*Cox Toner (International) Ltd* v *Crook* (1981)).

(b) In relation to a successful claim for unfair dismissal, an Employment Tribunal may award any one of the following remedies:

(i) reinstatement,

(ii) re-engagement or

(iii) compensation.

Reinstatement is where the dismissed employee is treated as not having been dismissed in the first place.

Re-engagement means that the dismissed employee is re-employed under a new contract of employment.

The calculation of a *basic* award of compensation is calculated in the same way as for redundancy payments and is subject to the same maximum level of payment. The actual figures are calculated on the basis of the person's age, length of continuous service and weekly rate of pay subject to statutory maxima. Thus employees between the ages of 18 and 21 are entitled to 1/2 week's pay for each year of service, those between 22 and 40 are entitled to 1 week's pay for every year of service, and those over 41 are entitled to 1 1/2 weeks' pay for every year of service. The maximum number of years of service that can be claimed is 20 and as the maximum level of pay that can be claimed is £350, the maximum total that can be claimed is £10,500 (i.e. $1.5 \times 20 \times 350$).

In addition, however, a *compensatory* award of up to £66,200 may be made at the discretion of the tribunal and an *additional* award may be made where the employer ignores an order for re-employment or re-engagement, or the reason for dismissal was unlawful discrimination.

34 GROUNDS FOR DISMISSAL *Walk in the footsteps of a top tutor*

Key answer tips

This question requires candidates to explain the grounds on which dismissal is fair in part (a) and the grounds on which dismissal is automatically unfair in part (b). Candidates should have good knowledge of the Employment Rights Act 1996 to answer this question and should refer to the relevant sections in their answer. The highlighted words are key phrases that markers are looking for.

(a)   The grounds on which dismissal may be fair are set out in s.98 Employment Rights Act (ERA) 1996. The Act places the burden of proof on the employer to show that the grounds for dismissal are fair. There are five categories as follows:

    (i)   **Lack of capability or qualifications**

        The employee does not have the capability or qualifications necessary to do the job. Capability is defined in s.98 in terms of 'skill, aptitude, health or any other physical or mental quality', and qualifications relate to 'any degree, diploma, or other academic, technical or professional qualification relevant to the position which the employee held.' However, even in this situation, the employer must show that not only was the employee incompetent, but that it was reasonable to dismiss them.

    (ii)   **Misconduct**

        The employee is guilty of misconduct. To warrant instant dismissal, the employee's conduct must be more than merely trivial and must be of sufficient seriousness to merit the description 'gross misconduct'. Examples of such conduct might involve assault, drunkenness, dishonesty or a failure to follow instructions or safety procedures, or persistent lateness.

(iii) Redundancy

This is, *prima facie*, a fair reason for dismissal as long as the employer has acted reasonably in introducing the redundancy programme.

(iv) In situations where continued employment would constitute a breach of a statutory provision

If the continued employment of the person dismissed would be a breach of some statutory provision then the dismissal of the employee is again, *prima facie*, fair. For example, if a person is employed as a driver and is banned from driving then they may be fairly dismissed.

(v) Some other substantial reason

The above particular situations are not conclusive and are supported by a general provision that allows the employer to dismiss the employee for 'some other substantial reason'. Consequently, it is not possible to provide an exhaustive list of all grounds for 'fair dismissal'. Examples that have been held to be substantial reasons have included: conflicts of personalities, failure to disclose material facts, refusal to accept necessary changes in terms of employment, and legitimate commercial reasons.

It has to be emphasised that the above reasons are not sufficient in themselves to justify dismissal and, under all instances, the employer must act as would be expected of a 'reasonable employer'. In determining whether the employer has acted reasonably, the Employment Tribunal will consider whether, in the circumstances 'including the size and administrative resources of the employer's undertaking, the employer acted reasonably or unreasonably in treating the reason given as sufficient reason for dismissing the employee' (s.98(4) ERA 1996). In this case the burden of proof is neutral.

Reasonable employers should follow the **ACAS 'Code of Practice on Disciplinary Practice and Procedures in Employment'** in relation to the way they discipline and dismiss their employees. Thus it would usually be inappropriate to dismiss someone for lack of capability without providing him with the opportunity to improve his skills. Nor would redundancy, *per se*, provide a justification for fair dismissal, unless the employer had introduced and operated a proper redundancy scheme, which included (preferably) objective criteria for deciding who should be made redundant, and provided for the consideration of redeployment rather than redundancy.

(b) The following are situations where dismissal is automatically unfair:

(i) Dismissal for trade union reasons

This applies where an employee has been dismissed for actual, or proposed, membership of a trade union, or is dismissed for taking part in trade union activities. It applies equally where an individual has refused to join a trade union.

Dismissal of individuals involved in a strike, lock out, or other industrial action is not unfair as long as all of those engaged in the action are dismissed. The employer cannot select which individuals to dismiss from the general body of strikers.

(ii) **Dismissal on grounds of pregnancy or childbirth**

Section 99 ERA 1996 provides that dismissal is automatically unfair where the principal reason for the dismissal is related to the employee's pregnancy or other reasons connected to her pregnancy; or following her maternity leave period, for childbirth or any reason connected with childbirth.

(iii) **Dismissal in relation to health and safety issues**

Section 100 ERA 1996 provides that employees have a right not to be dismissed for carrying out any health and safety-related activities for which they have been appointed by their employer; or for bringing to the employer's attention any reasonable concern related to health and safety matters. Nor can they be dismissed for leaving their place of work in the face of a reasonably-held belief that they faced serious danger.

(iv) **Dismissal for making a protected disclosure**

This is covered by s.103A ERA and protects 'whistle-blowing' employees who have reported their employer for engaging in certain reprehensible activity. Such protected activity is set out in s.43 ERA and covers criminal activity, breach of legal obligations, breach of health and safety provisions, and activity damaging to the environment.

(v) **Dismissal for asserting a statutory right**

Section 104 ERA provides that a dismissal is automatically unfair where the principal reason for it is victimisation of the employee for having taken action against the employer to enforce his or her statutory rights. Rights under the Working Time Regulations 1998 and the National Minimum Wage Act 1998 are specifically covered in ss.101(A) and 104(A) ERA.

35 REDUNDANCY

Key answer tips

This is a straightforward question on the rules relating to redundancy. A good answer will explain the circumstances in which an employee will be considered to have been made redundant and then move on to discuss how redundancy pay will be calculated.

Redundancy is defined in s.139(1) of the Employment Rights Act (ERA) 1996 as being: 'dismissal attributable wholly or mainly to:

(a) the fact that his employer has ceased, or intends to cease, to carry on the business for the purposes of which the employee was employed by him, or has ceased, or intends to cease to carry on that business in the place where the employee was so employed, or

(b) the fact that the requirements of that business for employees to carry out work of a particular kind, or for employees to carry out work of a particular kind in the place where they were so employed, have ceased or diminished or are expected to cease or diminish.'

In order to qualify for redundancy payments an employee must have been continuously employed by the same employer or associated company for a period of two years. At the outset of redundancy proceedings the onus is placed on the employee to show that they have been dismissed which they do by demonstrating that they are covered by s.136 of ERA 1996, which provides four types of dismissal. These are:

(i)   the contract of employment is terminated by the employer with or without notice;

(ii)   a fixed-term contract has expired and has not been renewed;

(iii)   the employee terminates the contract with or without notice in circumstances which are such that he or she is entitled to terminate it without notice by reason of the employer's conduct;

(iii)   the contract is terminated by the death of the employer, or the dissolution or liquidation of the firm.

Once dismissal has been established a presumption in favour of redundancy operates and the onus shifts to the employer to show that redundancy was not the reason for the dismissal. Employees who have been dismissed by way of redundancy are entitled to claim a redundancy payment from their former employer. Under the ERA 1996 the actual figures are calculated on the basis of the person's age, length of continuous service andweekly rate of pay subject to statutory maxima. Thus employees between the ages of 18 and 21 are entitled to $1/2$ weeks pay foreach year of service, those between 22 and 40 are entitled to 1 weeks pay for every year of service, and those over 41 are entitled to $1\frac{1}{2}$ weeks pay for every year of service. The maximum number of years service that can be claimed is 20 and as the maximum level of pay that can be claimed is £350, the maximum total that can be claimed is £10,500 (i.e. 1.5 x 20 x 350). Disputes in relation to redundancy claims are heard before an Employment Tribunal and on appeal go to the Employment Appeal Tribunal. The employer must act as would be expected of a 'reasonable employer' and in determining whether the employer has acted reasonably, the Employment Tribunal will consider whether, in the circumstances 'including the size and administrativeresources of the employer's undertaking, the employer acted reasonably or unreasonably in treating the reason given as sufficient reason for dismissing the employee.' (s.98(4) ERA 1996). Reasonable employers should follow the ACAS 'Code of Practice on Disciplinary Practice and Procedures in Employment' in relation to the way they discipline and dismiss their employees. Thus redundancy, *per se*, does not provide a justification for dismissal, unless the employer had introduced and operated a proper redundancy scheme, which included preferably objective criteria for deciding who should be made redundant, and provided forthe consideration of redeployment rather than redundancy.

Examiner's Report

This question required candidates to explain the meaning of the term redundancy and the legal rules relating to it.

The question enabled candidates who knew the law on redundancy to perform well since there are marks available for a large number of legal points/range of relevant legal information e.g. the definition of redundancy; the meaning of 'dismissal'; qualification; the effect of offers of alternative employment and trial periods; remedies and so on. Candidates who could clearly and accurately state these points with reference to some case-law examples scored well.

Candidates also were able to score by referring to the collective provisions on trade union consultation and particularly if they were able to identify the relationship of the individual redundancy payment with individual claims for unfair dismissal arising out of unfair selection.

Many candidates were able to accurately state the basic rules and some to describe the relationship with other rules such as dismissal and trade union consultation.

However, there were common basic errors in that candidates were unable to correctly state e.g. the length of the qualifying periods or time limits for claims. Others seemed unable to comprehend the distinction between a claim for a redundancy payment and other claims (e.g. common law for wrongful dismissal) or statutory (notice entitlement and unfair dismissal).

Thus some scripts made no distinction between the statutory rules on notice and those or redundancy. A significant number seemed to have no awareness that unfair dismissal and redundancy provide separate remedies e.g. some stated that an employee would only be redundant if the selection was unfair, or that an employee would be redundant if they e.g. lacked qualification or competence for the job. The remedy, it seems to some, for redundancy is re-instatement, re-engagement or an award of £60,000. Others thought that the employee could claim 'damages' for loss or earnings. In other cases redundancy was described as a wrongful dismissal.

ACCA marking scheme	
	Marks
Thorough to complete answers, showing a detailed understanding of the concept of redundancy, the rules for calculating payment and probably making reference to the legislation.	8–10
A clear understanding of the topic, but perhaps lacking in detail. Alternatively an unbalanced answer showing good understanding of one part but less in the other.	5–7
Some knowledge, although perhaps not clearly expressed, or very limited in its knowledge and understanding of the topic.	2–4
Little or no knowledge of the topic.	0–1

36 REMEDIES

Key answer tips

This question deals with remedies available to employees on termination of contract. Candidates should ensure they deal with each of the three parts of the requirement in turn and not try to answer all three parts at the same time.

(a) Employees who have been dismissed by way of redundancy are entitled to claim a redundancy payment from their former employer. Under the Employment Rights Act (ERA) 1996 the actual figures are calculated on the basis of the person's age, length of continuous service and weekly rate of pay subject to statutory maxima. Thus employees between the ages of 18 and 21 are entitled to $\frac{1}{2}$ week's pay for each year of service, those between 22 and 40 are entitled to 1 week's pay for every year of service, and those over 41 are entitled to $1\frac{1}{2}$ weeks' pay for every year of service.

The maximum number of years service that can be claimed is 20 and as the maximum level of pay that can be claimed is £350, the maximum total that can be claimed is £10,500, (i.e. $1.5 \times 20 \times 350$).

(b) In relation to a successful claim for unfair dismissal, the Employment Tribunal may award any one of the following remedies:

(i) reinstatement;

(ii) re-engagement; or

(iii) compensation.

Reinstatement is where the dismissed employee is treated as not having been dismissed in the first place. Re-engagement means that the dismissed employee is re-employed under a new contract of employment.

The calculation of a *basic* award of compensation is calculated in the same way as for redundancy payments and is subject to the same maximum level of payment. In addition, however, a *compensatory* award of up to £66,200 may be made at the discretion of the tribunal and an *additional* award may be made where the employer ignores an order for re-employment or re-engagement, or the reason for dismissal was unlawful discrimination.

(c) Generally the only effective remedy for the common law action of wrongful dismissal is the award of damages representing the loss of earnings sustained by the dismissed employee. The employee will nonetheless be expected to mitigate their loss by accepting suitable alternative employment. It is possible, in very limited circumstances, for the dismissed employee to seek an injunction to prevent the dismissal (see *Ridge* v *Baldwin* (1964) and *Irani* v *South West Hampshire Health Authority* (1985)).

37 FINE LTD

Key answer tips

This is a scenario question based on constructive dismissal. Part (a) requires a discussion of how Gus's resignation constitutes constructive dismissal and in part (b) candidates should explain that to be successful for a claim in unfair dismissal Gus must show that he was dismissed which will be the case if he can prove constructive dismissal.

(a) **Constructive dismissal**

Normally, employees who resign deprive themselves of the right to make a claim for unfair dismissal or other payments such as redundancy. Section 95 Employment Rights Act 1996 covers situations where 'the employee terminates the contract with, or without notice in circumstances which are such that he or she is entitled to terminate it without notice by reason of the employer's conduct'. This provision relates to what is known as 'constructive dismissal' which covers the situation where an employer has made the situation of the employee such that the employee has no other option than to resign. In other words the actions of the employer force the employee to resign. The rule is that there must be a fundamental breach of contract by the employer. In such a situation the employee is entitled to make a claim for unfair dismissal even if they actually resigned. In *Simmonds v Dowty Seals Ltd* (1978) Simmonds had been employed to work on the night shift. When his employer attempted to force him to work on the day shift he resigned. It was held that he could treat himself as constructively dismissed because the employer's conduct had amounted to an attempt to unilaterally change an express term of his contract.

An employee may also be able to claim constructive dismissal where the employer is in breach of an implied term in the contract of employment (*Gardner Ltd v Beresford* (1978)). And in *Woods v WM Car Services (Peterborough)* (1982) it was further held that there is a general implied contractual duty that employers will not, without reasonable or proper cause, conduct themselves in a manner that is likely to destroy the relationship of trust and confidence between employer and employee and that such obligation is independent of, and in addition to, the express terms of the contract (see also *Malik v BCCI* (1997)).

The action of the employer, however, must go to the root of the employment contract if it is to allow the employee to resign. In other words it must be a breach of some significance. In *Western Excavating Ltd v Sharp* (1978), Sharp was dismissed for taking time off from work without permission. On appeal to an internal disciplinary hearing, he was reinstated but was suspended for five days without pay. He agreed to accept this decision but asked his employer for an advance on his holiday pay as he was short of money: this was refused. He then asked for a loan of £40: that was also refused. Consequently Sharp decided to resign in order to get access to his holiday pay. Sharp instituted a claim for unfair dismissal on the basis that he had been forced to resign because of his employer's unreasonable conduct. The employment tribunal found in Sharp's favour on the grounds that his employer's conduct had been so unreasonable that Sharp could not be expected to continue working there. However, on appeal the Court of Appeal held that before a valid constructive dismissal can take place the employer's conduct must amount to a breach of contract which is such that it entitles the employee to resign. In Sharp's case there was no such breach and therefore there was no constructive dismissal. However, in *British Aircraft Corporation v Austin* (1978) a failure to investigate a health and safety complaint was held to be conduct amounting to a breach of contract on the part of the employer which was sufficient to entitle the employee to treat the contract as terminated.

If the employee does not resign in the event of a breach by the employer the employee will be deemed to have accepted the breach and waived any rights. However, they do not need to resign immediately and may, legitimately, wait until they have found another job (*Cox Toner (International) Ltd v Crook* (1981)).

Finally, the movement of an employer to some new distant location will normally give rise to redundancy claims for those employees who do not wish to move (*O'Brien v Associated Fire Alarms Ltd* (1969)). However, the compulsory move of employees such as is this scenario may well give rise to a claim for unfair dismissal and the employee may be able to resign and claim constructive dismissal. Such a claim could not arise where the employee's contract contained an express mobility clause.

(b) **Unfair dismissal**

Under the Employment Rights Act 1996 employees have a right not to be unfairly dismissed and it would appear that Gus would have an action for unfair dismissal.

All that the employee has to show is that they were dismissed, as Gus can demonstrate on the basis of constructive dismissal, and then the onus is placed on the employer to show it was <u>not</u> 'unfair'. In relation to unfair dismissal, a dismissal will not be regarded as unfair if the reason for the dismissal is one of those regarded as statutorily acceptable and the employer acted reasonably in dismissing the employee for that reason. Under ss.98(1) and 98(2) of the Employment Rights Act

1996 there are five reasons set out on which an employer may rely as justifying a fair dismissal. These are dismissals for:

(i)   Lack of capability or qualifications

(ii)   Misconduct

(iii) Redundancy

(iv)   Where continued employment would be a breach of a statutory provision

(v)   Some other substantial reason of a kind which justifies dismissal.

As well as the employee having to prove the fact of dismissal, as defined above, and the employer having to establish that the reason for the dismissal fell within one of the statutorily acceptable categories, the employment tribunal will still have to adjudicate on the fairness of the employer dismissing the employee for the reason given.

In order to take such an action the employee must have been employed for at least one year, which requirement Gus meets. He has a strict time limit of three months after the effective date of termination within which to bring the complaint before the Employment Tribunal.

Under the circumstances there is clearly no grounds for Fine Ltd to dismiss Gus and it would appear that he has good grounds for an action for unfair dismissal.

38   UNFAIR DISMISSAL

Key answer tips

This is a fairly straightforward question on unfair dismissal.   Part (a) requires an explanationof the grounds upon which a dismissal may be fair, and therefore candidates need to state the statutory fair reasons. Part (b) requires an explanation of constructive dismissal and candidates should refer to relevant case law when answering this part.

(a)   This question requires candidates to explain the provisions of the Employment Rights Act (ERA) 1996 relating to the statutory grounds covering fair dismissal. The grounds on which dismissal is capable of being fair are set out in s.98 ERA 1996. The Act places the burden of proof on the employer to show that the grounds for dismissal are fair. There are five categories as follows:

(i)   **Lack of capability or qualifications**

Capability is defined in s.98 in terms of 'skill aptitude, health or any other physical or mental quality', and qualifications relate to 'any degree, diploma, or other academic, technical or professional qualification relevant to the position which the employee held'. However, even in this situation, the employer must show that not only was the employee incompetent but that it was reasonable to dismiss them.

(ii)   **Misconduct**

To warrant instant dismissal the employee's conduct must be more than merely trivial and must be of sufficient seriousness to merit the description 'gross misconduct'. Examples of such conduct might involve assault, drunkenness, dishonesty or a failure to follow instructions, or safety procedures, or persistent lateness.

(iii) **Redundancy**

This is, *prima facie*, a fair reason for dismissal as long as the employer has acted reasonably in introducing the redundancy programme.

(iv) **In situations where continued employment would constitute a breach of a statutory provision**

If the continued employment of the person dismissed would be a breach of some statutory provision then the dismissal of the employee is again, *prima face*, fair. For example, if a person is employed as a driver and is banned from driving then they may be fairly dismissed.

(v) **Some other substantial reason**

The above particular situations are not conclusive and are supported by this general provision which allows the employee to dismiss the employee for 'some other substantial reason'. As a consequence, it is not possible to provide an exhaustive list of all grounds for 'fair dismissal'. Examples that have been held to be substantial reasons have included: conflicts of personalities, failure to disclose material facts, refusal to accept necessary changes in terms of employment, and legitimate commercial reasons.

It has to be emphasised that the above reasons are not sufficient in themselves to justify dismissal and under all instances the employer must act as would be expected of a 'reasonable employer'. In determining whether the employer has acted reasonably, the Employment Tribunal will consider whether, in the circumstances 'including the size and administrative resources of the employer's undertaking, the employer acted reasonably or unreasonably in treating the reason given as sufficient reason for dismissing the employee' (s.98(4) ERA 1996). In this case the burden of proof is neutral.

Reasonable employers should follow the ACAS 'Code of Practice on Disciplinary Practice and Procedures in Employment' in relation to the way they discipline and dismiss their employees. Thus it would usually be inappropriate to dismiss someone for lack of capability without providing them with the opportunity to improve their skills. Nor would redundancy, per se, provide a justification for fair dismissal, unless the employer had introduced and operated a proper redundancy scheme, which included preferably objective criteria for deciding who should be made redundant, and provided for the consideration of redeployment rather than redundancy.

(b) Normally employees who resign deprive themselves of the right to make a claim for redundancy or other payments. However, s.136 ERA covers situations where 'the employee terminates the contract with, or without, notice in circumstances which are such that he or she is entitled to terminate it without notice by reason of the employer's conduct'. This provision relates to what is known as 'constructive dismissal', which covers the situation where an employer has made the situation of the employee such that the employee has no other action than to resign. In other words the unreasonable actions of the employer force the employee to resign. In such a situation the employee is entitled to make a claim for unfair dismissal, no matter the fact that they actually resigned. In *Simmonds v Dowty Seals Ltd* (1978) Simmonds had been employed to work on the night shift. When his employer attempted to force him to work on the day shift he resigned. It was held that he could treat himself as constructively dismissed because the employer's conduct had amounted to an attempt to unilaterally change an express term of his contract. An employee may also be able to claim constructive dismissal where the employer is in breach of an implied term in the contract of employment (*Gardner Ltd v Beresford* (1978)). In *Woods v WM Car Services (Peterborough)* (1982) it was further held that there is a general implied contractual duty that employers will not, without reasonable or proper cause, conduct themselves in a manner that is likely to destroy the relationship of trust and confidence between employer and employee, and that such an obligation is independent of and in addition to the express terms of the contract.

The action of the employer, however, must go to the root of the employment contract if it is to allow the employee to resign. In other words it must be a breach of some significance. In Western Excavating Ltd v Sharp (1978), Sharp was dismissed for taking time off from work without permission. On appeal to an internal disciplinary hearing, he was reinstated but was suspended for five days without pay. He agreed to accept this decision but asked his employer for an advance on his holiday pay as he was short of money: this was refused. He then asked for a loan of £40: that was also refused. Consequently Sharp decided to resign in order to get access to his holiday pay. Sharp instituted a claim for unfair dismissal on the basis that he had been forced to resign because of his employers' unreasonable conduct. The employment tribunal found in Sharp's favour on the grounds that his employer's conduct had been so unreasonable that Sharp could not be expected to continue working there. However, on appeal the Court of Appeal held that before a valid constructive dismissal can take place the employer's conduct must amount to a breach of contract which is such that it entitles the employee to resign. In Sharp's case there was no such breach and therefore there was no constructive dismissal. However, in *British Aircraft Corporation v Austin* (1978) a failure to investigate a health and safety complaint was held to be conduct amounting to a breach of contract on the part of the employer, which was sufficient to entitle the employee to treat the contract as terminated.

If the employee does not resign in the event of a breach by the employer, the employee will be deemed to have accepted the breach and waived any rights. However, the employee need not resign immediately and may, legitimately, wait until they have found another job (*Cox Toner (International) Ltd v Crook* (1981)).

Examiner's Report

This question was on of the few, it has to be said, where candidates performed most satisfactorily. Sound answers to 7(a) precisely identified the statutory grounds covering fair dismissal under Employment Rights Act 1996, viz. capability or qualification, misconduct, redundancy, breach of statutory provision and other substantial reasons. The very best also referred to dismissal upon retirement. All too frequently, however, candidates listed a range of possible fair dismissal scenarios without tying them into the statutory headings, e.g. theft, fraud, violence, making secret profits, failing professional qualifications absenteeism and a range of other possibilities. Many of these overlapped and could have been cited as instances of one of the general headings. Marks awarded depended on the comprehensive nature of these instances, but a number merely cited examples of misconduct and consequently did not gain the level of marks available.

The answers to part (b) were well done. Many candidates were able to adequately define constructive dismissal and to offer one or two case examples.

Simmos v Dowty Seals Ltd (1978) was often referred to. The best answers went on to discuss the contractual basis of constructive dismissal, citing *Western Excavating v Sharp* (1978) and went on to mention possible remedies.

Some answers completely misinterpreted the concept of constructive dismissal, often portraying it as an extra weapon in the employer's armoury in the defence of an unfair dismissal claim. A number of candidates adequately defined constructive dismissal but appeared to believe that it only related to redundancy dismissal.

	ACCA Marking Scheme	Marks
(a)	Some awareness of the area but lacking in detailed knowledge.	0-2
	A good explanation of the grounds upon which dismissal may be fair.	3-5
(b)	Unbalanced, or may not deal with all of the required aspects of the topic. Alternatively the answer will demonstrate very little understanding of what is actually meant by constructive dismissal.	0-2
	Candidates must show an understanding of what is meant by constructive dismissal, perhaps citing cases or examples.	3-5

THE FORMATION AND CONSTITUTION OF BUSINESS ORGANISATIONS

39 AGENT'S AUTHORITY

Key answer tips

This question requires candidates to explain the three forms of how authority of an agent can arise. Candidates should explain the agent/principal relationship as an introduction in their answer.

An agent is a person who is empowered to represent another legal party, called the principal, and to bring the principal into a legal relationship with another party. Any contract entered into and arranged by an agent is between the principal and the other party, each of whom may enforce it. In the normal course of events, the agent has no personal rights or liabilities in relation to the contract.

The principal/agent relationship can be created in a number of ways. It may arise as the outcome of a distinct contract, which may be made either orally or in writing, or it may be established purely gratuitously where some person simply agrees to act for another.

In establishing a relationship of principal/agent, however, the principal does not give the agent unlimited power to enter into any contract whatsoever, but is likely to place strict limits on the nature of the contracts that the agent can enter into on his behalf. In other words, the authority of the agent is limited and, in order to bind a principal, any contract entered into by the agent must be within the limits of the authority extended to the agent. The authority of an agent can take a number of distinct forms.

(a)   **Express authority**

In this instance, when the principal/agency relationship is established, the agent is instructed as to what particular tasks are required to be performed and is informed of the precise powers given in order to fulfil those tasks. If the agent subsequently enters a contract outside his express authority, he will be liable to the principal and to the other party for breach of warrant of authority. The consequences for the relationship between the principal and the other party depend on whether the other party knew that the agent was acting outside the scope of his authority.

For example, an individual director of a company may be given the express power by the board of directors to enter into a specific contract on behalf of the company. In such circumstances the company would be bound by the subsequent contract, but the director would have no power to bind the company in other contracts.

(b)   **Implied authority**

Other parties are entitled to assume that agents holding a particular position have all the powers that are usually provided to such an agent. Without actual knowledge to the contrary, they may safely assume that the agent has the usual authority that goes with their position.

In *Watteau v Fenwick* (1893) the new owners of a hotel continued to employ the previous owner as its manager. They expressly forbade him to buy certain articles including cigars. The manager, however, bought cigars from a third party who later sued the owners for payment as the manager's principal. It was held that the purchase of cigars was within the usual authority of a manager of such an establishment and that for a limitation on such usual authority to be effective it must be communicated to any third party.

Directors of companies can also bind their companies on the basis of implied authority. In *Hely-Hutchinson v Brayhead Ltd* (1968) although the chairman and chief executive of a company acted as its de facto managing director he had never been formally appointed to that position. Nevertheless, he purported to bind the company to a particular transaction. When the other party to the agreement sought to enforce it, the company claimed that the chairman had no authority to bind it. It was held that although the director derived no authority from his position as chairman of the board, he did acquire such authority from his position as chief executive and thus the company was bound by the contract he had entered into on its behalf as it was within the implied authority of a person holding such a position.

(c)   **Ostensible/apparent authority**

Ostensible authority, an aspect of agency by estoppel, can arise in two distinct ways:

(i)   Where one person makes a representation to third parties that another person has the authority to act as his agent, but without actually appointing him as his agent, the person making the representation is bound by the actions of the ostensible/apparent agent. The principal is also liable for the actions of the agent where he is aware that the agent claims to be his agent and yet does nothing to correct that impression.

In *Freeman & Locker v Buckhurst Park Properties (Mangal) Ltd* (1964), although a particular director had never been appointed as managing director, he acted as such with the clear knowledge of the other directors and entered into a contract with the plaintiffs on behalf of the company. When the plaintiffs sought to recover fees due to them under the contract it was held that the company was liable: a properly appointed managing director would have been able to enter into such a contract and the third party was entitled to rely on the representation of the other directors that the person in question had been properly appointed to that position.

(ii) Where a principal has previously represented to a third party that an agent has the authority to act on their behalf. Even if the principal has subsequently revoked the agent's authority he may still be liable for the actions of the former agent unless he has informed third parties who had previously dealt with the agent about the new situation (*Willis Faber & Co Ltd v Joyce* (1911)).

If an agent contracts with a third party on behalf of a principal, the agent implicitly guarantees that the principal exists and has contractual capacity. The agent also implies that he or she has the authority to make contracts on behalf of that principal. If any of these implied warranties prove to be untrue then the third party may sue the agent in quasi-contract for breach of warrant of authority. Such an action may arise even though the agent was genuinely unaware of any lack of authority (*Yonge v Toynbee* (1910)).

40 AGENCY RELATIONSHIP

Key answer tips

This question requires candidates to explain the various ways in which the relationship of principal and agent can be created. No one can act as an agent without the consent of the principal, although consent need not be expressly stated.

The principal/agent relationship can be created in a number of ways.

(a) **Express appointment**

This is the most common manner in which a principal/agent relationship comes into existence. In this situation, the agent is specifically appointed by the principal to carry out a particular task or to undertake some general function. In most situations, the appointment of the agent will itself involve the establishment of a contractual relationship between the principal and the agent, but need not necessarily depend upon a contract between the parties. For the most part, there are no formal requirements for the appointment of an agent, although, where the agent is to be given the power to execute deeds in the principal's name, they must themselves be appointed by way of a deed (that is, they are given power of attorney).

(b) **Ratification**

An agency is created by ratification when a person who has no actual authority purports to contract with a third party on behalf of a principal and the principal subsequently accepts the contract. Where the principal elects to ratify the contract, it gives *retrospective validity* to the action of the purported agent. In order for ratification to be effective, the principal must have been in existence at the time when the agent entered into the contract (*Kelner v Baxter* (1866)) and the principal must have had legal capacity to enter into the contract when it was made. An undisclosed principal cannot ratify a contract, so if the agent appears to be acting their own account, then the principal cannot later adopt the contact (see *Keighley,*

Maxsted and Co v *Durant* (1901)). The principal must adopt the whole of the contract and cannot pick and choose which parts of the contract to adopt. Finally, ratification must take place within a reasonable time.

(c) **Necessity**

Agency by necessity occurs under circumstances where, although there is no agreement between the parties, an emergency requires that an agent take particular action in order to protect the interests of the principal. The usual situation which gives rise to agency by necessity occurs where the agent is in possession of the principal's property and, due to some unforeseen emergency, the agent has to take action to safeguard that property. In order for agency by necessity to arise, there needs to be a genuine emergency *(Great Northern Railway Co* v *Swaffield* (1874)) and there must also be no practical way of obtaining further instructions from the principal *(Springer* v *Great Western Railway Co* (1921). Also, the person seeking to establish the agency by necessity must have acted *bona fide* in the interests of the principal *(Sachs* v *Miklos* (1948)).

(d) **Estoppel**

This form of agency is also known as 'agency by holding out' and arises where the principal has led other parties to believe that a person has the authority to represent him. In such circumstances, even though no principal/agency relationship actually exists in fact, the principal is prevented (estopped) from denying the existence of the agency relationship and is bound by the action of his or her purported agent as regards any third party who acted in the belief of its existence. To rely on agency by estoppel, there must have been a representation by the principal as to the authority of the agent *(Freeman and Lockyer* v *Buckhurst Park Properties Ltd* (1964)) and the party seeking to rely on it must have relied on the representation.

41 TERMINATION OF PARTNERSHIP

Key answer tips

There are a number of possible reasons for bringing a partnership to an end. It may have been established for a particular purpose and that purpose has been achieved, or one of the partners might wish to retire from the business, or the good relationship between the members, which is essential to the operation of a partnership, may have broken down. In all such cases, the existing partnership is dissolved, although in the second case a new partnership may be established to take over the old business. Reference should be made to the Partnership Act 1890 (PA).

Grounds for dissolution

Partnerships are created by agreement and may be brought to an end in the same way. However, subject to any provision to the contrary in the partnership agreement, the Partnership Act 1890 (PA) provides for the dissolution of a partnership on the following grounds:

The expiry of a fixed term or the completion of a specified enterprise (s.32 (a) and (b))

It is possible for a partnership to be established for a stated period of time and at the end of that time the partnership will come to an end and the partnership will be dissolved. Alternatively, it is possible for the partnership to be established in order to achieve a particular goal and again once that goal has been attained the partnership will come to an end. However, it is possible for the partnership to continue beyond this stated period or the goal, provided that the partners agree. If the partnership does continue after the pre-set limit, it is known as a 'partnership at will' and it can be ended at any time thereafter at the wish of any of the partners.

The giving of notice (s.32(c))

If the partnership is of indefinite duration, then it can be brought to an end by any one of the partners giving notice of an intention to dissolve the partnership.

The death or bankruptcy of any partner (s.31 (1))

In English law the ordinary partnership has no legal personality in its own right, but merely exists as the collection of individuals. Consequently, the death of a member will bring about the end of the partnership. (**Note:** This is not the case with limited partnerships formed under the Limited Liability Partnerships Act 2000, which *does* provide legal capacity to such partnerships formed under its provisions). The bankruptcy of a partner has the same effect.

Although the occurrence of either of these events will bring the original partnership to an end, it is usual for partnership agreements to provide for the continuation of the business under the control of the remaining/solvent partners who will constitute a new partnership. The dead partner's interest will be valued and paid to his or her personal representative, and the bankrupt's interest will be paid to his or her trustee in bankruptcy.

Where a partner's share becomes subject to a charge (s.23 (s.33 (2))

Section 23(1) of the PA prevents action against partnership property in relation to any personal debt owed by a partner. However, s.23 (2) allows for the creation of a charge against the partner's interest in the property or profits in relation to any judgment debt. Such a situation may well prove unsatisfactory to the other partners and therefore s.33 (2) allows for the dissolution of the partnership in such circumstances. It should be noted, however, that dissolution in this instance is not automatic; it is merely open to the other partners to dissolve the partnership.

Illegality (s.34)

The occurrence of events making the continuation of the partnership illegal will bring it to an end. One case would be where the continuation of the partnership would result in trading with the enemy (see *R v Kupfer* (1915)). The principle applied equally, however, in a perhaps more relevant case *Hudgell, Yeates and Co v Watson* (1978). Practising solicitors are legally required to have a practice certificate. However, one of the members of a three-person partnership forgot to renew his practice certificate and so was not legally entitled to act as a solicitor. It was held that the failure to renew the practice certificate brought the partnership to an end, although a new partnership continued between the other two members of the old partnership.

By Court Order

In addition to the provisions listed above, the court may, mainly by virtue of s.35 of the PA 1890, order the dissolution of the partnership under the following circumstances:

(i)   Where a partner becomes a patient under the Mental Health Act 1893.

(ii)   Where a partner suffers some other permanent incapacity.

        This provision is analogous to the previous one. It should be noted that it is for the other partners to apply for dissolution and that the incapacity alleged as the basis of dissolution must be permanent.

(iii)   Where a partner engages in activity prejudicial to the business.

Such activity may be directly related to the business, such as the misappropriation of funds. Alternatively, it may take place outside the business but operate to its detriment. An example might be a criminal conviction for fraud.

(iv)   Where a partner persistently breaches the partnership agreement.

This provision also relates to conduct which makes it unreasonable for the other partners to carry on in business with the party at fault.

(v)   Where the business can only be carried on at a loss.

This provision is a corollary of the very first section of the PA 1890 in which the pursuit of profit is part of the definition of the partnership form. If such profit cannot be achieved, then the partners are entitled to avoid loss by bringing the partnership to an end.

(vi)   Where it is just and equitable to do so.

The courts have wide discretion in relation to the implementation of this power. A similar provision operates within company legislation (s.122 Insolvency Act 1986) and the two provisions come together in the cases involving quasi-partnerships (*Re Yenidje Tobacco Co Ltd* (1916) and *Ebrahimi v Westbourne Galleries Ltd* (1973)).

42   PARTNERSHIPS AND LIABILITY

Key answer tips

The question asks for an explanation of the **liability** of partners under each Act. The model answer below is more comprehensive than would be required in the exam to attain full marks, especially in answer to part (c), but is given for completeness.

(a)   **Partnership Act 1890**

Section 1 of the Partnership Act 1890, which governs ordinary partnerships, states that partnership is the relationship which subsists between persons carrying on a business in common with a view to profit. Ordinary partnerships do not benefit from any limitation on the liability of the various partners. Consequently the individual members of a partnership are **jointly and severally liable** for the debts of the partnership to the full extent of their personal wealth. This applies equally to 'sleeping' partners who take no active part in the day-to-day operation of the partnership business. Outsiders have the choice of taking action against the firm collectively or against the individual partners. Where damages are recovered from one partner only, the other partners are under a duty to contribute equally to the amount paid.

(b)   **Limited Partnership Act 1907**

The Limited Partnership Act 1907 allows for the formation of **limited partnerships**. For members of a partnership to gain the benefit of limited liability under this legislation, the following rules apply:

•   limited partners are not liable for partnership debts beyond the extent of their capital contribution, but in the ordinary course of events they are not permitted to remove their capital

- at least one of the partners must retain full, that is, unlimited, liability for the debts of the partnership

- a partner with limited liability is not permitted to take part in the management of the business enterprise and cannot usually bind the partnership in any transaction. If a partner acts in contravention of this rule they will lose the right to limited liability

- the partnership must be registered with the Companies Registry.

(c) **Limited Liability Partnerships Act 2000**

The main shortcoming with regard to the standard partnership is the lack of limited liability for its members. The Limited Liability Partnerships Act 2000 provides for a new form of business entity, the **limited liability partnership** (LLP). Although stated to be a partnership, the new form is a corporation, with a distinct legal existence apart from its members. As such it will have the ability:

- to hold property in its own right

- to sue and be sued in its own name.

It will have perpetual succession and consequently alterations in its membership will not have any effect on its existence. Most importantly however, the new legal entity will allow its members to benefit from **limited liability** in that they will not be liable for more than the amount they have agreed to contribute to its capital.

The Limited Liability Partnership Regulations 2001 extend the provisions relating to the insolvency and winding up of registered companies to LLPs. Thus the relevant sections of the Companies Act 2006, the Insolvency Act 1986, the Company Directors Disqualification Act 1986 and the Financial Services and Markets Act 2000 have been appropriately modified to apply to LLPs.

To form a Limited Liability Partnership:

- two or more persons must subscribe to an incorporation document

- the incorporation document must be delivered to the companies' registry

- a statement of compliance must be completed by a solicitor or subscriber to the incorporation document.

The **incorporation document** must include:

- the name of the LLP (subject to restrictions)

- the address of the registered office

- the names and addresses of those who will be members on incorporation of the LLP

- the names of at least two designated members, whose duty it is to ensure that the administrative and filing duties of the LLP are complied with. If no such members are designated then all members will be assumed to be designated members.

43 DOCTRINE OF SEPARATE PERSONALITY

Key answer tips

This question requires candidates in part (a) to consider the doctrine of separate personality, which is one of the key concepts of company law. In part (b) candidates must also consider occasions where the doctrine will be ignored and the veil of incorporation will be pulled aside. The latter part should require consideration of both statute and common law provisions.

(a)   **Separate personality**

Whereas English law treats a partnership as simply a group of individuals trading collectively, the effect of incorporation is that a company once formed has its own distinct legal personality, completely separate from its members.

The doctrine of separate or corporate personality is an ancient one, but the case usually cited in relation to separate personality is: *Salomon* v *Salomon & Co* (1897). Salomon had been in the boot and leather business for some time. Together with other members of his family he formed a limited company and sold his previous business to it. Payment was in the form of cash, shares and debentures. When the company was eventually wound up it was argued that Salomon and the company were the same, and, as he could not be his own creditor, his debentures should have no effect. Although earlier courts had decided against Salomon, the House of Lords held that under the circumstances, in the absence of fraud, his debentures were valid. The company had been properly constituted and consequently it was, in law, a distinct legal person, completely separate from Salomon. Prior to the Companies Act 2006 (CA 2006) true single person limited companies, with only one member, could be formed but these were exceptional and in the event of the membership of an ordinary company falling below one, the remaining member assumed liability for the debts of the company. Now under s.123 CA 2006, if the number of members of a limited company falls to one, all that is required is that the fact be entered in the company's register of members, with the name and address of the sole member.

A number of consequences flow from the fact that corporations are treated as having legal personality in their own right.

Limited liability

No one is responsible for anyone else's debts unless they agree to accept such responsibility. Similarly, at common law, members of a corporation are not responsible for its debts without agreement. However, registered companies, i.e. those formed under the Companies Acts, are not permitted unless the shareholders agree to accept liability for their company's debts. In return for this agreement the extent of their liability is set at a fixed amount. In the case of a company limited by shares the level of liability is the amount remaining unpaid on the nominal value of the shares held. In the case of a company limited by guarantee it is the amount that shareholders have agreed to pay in the event of the company being wound up.

Perpetual existence

As the corporation exists in its own right changes in its membership have no effect on its status or existence. Members may die, be declared bankrupt or insane, or transfer their shares without any effect on the company. As an abstract legal person the company cannot die, although its existence can be brought to an end through the winding up procedure.

Business property is owned by the company

Any business assets are owned by the company itself and not the shareholders. This is normally a major advantage in that the company's assets are not subject to claims based on the ownership rights of its members. It can, however, cause unforeseen problems as may be seen in *Macaura* v *Northern Assurance* (1925). The plaintiff had owned a timber estate and later formed a one-man company and transferred the estate to it. He continued to insure the estate in his own name. When the timber was lost in a fire it was held that Macaura could not claim on the insurance as he had no personal interest in the timber, which belonged to the company.

Legal capacity

The company has contractual capacity in its own right and can sue and be sued in its own name. The extent of the company's liability, as opposed to the members, is unlimited and all its assets may be used to pay off debts. The company may also be liable in tort for any injuries sustained as a consequence of the negligence of its agents or employees.

The rule in Foss v *Harbottle*

This states that where a company suffers an injury, it is for the company, acting through the majority of the members, to take the appropriate remedial action. Perhaps of more importance is the corollary of the rule which is that an individual cannot raise an action in response to a wrong suffered by the company.

(b) **Lifting the veil of incorporation**

There are a number of occasions, both statutory and at common law, when the doctrine of separate personality will not be followed. On these occasions it is said that the veil of incorporation, which separates the company from its members, is pierced, lifted or drawn aside. Such situations arise as follows:

Under the companies legislation

Section 399 of the Companies Act 2006 requires accounts to be prepared by a group of related companies, thus recognising the common link between them as separate corporate entities. Section 213 of the Insolvency Act 1986 provides for personal liability in relation to fraudulent trading and s.214 does the same in relation to wrongful trading.

At common law

As in most areas of law that are based on the application of policy decisions it is difficult to predict when the courts will ignore separate personality. What is certain is that the courts will not permit the corporate form to be used for a clearly fraudulent purpose or to evade a legal duty. Thus in *Gilford Motor Co Ltd* v *Horne* (1933) an employee had covenanted not to solicit his former employer's customers. After he left their employment he formed a company to solicit those customers and it was held that the company was a sham and the court would not permit it to be used to avoid the contract.

As would be expected the courts are prepared to ignore separate personality in times of war to defeat the activity of shareholders who might be enemy aliens. See *Daimler Co Ltd* v *Continental Tyre and Rubber Co (GB) Ltd* (1917).

Where groups of companies have been set up for particular business ends the courts will usually not ignore the separate existence of the various companies unless they are being used for fraud. There is authority for treating separate companies as a single group as in *DHN Food Distributors Ltd* v *Borough of Tower Hamlets* (1976) but later authorities have cast extreme doubt on this decision. See *Woolfson* v *Strathclyde RC* (1978) and *National Dock Labour Board* v *Pinn & Wheeler* (1989). The later cases would appear to suggest that the courts are becoming more reluctant to ignore separate personality where the company has been properly established (*Adams* v *Cape Industries plc* (1990) and *Ord* v *Belhaven Pubs Ltd* (1998)).

Examiner's Report

The question required an analysis of one of the main concepts of company law, the doctrine of separate personality. There was a 60/40 split on the 10 mark total available and this indicated the weight that should have been given to each section. As a whole candidates performed well on this question. However, once again it has to be stated that a significant number of candidates did not even attempt this question on one of the most fundamental principles of company law. As with question 2 a failure to do this question or a failure to answer adequately was an indication that such candidates were not sufficiently prepared to take the exam.

Part (a) required an explanation of the doctrine and its consequences and the majority of candidates were able to demonstrate understanding by reference to the seminal case of *Saloman v Saloman & Co (1897)*. Others illustrated this distinction further using *Macaura v Northern Assurance Co Ltd (1925) and Lee v Lee's Air Farming Ltd (1961)*. The consequences of this separation of the company and its members included limited liability whereby the members are limited only to the nominal amount of their shares, perpetual existence of the company separate from its members, ownership of property by the company in its own right and the capacity to contract and sue in its own name. Most candidates were able to explain these or other examples to gain a reasonable amount of marks.

Having discussed the veil that separates the members from the company part (b) required an analysis of the circumstances under which the veil will be lifted to make the members liable. This falls into statutory and common law situations with most students recognising this distinction. Under statute *S399* of the Companies Act 2006 requires groups of related companies to recognise the link between them when preparing accounts, whilst *s213 & 214* of the *Insolvency Act 1986* impose liability where there is evidence of either fraudulent or wrongful trading. These were the common examples given but others used were given credit. From a common law position, examples such as *Gilford Motor Co Ltd v Horne (1933)* to illustrate the evasion of a legal duty, Daimler *Co Ltd v Continental Tyre & Rubber Co (GB) Ltd (1917)* possible trading with enemy aliens at time of war and an examination of the courts treatment of groups of companies as a single entity where they are considered to be trying to evade a liability, reference was made here to cases such as *DHN Food Distributors Ltd v Borough of Tower Hamlets (1976)* and the later case *of Adams v Cape industries plc (1990)*. Again candidates were able to relate these or other circumstances to gain reasonable marks.

ACCA Marking Scheme		Marks
(a)	Very little or no understanding whatsoever.	0-1
	Some but limited knowledge of the topic. Perhaps uncertain as to meaning or lacking in detailed explanation or authority.	2-4
	A thorough to complete answer explaining the meaning and effect of separate personality. It is likely that cases will be cited as authority although examples will be acceptable as an alternative.	5-6
(b)	No understanding whatsoever.	0
	Some understanding perhaps lacking in explanation or examples of when the doctrine will be ignored.	1-2
	A thorough to full explanation detailing the situations under which separate personality will be ignored.	3-4

44 TYPES OF COMPANY

Key answer tips

This question requires candidates to consider three alternative categories of company: the first unlimited in nature, whilst the second and third are limited in different ways. In this context, liability refers to the extent to which shareholders in companies are responsible for the debts of their companies and limited liability indicates that a limit has been placed on such liability. The key point is that the limitation on liability is enjoyed by the member shareholders rather than the company.

As will be considered further below, one of the major advantages of forming a company is limited liability. Companies can, however, be formed without limited liability. Such companies are incorporated under the Companies Acts and receive all the benefits that flow from incorporation except limited liability. Consequently the shareholders in such unlimited companies remain liable to the full extent of their personal wealth for any unpaid debt of the company. It should be noted that, in line with the doctrine of separate personality, even in the case of unlimited companies any subsequent debt is owed to the company and not directly to the creditors of the company. The compensating benefit enjoyed by such companies is that they do not have to submit their accounts and make them available for public inspection. Such advantage in terms of confidentiality as this once represented has been undermined by the fact that both small and medium sized private companies are now permitted to submit abbreviated annual accounts to the registrar.

The great majority of companies, however, are limited liability companies. This means that the maximum liability of shareholders is fixed and cannot be increased without their agreement. There are two ways of establishing limited liability. One such is the company limited by guarantee. This type of limited liability is usually restricted to non-trading enterprises such as charities and professional and educational bodies. It limits the shareholders' liability to an agreed amount which is only called on if the company cannot pay its debts on being wound up. In reality, the sum guaranteed is usually a nominal sum, so no real risk is involved on the part of the guarantor.

The more common procedure is to limit liability by reference to shares. The effect of this is to limit liability to the amount remaining unpaid on shares held. If the shareholder has paid the full nominal value of the shares to the company, then that is the end of responsibility with regard to company debts. Consequently, if the company should subsequently go into insolvent liquidation the shareholders cannot be required to contribute to its assets in order to pay off its outstanding debts.

45   INCORPORATION AS A PRIVATE COMPANY *Walk in the footsteps of a top tutor*

Key answer tips

This question requires you to explain briefly the likely advantages and disadvantages of incorporating a business as a private company. Consider also incorporation as a public limited company and non-incorporation as alternatives. The highlighted words are key phrases that markers are looking for.

In a legal sense there are a number of different forms of business organisation. Two of the most common, particularly in the case of small businesses, are where a businessman or businesswoman operates as a sole trader and where the business consists of a partnership. Both of these forms of organisation are appropriate to an enterprise which is small and wishes to remain that way, or to an enterprise which may grow into something more substantial. If the enterprise is successful, the point will often come where those who own the business will wish to consider whether there is some advantage in converting it into a private company.

The process by which a company is created is known as incorporation, and this process carries with it both advantages and disadvantages, and also involves a number of procedural steps. However, the key feature of incorporation of a business as a company is that, once incorporated, the company becomes a legal entity quite separate from that of those who have formed, or own, the company. This separate and distinct legal personality was clearly established in the well known case of *Salomon v Salomon & Co Ltd* (1897) and has been recognised in many subsequent decisions: see, for example, *Lee v Lee's Air Farming* (1960). The separate legal identity of a company is fundamental to much of modern company law.

This question does not require a discussion of the process by which a private company is formed, but the actual process of formation is a relatively straightforward one (as compared with, for example, incorporation of a business as a public company). Thus, there is no minimum level of share capital needed to either register the company or to begin trading and, following the Companies (Single Member Private Limited Companies) Regulations 1992 it is now possible to incorporate and operate private limited companies with a single member.

There are a number of significant advantages for a businessman or businesswoman in trading as a private limited company.

(i)   **Limited liability**

Once a company has been incorporated as a limited company, its members enjoy limited liability. Liability is limited to any amount which is unpaid on shares, unlike in the case of a sole trader or member of a partnership, where liability is unlimited. In practice of course, the protection of limited liability may be more apparent than real in that financial institutions which lend money to private companies will usually require personal guarantees as security from the principal shareholder.

(ii)   **Perpetual succession**

Once a company is formed it will continue in being until it is wound up. Unlike in the case, for example, of a sole trader or a partnership, the death of a shareholder does not mean that the business comes to an end, and this is so irrespective of the number or proportion of shares held by the shareholder. One of the advantages of this is that the directors of the company will continue to run the business and the contracts of employment of the company's workforce continue.

(iii)   **Flexibility in raising capital**

One of the consequences of limited liability is that potential investors in a company can invest knowing that they will carry no liability for the unpaid debts of the company. Of particular significance is the fact that a company can raise capital by means of a floating charge; this is a useful possibility which allows the company to deal with the assets of the company over which the charge floats until such time as it crystallises. Neither sole traders nor partnerships can use floating charges as a way of raising money.

(iv)   **Advantages over incorporation as a public company**

Private companies involve a number of advantages over public companies. These include the fact that the directors of a private company have more freedom in their dealings with the company than in the case of a public company; depending on its size it may be excluded from some of the publication requirements on accounts and some of the requirements relating to company meetings do not apply to private companies if they take advantage of the written resolution and elective resolution procedures.

There are, however, a number of disadvantages of incorporating a business as a private company. Depending on its size, one of the most significant may be that it cannot raise capital through the public issue of shares and this may be a significant problem if the company is at a state in its growth where it needs large amounts of further capital to finance further expansion. Other disadvantages of incorporation as a private company are:

Legal formalities   The process of incorporation and the subsequent operation of the company both attract considerably more regulation than a sole trader or partnership, and also incur compliance costs;.

Loss of privacy   Private companies are required to file accounts annually with the Registrar of Companies which are open to public scrutiny, whereas the affairs of unincorporated businesses and partnerships may remain private;

Capital must be maintained   Strict rules regulate the withdrawal of capital or profits from the company by the shareholders, unlike the case for sole traders and partnerships.

Winding up of the company   Unlike in the case of sole traders and partnerships, if a company ceases trading it needs to be formally wound up.

46 PLC DOCUMENTS

Key answer tips

This question specifically refers to the registration of public limited companies and therefore reference must be made to the requirement for such companies to acquire a s.761 certificate before they can commence trading.

Incorporation under the Companies Act 2006 requires companies to register certain documents with the Registrar of Companies and pay the registration fee. The necessary documents are as follows:

Memorandum of Association

This document must be signed by all the subscribers. It states that one or more persons wish to form a company, that they agree to become members of that company and to take at least one share in the company each.

Application

The application form must include the proposed name of the company; whether, and if so how, the liability of the members is to be limited; a statement as to whether the company is private or public; the details and address of the registered office.

Articles of Association

The articles of association, form part of the company's internal constitution, along with other agreements or special resolutions (s.17).

They set out the manner in which the company is to be governed and regulate the relationship between the company and its shareholders.

If no articles are submitted, the company will be governed by the model articles prescribed by the Secretary of State.

Statement of capital and initial shareholdings

This must state the number of shares, their aggregate nominal value and how much has been paid up on each share.

Statement of proposed officers

This gives details of the first directors and company secretary and their consent to act.

Statement of compliance

This provides confirmation that the provisions of Companies Act 2006 have been complied with.

Trading certificate

A private company can commence trading immediately. However, a public limited company cannot commence trading until the registrar has issued a trading certificate (s.761 CA 2006). To obtain a trading certificate, there must be at least £50,000 of allotted share capital with at least one quarter of the nominal value and all of the premium being paid up.

It is a criminal offence for a plc to carry on a business without a certificate. If it does so, the company and any officers are liable to a fine.

47 PROMOTER AND PRE-INCORPORATION CONTRACT

Key answer tips

This question requires candidates to explain in part (a) who is a promoter and in part (b) what is a pre-incorporation contract. It is important in their answer to part (a) that candidates explain that promoters have a 'fiduciary relationship' with the company that they are a promoter for.

(a)   There is no general statutory definition of a promoter in company law and as yet the courts have not given a comprehensive judicial definition. In *Twycross v Grant* (1877) Cockburn C J defined a promoter as '... one who undertakes to form a company with reference to a given project and to set it going, and who takes the necessary steps to accomplish that purpose'. In *Whaley Bridge Calico Printing Co v Green* (1880) Bowen L described the term promoter as 'a term not in law but of business, usefully summing up in a single word a number of business operations, familiar to the commercial world, by which a company is generally brought into existence'. The consequence of the above two statements is that the answer to the question of whether a person is a promoter or not is a question of fact and the determining factor is whether the individual in question will be a person who exercises some control over the affairs of the company both before and after it is formed up until the process of formation is completed. The following are typical acts which promoters perform:

(i)   taking the procedural steps necessary to form a company;

(ii)   inviting other persons to become directors; and

(iii)   issuing a prospectus.

Persons are not to be treated as a promoter of a company simply on the basis that they act in a professional capacity with respect to the establishment of a company. Thus, solicitors and accountants employed purely in their professional capacity in order to establish a company will not be considered to be promoters.

As with directors, promoters are said to be in a 'fiduciary relationship' with the company they are establishing. This is a position similar to that of a trustee and the most important consequence that flows from it is that the promoter is not entitled to make a profit from establishing the company, without full disclosure of that profit to either an independent board of directors, or to the existing and prospective shareholders in the company. Such a situation usually arises in situations where the promoters sell assets to the company they are in the process of forming. Failure to make such a disclosure will enable the company to:

(i)   rescind the contract;

(ii)   claim damages; and

(ii)   hold the promoter liable to account for any profit made (*Erlanger v New Sombrero Phosphate Co* (1878), *Gluckstein v Barnes* (1990); *Re Leeds & Hanley Theatres of Varieties* (1902)).

Although problems in relation to the promotion of companies have been greatly diminished by the introduction of rigorous rules relating to the provision of information in company prospectuses, nevertheless the Company Directors Disqualification Act 1986 also provides for the disqualification of anyone who has been convicted of an indictable offence in relation to the promotion or formation of a company.

(b)   A **pre-incorporation contract** is a contract which promoters enter into, naming the company as a party, prior to the date of the certificate of incorporation and hence prior to the company's existence as a separate legal person. The legal difficulty is that the company cannot enter into a binding contract until it has become incorporated, and it is not bound by any contract made on its behalf prior to incorporation. The legal consequences of the above propositions are that the company, when formed, is not bound by the contract even if it has taken some benefit under the contract. In *Kelner* v *Baxter* (1866) a contract was entered into supposedly on behalf of a company, but before it was actually registered. Although goods were supplied to the company under the contract it was held that it could not be held liable under the contract, as it had not been in existence at the time the contract had been entered into. The parties who had purported to act as its agents were liable on the contract but the company itself could not be held responsible. Similarly the company cannot ratify the agreement even after it has become incorporated.

One of the main consequences of the principles outlined above is that someone who contracts on behalf of a company in respect of a pre-incorporation contract is treated as if he had contracted on his own behalf. Such was the consequence of ordinary agency law as stated in *Kelner* v *Baxter* above, but that position has been reinforced by statutory authority. Section 51 Companies Act 2006 provides that, subject to any agreement to the contrary, the person making the contract is personally liable. Clear and express words are needed to negate liability. Thus in *Phonogram Ltd* v *Lane* (1982) it was proposed to form a company, FM Ltd to run a pop group. Lane made a contract with Phonogram Ltd 'for and on behalf of FM Ltd'. However FM Ltd was never actually incorporated. Consequently the court held that Lane was personally liable for the money advanced to FM Ltd by Phonogram Ltd. The Court of Appeal held that the fact that Lane had signed 'for and on behalf of FM' made no difference to his personal liability. To give effect to the words 'subject to any agreement to the contrary' the words used would need to amount to an express exclusion of liability.

Promoters can avoid liability for pre-incorporation contracts in a number of ways. For example, it is possible to avoid entering the contract until the company has actually been incorporated. Alternatively, the promoter may enter into an agreement 'subject to contract' with the effect that there is no binding agreement until the company itself enters into one. As the promoters are usually the first directors of the company, they can ensure that the company does in fact enter into the pre-arranged contract. Finally, the promoters can enter into an agreement of 'novation', which involves discharging the original contract and replacing it with a new one.

48   CLARE, DAN AND EVE   *Walk in the footsteps of a top tutor*

Key answer tips

This scenario question deals with a partnership where one partner is a sleeping partner and another has retired. Candidates should deal with each partner in turn when structuring their answer and ensure they make a clear conclusion as to whether each partner is liable or not. The highlighted words are key phrases that markers are looking for.

Clare

The first thing to establish is the status of Clare. Although the question states that she is a sleeping partner, it has to be stated that the law does not recognise any such category. A dormant or sleeping partner is a person who merely invests money in a partnership enterprise but, apart from receiving a return on capital invested, takes no active part in the day-to-day running of the business. Although a limited partner in a limited partnership formed under the Limited Partnerships Act 1907 may be seen as a dormant partner, the term is used more generally to refer to people who simply put money into partnership enterprises without taking an active part in the business and yet do not comply with the formalities required for establishing a limited partnership (as this partnership was formed 10 years ago the requirements, and benefits of the Limited Liability Partnerships Act 2000 do not apply to it). The essential point that has to be emphasised with regard to Clare is that she has placed herself at great risk. The law considers her in the same way as it does a general partner in the enterprise and consequently she will be held personally and fully liable for the debts of the partnership to the extent of her ability to pay. By remaining outside the day-to-day operation of the business, Clare has merely surrendered her personal unlimited liability into the control of the active parties in the partnership.

Dan

The rules relating to the residual responsibility of retired partners for partnership debts depends on when the debts were contracted and the action taken by the former partner to announce their retirement from the business.

A retired partner remains liable for any debts or obligations incurred by the partnership prior to retirement. Thus the date of any contract determines responsibility: if the person was a partner when the contract was entered into, then they are responsible, even if the contract is completed after their retirement. It is possible for the retiring partner to be discharged from existing liability as a consequence of a contract of novation. Novation is essentially a tripartite contract involving the retiring partner, the remaining members of the continuing partnership and the existing creditors. Under such an agreement any liability of the retiring partner is passed to the remaining partners. As creditors effectively give up rights against the retiring partner, their approval is required. Such approval may be express, or it may be implied from the course of dealing between the creditor and the firm.

Where someone deals with a partnership after a change in membership, they are entitled to treat all the apparent members of the old firm as still being members until they receive notice of any change in the membership. In order to avoid liability for future contracts, a retiring partner must ensure that individual notice is given to **existing customers** of the partnership; and advertise the retirement in the London Gazette. This serves as general notice to people who were not customers of the firm prior to the partner's retirement, but knew that the person had been a partner in the business. Such an advert is effective whether or not it comes to the attention of third parties.

As regards **new customers** a retired partner owes no responsibility to someone who had no previous dealings with the partnership nor previous knowledge of their membership (*Tower Cabinet Co Ltd v Ingram (1949)*).

It follows from this that Dan could be liable for any debts towards the longstanding customer Greg, unless he has taken steps to notify Greg of his retirement from the partnership, which does appear likely. However, Dan's liability as regards any partnership debts to Hugh, who has never dealt with the partnership when Dan was a member, depends on whether the appropriate notice was issued in the London Gazette. If it was, then Dan is not liable to Hugh. If it was not, he will be liable.

Eve

She is the last remaining active partner in the business and has full responsibility for any partnership debts.

Under s.9 of the Partnership Act 1890 (PA), the liability of partners as regards debts or contract is joint. The effect of joint liability used to be that, although the partners were collectively responsible, a person who took action against one of the partners could take no further action against the other partners, even if they had not recovered all that was owing to them. That situation was remedied by the Civil Liability (Contributions) Act 1978, which effectively provided that a judgement against one partner does not bar a subsequent action against the other partners. This means that as regards Greg's debt, Clare, Dan, and Eve are all personally responsible for any shortfall and he may take action against any one of them. The one against whom the action is taken will be able to claim a proportionate indemnity from the others. In the case of Hugh's debt, Dan would not be liable if the appropriate notice had been issued in the London Gazette and hence the loss would be borne by Clare and Eve proportionally.

Examiner's Report

This question required candidates to analyse a problem scenario that raised issues relating mainly to partnerships but which also involves agency law.

On the whole the majority of candidates recognised the specific underlying issues within the general context of partnership law, although the manner in which they applied the law to the issues differed significantly depending on their knowledge of partnership law. The question concerned three distinct characters; Clare, Dan and Eve and most candidates dealt with in turn although not always appropriately.

In relation to Clare, the majority of candidates explained what is meant by a sleeping partner and correctly recognised that she could not avoid liability even if she took no part in the operation of the partnership business. Some explained that she might have been able to limit her liability if the partnership was registered under the Limited Partnerships Act 1907 or the Limited Liability Partnerships Act 2000. However, some candidates wrongly assumed that she had limited liability or that the partnership was a limited liability partnership.

In relation to Dan, most candidates recognised the issue involved and recognised the general law, but fewer succeeded in distinguishing the situations of the two customers Greg and Hugh and dealing with them appropriately.

Once again, in relation to Eve's situation, the majority were able to explain her unlimited liability for the partnership debts, but only a minority raised the issue of her authority to bind the other partners to the contract.

ACCA marking scheme	
	Marks
Very weak answer showing little analysis, appropriate knowledge or application.	0-2
Unbalanced answer perhaps showing some appropriate knowledge but weak in analysis or application.	3-4
Sound analysis of the problem – recognition of the major principles involved and a fair attempt at applying them. Perhaps sound in knowledge but lacking in analysis and application.	5-7
Clear analysis of the problem scenario – recognition of the issues raised and a convincing application of the legal principles to the facts. Appropriate case authorities may be cited, but are not necessary if the principles are understood.	8-10

49 HAM, SAM AND TAM

Key answer tips

This is a question which requires candidates to explain key issues relating to powers, authority and liability of partners. A good answer would explain the law relating to implied authority and how if it can be shown to exist can make all the partners liable for the contract.

Sam has clearly used his powers for an unauthorised purpose. Unfortunately for the other partners they cannot repudiate his transaction with the bank, even although it was outside his actual authority. The reason being that it is within his implied authority as a partner to enter into such a transaction. As a trading partnership, all the members have the implied authority to borrow money on the credit of the firm and the bank would be under no duty to investigate the purpose to which the loan was to be put. As a result the partnership cannot repudiate the debt to the bank and each of the partners will be liable for its payment. It has to be stated, however, that Sam will be personally liable to the other partners for the £10,000 and as a further consequence of his breach of his duty not to act in any way prejudicial to the partnership business, the partnership could be wound up.

Tam's purchase of the used cars was also clearly outside of the express provision of the partnership agreement. Nonetheless the partnership would be liable as the transaction would be likely to be held to be within the implied authority of a partner in a garage business (*Mercantile Credit v Garrod* (1962)). Once again Tam, the partner in default of the agreement, would be liable to the other members for any loss sustained in the transaction.

As regards the payment for the petrol, that is clearly within the ambit of the partnership and the members are all liable for non-payment.

If the partnership cannot pay the outstanding debts then the individual partners will become personally liable for any outstanding debt. Although under s.9 of the Partnership Act 1890 partnership debts are said to be joint, the Civil Liability Act 1978 provides that a judgement against one partner does not bar a subsequent action against the other partners. Once the debts owed to outsiders have been dealt with, then the internal financial relationships of the partners amongst themselves will be dealt with according to the partnership agreement.

Examiner's Report

This question required candidates to consider key issues relating to the powers, authority and liability of partners. Candidates were required to exhibit a thorough knowledge of partnership law together with the ability to analyse the problems contained in the question and apply the law accurately. While there were many decent answers to the question, with candidates demonstrating a reasonable understanding of partnership law, once again it has to be said that some candidates simply did not recognise the issues involved in the problem scenario. As has been said a small number of candidates appeared to take the fact that the business of the partnership was limited to the sale of petrol as an indication that it was a limited partnership and produced answers explaining that business form. Others presented general answers on the different possible partnership forms without making any real attempt to deal with the question, a clear indication that they prepared an answer and were going to reproduce it whether it was relevant or not.

ACCA Marking Scheme	
	Marks
This question refers to key issues relating to the powers, authority and liability of partners.	
Very weak answers which might recognise what the question is about but show no ability to analyse or answer the problem as set out.	0-2
Identification of some of the central issues in the question and an attempt to apply the appropriate law. Towards the bottom of this range of marks there will be major shortcomings in analysis or application of law.	3-4
Candidates will exhibit a sound knowledge of partnership law together with the ability to recognise the issues contained in the question. Knowledge may be less detailed or analysis less focused.	5-7
Candidates will exhibit a thorough knowledge of partnership law together with the ability to analyse the problems contained in the question.	8-10

50 COMPANY NAMES

Key answer tips

This is a straightforward question linking the law of torts and Companies Act 2006 relating to company names.

(a)   Except in relation to specifically exempted companies, such as those involved in charitable work, companies are required to indicate that they are operating on the basis of limited liability. Thus private companies are required to end their names, either with the word 'limited' or the abbreviation 'ltd', and public companies must end their names with the words 'public limitedcompany' or the abbreviation 'plc'. Welsh companies may use the Welsh language equivalents (Companies Act (CA)2006 ss.58, 59 & 60). Companies Registry maintains a register of business names, and will refuse to register any company with a name that is the same as one already on that index (CA 2006 s.66). Certain categories of names are, subject to the decision of the Secretary of State, unacceptable *per se*, as follows:

(i)   names which in the opinion of the Secretary of State constitute a criminal offence or are offensive (CA 2006 s.53)

(ii)   names which are likely to give the impression that the company is connected with either government or local governmentauthorities (s.54).

(iii)   names which include a word or expression specified under the Company and Business Names Regulations 1981 (s.26(2)(b)). This category requires the express approval of the Secretary of State for the use of any of the names orexpressions contained on the list, and relates to areas which raise a matter of public concern in relation to their use.

Under s.67 of the Companies Act 2006 the Secretary of State has power to require a company to alter its name under thefollowing circumstances:

(i)   where it is the same as a name already on the Registrar's index of company names.

(ii)   where it is 'too like' a name that is on that index.

The name of a company can always be changed by a special resolution of the company so long as it continues to comply with the above requirements (s.77).

(b)   The tort of passing off was developed to prevent one person from using any name which is likely to divert business their way by suggesting that the business is actually that of some other person or is connected in any way with that other business. It thus enables people to protect the goodwill they have built up in relation to their business activity. In Ewing v Buttercup Margarine Co Ltd (1917) the plaintiff successfully prevented the defendants from using a name that suggested a link with his existing dairy company. It cannot be used, however, if there is no likelihood of the public being confused, where for example the companies are conducting different businesses (Dunlop Pneumatic Tyre Co Ltd v Dunlop Motor Co Ltd (1907) and Stringfellow v McCain Foods GB Ltd (1984). Nor can it be used where the name consists of a word in general use (Aerators Ltd v Tollitt (1902)).

Part 41 of the Companies Act (CA) 2006, which repeals and replaces the Business Names Act 1985, still does not prevent one business from using the same, or a very similar, name as another business so the tort of passing off will still have an application in the wider business sector. However the Act introduced a new procedure to deal specifically with company names. As previously under the CA 1985, a company cannot register with a name that was the same as any already registered (s.665 Companies Act (CA) 2006) and under CA s.67 the Secretary of State may direct a company to change its name if it has been registered in a name that is the same as, or too like a name appearing on the registrar's index of company names. In addition, however, a completely new system of complaint has been introduced.

(c)   Under ss.69–74 of CA 2006 a new procedure has been introduced to cover situations where a company has been registered with a name

(i)   that it is the same as a name associated with the applicant in which he has goodwill, or

(ii)   that it is sufficiently similar to such a name that its use in the United Kingdom would be likely to mislead by suggestinga connection between the company and the applicant (s.69).

Section 69 can be used not just by other companies but by any person to object to a company names adjudicator if acompany's name is similar to a name in which the applicant has goodwill. There is list of circumstances raising a presumptionthat a name was adopted legitimately, however even then, if the objector can show that the name was registered either, to obtain money from them, or to prevent them from using the name, then they will be entitled to an order to require thecompany to change its name.

Under s.70 the Secretary of State is given the power to appoint company names adjudicators and their staff and to financetheir activities, with one person being appointed Chief Adjudicator. Section 71 provides the Secretary of State with power to make rules for the proceedings before a company names adjudicator. Section 72 provides that the decision of an adjudicator and the reasons for it, are to be published within 90 days of thedecision.

Section 73 provides that if an objection is upheld, then the adjudicator is to direct the company with the offending name to change its name to one that does not similarly offend. A deadline must be set for the change. If the offending name is not changed, then *the adjudicator will decide* a new name for the company.

Under s.74 either party may appeal to a court against the decision of the company names adjudicator. The court can either uphold or reverse the adjudicator's decision, and may make any order that the adjudicator might have made.

Examiner's Report

This question, divided into three parts, required candidates to explain the limitations on the use of company names, the tort of 'passing off' and finally the role of the company names adjudicators under the Companies Act 2006.

It has to be said that this question, and in particular part (a) was extremely well done. The great majority of candidates were well able to cite most of the rules governing what names can and can't be used by companies. Part (b) was also done fairly well with many candidates able to cite cases in support of their explanation of the law. Part (c), which introduced the new concept of the company names adjudicator was also done fairly well. It is pleasing to see that candidates are now coming to terms with the 'new' companies legislation.

	ACCA marking scheme	
		Marks
(a)	Good explanation of the rules relating to company names.	3–4
	Some but limited knowledge of the control over company names.	0–2
(b)	Good explanation of the tort of 'passing off' with case authority to support the explanation.	3–4
	Some but limited knowledge of 'passing off' or control over company names.	0–2
(c)	Good explanation of the role of the company names adjudicators and why they are necessary.	2
	Little if any knowledge of the concept.	0–1

51 ELEANOR

Key answer tips

Part (a) is only asking for information about the registers, not the documents which are kept at the registered office. Part (b) requires knowledge of the concept of domicile or nationality and the procedure for changing the registered office.

(a) **The statutory registers of a company**

There are a number of important registers which companies have a statutory obligation to keep. These are:

(i) Register of Members: Under s.113 of the Companies Act 2006 every company is under an obligation to keep a register of its members and to enter in it the following particulars: the names and addresses of the members, the date on which each person was registered as a member and the date at which any person ceased to be a member.

(ii) Register of Charges: All limited companies are obliged to keep at their registered office a register of all charges affecting the property of the company and all floating charges on the undertaking or property of the company. The register must contain a short description of the property which has been charged, the amount of the charge and the names of the persons who are entitled to the charge.

(iii) Register of directors (and, if applicable, company secretaries): This must include the name, occupation, nationality and date of birth if the director is an individual. If the director is a corporate body, the corporate name and registered office must be stated.

The register should now contain service addresses rather than details of the directors' residential addresses. The service address can be simply 'the company's registered office'.

The company must also keep a separate register of the directors' residential addresses. Both the service and the residential addresses will need to be supplied to the Registrar of Companies.

The residential addresses will be withheld from the public register. However, they will generally remain available to the Registrar and certain specified public bodies and credit reference agencies.

(iv) Other documents: Resolutions and minutes of general meetings must be kept for ten years.

(b) **The meaning of a company's 'registered office' and changing its address**

Under s.86 Companies Act 2006 it is required that a company shall at all times have a registered office to which all communications and notices may be addressed. The application submitted to form a company states the address of the company's first registered office.

The situation of the registered office of a company determines its nationality and its domicile: these are important matters in the case of serving legal documents on the company which may be served by leaving them or sending them by post to the registered office of the company.

Changes in the registered office of a company may be effected under s.87. This provides that a company may change the situation of its registered office from time to time by giving notice in the prescribed form to the Registrar of Companies. The company must notify the Registrar of the change within 15 days of the change of address, and the change is effective once registered. The Registrar must publish notice of the change in the London Gazette. Until 14 days after the notification has appeared in the Gazette, the company cannot rely on the change of address against a person who was unavoidably prevented from knowing of it.

52   DON

Key answer tips

This is a scenario question dealing with the concept of a promoter in company law. Candidates should address three things in their answer, firstly is Don a promoter, secondly has there been a breach of a 'fiduciary relationship', and thirdly the consequence of the pre-incorporation contract.

There is no general statutory definition of a promoter in company law. The courts have not given a comprehensive judicial definition. In *Twycross* v *Grant* (1877) Cockburn C. J. defined a promoter as '. . . one who undertakes to form a company with reference to a given project and to see it going, and who takes the necessary steps to accomplish that purpose'. In *Whaley Bridge Calico Printing Co* v *Green* (1880), Bowen L described the term promoter as 'a term not of law but of business, usefully summing up in a single word a number of business operations, familiar to the commercial world, by which a company is generally brought into existence'.

The consequence of the above two statements is that the answer to the question of whether a person is a promoter or not, is a question of fact and the determining factor is whether the individual in question will be a person who exercises some control over the affairs of the company both before and after it is formed up until the process of formation is completed. A person is not to be treated as a promoter of a company simply on the basis that they act in a professional capacity with respect to the establishment of a company. Thus solicitors and accountants employed purely in their professional capacity in order to establish a company will not be considered to be promoters. The question expressly states that Don 'was instrumental in forming Eden plc', it is apparent, therefore, that he assumed the role of a promoter and is subject to the rules that govern that position.

Promoters are said to be in a 'fiduciary relationship' with the company they are establishing. This is a position akin to that of a trustee and the most important consequence that flows from it is that the promoter is not entitled to make a profit from establishing the company, without full disclosure of that profit to either an independent board of directors, or to the existing and prospective shareholders in the company. Such a situation usually arises where the promoters sell assets to the company they are in the process of forming. Failure to make such a disclosure will enable the company to: rescind the contract; claim damages or hold the promoter liable to account for any profit made (*Erlanger* v *New Sombrero Phosphate Co* (1878), *Gluckstein* v *Barnes* (1900); *Re Leeds & Hanley Theatres of Varieties* (1902)).

A pre-incorporation contract is a contract which promoters enter into, naming the company as a party, prior to the date of the certificate of incorporation and hence prior to its existence as a separate legal person. The legal difficulty, of course, is that the company cannot enter into a binding contract until it has become incorporated, and it is not bound by any contract made on its behalf prior to incorporation. The legal consequences of the above propositions are that the company, when formed, is not bound by the contract even if it has taken some benefit under the contract. In *Kelner* v *Baxter* (1866) a contract was entered into supposedly on behalf of a company, but before it was actually registered. Although goods were supplied to the company under the contract, it was held that it could not be held liable under the contract, as it had not been in existence at the time the contract had been entered into. The parties who had purported to act as its agents were liable on the contract, but the company itself could not be held responsible. Similarly, the company cannot ratify the agreement even after it has become incorporated.

One of the main consequences of the principles outlined above is that someone who contracts on behalf of a company in respect of a pre-incorporation contract is treated as if he had contracted on his own behalf. Such was the consequence of ordinary agency law as stated in *Kelner* v *Baxter* above, but that position has been bolstered by statutory authority. Thus s.51 CA 2006 reinforces the common law position. It provides that, subject to any agreement to the contrary, the person actually making the contract is personally liable. Clear and express words are needed to negate liability. Thus in *Phonogram Ltd* v *Lane* (1982) it was proposed to form a company, FM Ltd, to run a pop group. L made a contract with Phonogram Ltd 'for and on behalf of FM Ltd'. However, FM Ltd was never actually incorporated. Consequently the court held that Lane was personally liable for the money advanced to FM Ltd by Phonogram Ltd. The Court of Appeal held that the fact that Lane had signed 'for and on behalf of FM' made no difference to his personal liability.

Applying the preceding rules to the facts in the problem produces the following results:

(i) Don has clearly breached his fiduciary duty to the company he is promoting by making a secret profit from this contract with it. Consequently, if the possibility still exists, the company may rescind the contract. However, it is more likely that Don would be required to reimburse the profit he made on the transaction to the company.

(ii) In this situation it is apparent that a contract in the company's name was purportedly entered into before the company had come into existence. In such circumstances the company cannot be bound by the contract (*Kelner* v *Baxter*). Consequently, the provider of the computer equipment cannot take any action against Eden plc, but will have recourse to action against Don for any losses suffered by virtue of s.51 CA 2006.

53 FORM OF BUSINESS

Key answer tips

This question requires candidates to consider the most suitable business form and in doing so consider the advantages and disadvantages of setting up a limited company compared to a partnership.

A company is defined in *Salomon v Salomon & Co Ltd* as a person in law whereas **S1 Partnership Act 1890** defines a partnership as a relation which subsists between persons carrying on a business in common with a view to profit.

As a consequence of the fact that it is a corporation a registered company has the following advantages over a partnership:

(i) **Perpetual succession**

A company will continue regardless of any changes in its membership. Shareholders may transfer their shares, or be declared bankrupt or even die, without in any way affecting the company's existence or the day-to-day operation of the company's business. A partnership does not benefit from perpetual succession and exists only as long as the partners agree that it should continue. Resignation, death or bankruptcy of a partner could lead to the end of the partnership.

(ii) **Debts and limited liability**

Any business debts owed by a limited company are owed by the company as a distinct legal person, rather than by the shareholders in the company. Shareholders in limited liability companies are only liable for the amount remaining unpaid on their shares. Membership of a partnership, in contrast, usually renders any partner jointly and severally liable for the total debts of the partnership, and any such debt extends to the full extent of the partner's personal wealth.

(iii) **Contracts**

When a company enters into contracts, the company itself can sue and be sued on such contracts. The directors as the agents of the company generally incur on personal liability. In a partnership, when a partner enters into a contract, he is acting as the agent of all partners. All partners are jointly and severally liable.

(iv) **Transferability of title and liquidity of investments**

Shares in a company can be transferred to a new owner without the need to acquire the approval of the other members of the company, although there are usually controls on transferability in private companies. Partners are not at liberty to transfer their interests without the approval of the other partners.

(vi) **Loan capital**

A further advantage that the company has over the partnership in raising capital is the fact that the company is permitted to borrow capital via debentures, or loan stock. This facility is not open to partnerships. With regard to borrowing, companies are in the advantageous position of being able to give security for its debts by means of a floating charge, whereas partnerships cannot use floating charges to secure loans.

(vii) **Separation of ownership from management**

In companies, the directors and the members can be two distinct groups of persons. Therefore if a person becomes a member of the company, he is not automatically entitled to take part in the management of the company. This means that if a company wishes to raise capital, the existing directors can retain control of management. In partnerships, the partners both own and manage the business. Any new partner has the right to participate in management.

Disadvantages of trading as a company as opposed to partnership:

(i) **Formalities**

In order to form a company, however, it is necessary to comply with the procedure for registration as set out in the Companies Acts, and to ensure that the appropriate documents are provided.

The major advantage of a partnership is the lack of formality involved in forming and running the business enterprise. Although it is usual for a formal Deed of Partnership to be drawn up, which states the conditions of the partnership, such procedure is not compulsory, and partnerships can be formed on the basis of an oral agreement. The existence of a partnership can even be inferred from the conduct of the parties where otherwise there is no express agreement.

(iv)   **Publicity requirements**

Limited companies are required to file accounts and comply with other publicity requirements under CA 2006. Partnerships are not subject to such requirements.

In conclusion, it would seem that the individuals in the question might be best advised to form a private limited company.

CAPITAL AND THE FINANCING OF COMPANIES

54   TYPES OF SHARES

Key answer tips

This is a fairly straightforward factual question requiring explanation of share and loan capital. Candidates should ensure they deal with each part of the requirement in isolation. It should be noted that the requirement does not ask for comparisons.

(a)   **Ordinary shares**

As defined in *Borland's Trustees* v *Steel* (1901) a share: '...is the interest of a shareholder in the company measured by a sum of money, for the purpose of liability in the first place, and of interest in the second...'

The nominal value of the shares held represents the maximum liability of a shareholder in a limited liability company. However, the actual liability of a shareholder is the amount remaining unpaid on any shares held. This difference arises in the following circumstances. When companies issue shares they may not require the full nominal value of the shares to be paid at once. This allows the company the possibility of raising further capital from its members as it becomes necessary in the future. The amount already paid to the company is referred to as called-up capital. Any uncalled capital represents the amount of potential liability. If the shares are fully paid up then the shareholder has no further liability towards meeting the company's debts. In regard to return, shares enjoy an advantage of other securities. If the company is profitable, not only will they enjoy dividend payments but the market value of their shares will go up. On the other hand if the company does not do well, they may well not receive any payment and the value of their shares will diminish.

(b)   **Preference shares**

Preference shares represent a more secure form of investment than the ordinary share. The reason for this is that preference shares receive a fixed rate of dividend before any payment is made to the ordinary shareholders and usually they enjoy priority over ordinary shares with regard to repayment of capital. The actual rights enjoyed by the preference will be stated in the company's articles of association. Dividend rights in relation to preference shares are usually cumulative, which means that a failure to pay the dividend in one year has to be made good in subsequent years. Although, as with ordinary shares, the holders of preference shares are members of the company, their voting rights are restricted to any period when their dividends are in arrears.

(c) **Debentures**

Debentures are documents that acknowledge a company's borrowing, although the term has been extended to cover the loan itself. As debenture holders lend money to the company they are its creditors, they are not members. As creditors they are entitled to receive interest, whether the company is profitable or not. It may even be necessary to use the company's capital to pay the debenture interest. Share dividends on the other hand must never be paid from capital. It is usual for the company to provide security for the amount it has borrowed by issuing debentures. There are two methods of securing debentures: by means of a floating charge, or by means of a fixed charge, both of which have to be properly registered. In the case of a floating charge the security is provided by all of the company's property, some of which may be continuously changing, such as stock-in-trade. The charge only crystallises, i.e. fixes on the specific property, when the company commits some act of default, and until then it is free to deal with the property in its ordinary course of business. The disadvantage of floating charges are that they come after fixed charges when it comes to paying a company's debts, so if all the assets are used to pay off those prior debts, there may well be nothing left to pay the holders of the floating charges.

Examiner's Report

This question required candidates to consider the various investment mechanisms available to investors, namely ordinary shares, preference shares and debentures, with marks being divided 3, 3 for parts (a) and (b) and 4 for part (c) on debentures.

The majority of candidates dealt with the question well, indeed it was the best answered question in the paper, but some answers shared the error already mentioned in relation to question 2, that as regards ordinary and preference shares there was a tendency to define them in terms of each other and hence effectively to repeat information. Surprisingly candidates were less successful at defining the ordinary share, although those who made use of the definition in *Borland's Trustees* v *Steel* (1901) invariably produced reasonable answers.

Part (b) relating to preference share almost always gave rise to answers relating to priority rights although there was some confusion as to whether they provided membership and specifically voting rights.

Part (c) on debentures tended to produce thorough answers and many candidates were able, not just to explain debentures but to also consider fixed and floating charges.

ACCA marking scheme	
	Marks
Little if any knowledge of the topic.	0-2
Some, but little, knowledge of the topic.	3-4
Lacking in detail in some or all aspects of the possible investment forms. Unbalanced answer that only focuses on some of the forms.	5-7
Full understanding and explanation of the various forms of investment	8-10

55 SHARE ISSUES

Key answer tips

This question requires an explanation of the different types of share capital listed together with an explanation of the difference between the nominal value of shares and their market value.

The word 'capital' is used in a number of different ways in relation to shares.

(a)   Under the provisions of the Companies Act (CA) 1985 the memorandum of a limited company with a share capital was required to state the amount of the share capital with which the company proposed to be registered and the nominal amount of each of its shares. This was known as the 'authorised share capital' and set a limit on the amount of capital which the company could issue, subject to increase by ordinary resolution. Section 9 of the CA 2006 removes the concept of 'authorised capital' and replaces it with the requirement to submit a 'statement of capital and initial shareholdings' to the registrar in the application to register the company.

The statement of capital and initial shareholdings is essentially a 'snapshot' of a company's share capital at the point of registration.

Section 10 CA 2006 requires the statement of capital and initial shareholdings to contain the following information:

–   the total number of shares of the company to be taken on formation by the subscribers to the memorandum;

–   the aggregate nominal value of those shares;

–   for each class of shares: prescribed particulars of the rights attached to those shares, the total number of shares of that class and the aggregate nominal value of shares of that class; and

–   the amount to be paid up and the amount (if any) to be unpaid on each share (whether on account of the nominal value of the shares or by way of premium).

The statement must contain such information as may be required to identify the subscribers to the memorandum of association. With regard to such subscribers it must state:

–   the number, nominal value (of each share) and class of shares to be taken by them on formation; and

–   the amount to be paid up and the amount (if any) to be unpaid on each share. Where a subscriber takes shares of more than one class of share, the above information is required for each class.

(b)   Issued capital represents the nominal value of the shares actually issued by the company and public companies must have a minimum issued capital of £50,000 or the prescribed euro equivalent (s.763 CA 2006).

(c)   Paid-up capital. This is the proportion of the nominal value of the issued capital actually paid by the shareholder (s.547 CA 2006). It may be the full nominal value, in which case it fulfils the shareholder's responsibility to outsiders; or it can be a mere part payment, in which case the company has an outstanding claim against the shareholder. Shares in public companies must be paid up to the extent of at least a quarter of their nominal value (s.586 CA 2006).

(d)   Once established, the nominal value of the share remains fixed and does not normally change. However, the value of the shares in the stock market may be subject to daily fluctuation depending on a number of interrelated factors, such as the profitability of the company, the prevailing rate of interest or prospective take-over bids. Thus the market value of a share of £1 nominal value may as much as £5 or higher, or as low as one penny.

Examiner's Report

This question required an explanation of the different types of share capital listed together with an explanation of the difference between the nominal value of shares and their market value. Given that the examiner had provided an article on this very topic, the inadequate performance in this question gives ground for concern. This was the first question that required an understanding of the provision in the Companies Act 2006 and unfortunately the majority of candidates were simply unaware of the changes introduced by that piece of legislation. As a result part (a) was very inadequately done. Answers also indicated that many candidates still are of the opinion that the memorandum of association is still the most important constitutional document for companies and that it contains the company's 'authorised capital', a concept completely removed by the 2006 Act.

The three other parts of the question were done better, for the simple reason that they did not require any real knowledge of the Companies Act 2006 and any legal regulation required in the answers was not changed by it. On some occasions decent performance in the latter three parts was sufficient to compensate for an inadequateperformance in part (a).

ACCA Marking Scheme	Marks
Unbalanced to very unbalanced answer, focusing on only one element and ignoring the others, or one which shows little understanding of the subject matter of the question.	0–3
Thorough treatment of some of the elements, or a less complete treatment of all of them.	4–7
Thorough explanation of all of the elements in the question.	8–10

56   DEBENTURES, FIXED AND FLOATING CHARGES

Key answer tips

This factual question requires candidates to explain the meaning and purpose of a debenture. It also requires an explanation of a fixed and floating charge as security over a debt. Candidates should ensure they deal with all three parts of the requirement to achieve a well balanced answer.

Companies ordinarily raise the money they need to finance their operations through the issue of share capital, but it is equally common for companies to raise additional capital through borrowing. The essential difference between share capital and loan capital is that, whereas a share represents a proportionate interest in the business and the shareholder is a member of the company, a lender, even where they hold loan-stock, remains a creditor of the company rather than a member. Such borrowing on the part of the company does not give the lender any interest in the company but represents a claim against the company. The relationship between the company and the provider of loan capital is the ordinary relationship of debtor/creditor, although specific mechanisms exist to facilitate the borrowing of companies and secure the interests of their creditors.

(a) **Debentures**

A debenture is a document which acknowledges the fact that a company has borrowed money. The use of the term 'debenture', however, has been extended to cover the loan itself. A debenture may be issued to a single creditor or to a large number of people, in which case each of the creditors has a proportionate claim against the total 'debenture stock'.

As creditors of the company, debenture-holders receive interest on their loans and are entitled to receive payment whether the company is profitable or not. As regards repayment, debts rank in order of creation, so earlier debentures have to be paid before those created later. Where debentures are issued as part of a series, it is usual for a *pari passu* clause to be included in the document creating the debt, with the effect that all of the loans made within the series rank equally with regard to repayment.

Debentures which have no security are referred to as 'unsecured loan stock'. It is usual, however, for debentures to provide security for the amount loaned. 'Security' means that if the company is wound up, the secured creditor will have priority in terms of repayment over any unsecured creditor. There are two types of security for company loans; fixed charges and floating charges.

(b) **Fixed charge**

In this situation, a specific asset of the company is made subject to a charge in order to secure a debt. Once the asset is subject to the fixed charge, the company cannot dispose of it without the consent of the debenture-holders. The asset most commonly subject to fixed charges is land, although any other long-term capital asset may also be charged, as may such intangible assets as book debts. It would not be appropriate, however, to give a fixed charge against stock in trade as the company would be prevented from freely dealing with it without the prior approval of the debenture-holders. Such a situation would obviously prevent the company from carrying on its day-to-day business. If the company fails to honour the commitments set out in the document creating the debenture, such as meeting its interest payments, the debenture-holders can appoint a receiver who will, if necessary, sell the asset charged to recover the money owed. If the value of the asset that is subject to the charge is greater than the debt against which it is charged then the excess goes to pay off the rest of the company's debts. If it is less than the value of the debt secured then the debenture-holders will become unsecured creditors for the amount remaining outstanding.

(c) **Floating charge**

This category of charge is peculiar to companies and represents one of the advantages of the company over other business forms. The floating charge is most commonly made in relation to the 'undertaking and assets' of a company and does not attach to any specific property whilst the company is meeting its requirements as stated in the debenture document. The security is provided by all the property owned by the company, some of which may be continuously changing, such as stock-in-trade. Thus, in contrast to the fixed charge, the use of the floating charge permits the company to deal with its property without the need to seek the approval of the debenture holders. However, if the company commits some act of default such as not meeting its interest payments, or going into liquidation, the floating charge is said to 'crystallise'. This means that the floating charge becomes a fixed equitable charge over the assets detailed and their value may be realised in order to pay the debt owed to the floating charge-holder.

All charges, including both fixed and floating, have to be registered with the Companies' Registry within 21 days of their creation. Failure to register the charge as required has the effect of making the charge void, i.e. ineffective, against any other creditor or the liquidator of the company. The charge, however, remains valid against the company, which means in effect that the holder of the charge loses their priority as against other company creditors. In addition to registration at the Companies' Registry, companies are required to maintain a register of all charges on their property. Although a failure to comply with this requirement constitutes an offence, it does not invalidate the charge.

It is possible to obtain court permission for later registration of a charge e.g. where failure to register was by mistake or due to inadvertence. However, the court cannot allow the rights of subsequent charge-holders to be prejudiced. Thus, any charge that is registered late is registered subject to those charges already registered. In relation to properly registered charges of the same type, they take priority according to their date of creation. However, as regards charges of different types, a fixed charge takes priority over a floating charge even if it was created after it. Generally there is nothing to prevent the creation of a fixed charge after the issuing of a floating charge, and, as a legal charge against specific property, that fixed charge will still take priority over the earlier floating charge. It is possible, however, for the debenture creating the original floating charge to include a provision preventing the creation of a later fixed charge taking priority over that floating charge. Such a negative pledge clause is effective if the subsequent fixed charge holder has actual notice of it.

57   CRUMS LTD

Key answer tips

This scenario question requires candidates to rank the charges in order of priority. Before ranking the charges candidates should explain the general rules on the priority of charges.

Properly registered charges of the same type take priority according to their date of creation. However, as regards charges of different types, a fixed charge takes priority over a floating charge even if it was created after it. Generally there is nothing to prevent the creation of a fixed charge after the issuing of a floating charge, and, as a legal charge against specific property, that fixed charge will still take priority over the earlier floating charge. It is possible, however, for the debenture creating the original floating charge to include a provision preventing the creation of a later fixed charge taking priority over that floating charge.

As all the charges in the problem were properly registered it follows that all of the fixed charges take precedence over the floating charges, and within each category the charges take priority depending on date of creation, rather than the date of registration. Consequently the charges assume the following priority:

(i)   Flash Bank plc's loan, secured by a fixed charge created on 1 April;

(ii)   High Bank plc's loan, secured by a fixed charge created on 5 April;

(iii)   Don's loan, secured by a floating charge created on 1 February;

(iv)   Else's loan, secured by a floating charge created on the morning of 1 April;

(v)   Gus's loan, secured by a floating charge created on 3 April.

58   DIVIDENDS

Key answer tips

This factual question requires candidates to explain the rules relating to funding of dividends, the rules applicable to PLC's and consequences if rules are breached. Candidates should make reference to the Companies Act 2006 to score a reasonable mark.

(a)   Dividends are the return received by shareholders in respect of their investment in a company. Subject to any restriction in its articles, every company has the implied power to apply its profits in the distribution of dividend payments to its shareholders. Although the directors recommend the level of dividend payment, it is for the members to declare the dividend. If the directors decline to recommend a dividend then it is not open to the members to overrule that decision and declare a dividend.

The long standing common law rule is that dividends must not be paid out of capital (*Flitcroft's case* 1882). The current rules relating to the payment of dividends are contained in the Companies Act 2006. S.829 CA 2006 states that a distribution is 'every description or distribution of a company's assets to its members', except for the issue of bonus shares, the redemption of shares, authorised reductions of share capital and the distribution of assets on winding up.

Section 830 provides that a company can only make a distribution out of profits available for that purpose, i.e. distributable profits. Distributable profits are accumulated realised profits (which have not been previously distributed or capitalised), less accumulated realised losses (which have not previously been written off in a reduction of capital).

It is important to note that the use of the term 'accumulated' means that any previous years' losses must be included in determining the distributable surplus, and that the requirement that profits be realised prevents payment from purely paper profit resulting from the mere revaluation of assets.

(b)   In addition to the rules outlined above, s.831 CA 2006, provides that a plc can only declare a dividend if both before and after the distribution, its net assets are not less than the aggregate of its called-up share capital and undistributable reserves.

Undistributable reserves include the share premium account, the capital redemption reserve, unrealised profits such as the revaluation reserve and any other reserves that the company is forbidden to distribute.

(c)   Under the rule in *Flitcroft's case* any directors of a company who breached the distribution rules, and knowingly paid dividends out of capital, were held jointly and severally liable to the company to replace any such payments made. The fact that the shareholders might have approved the distribution did not validate the illegal payment (*Aveling Barford Ltd* v *Perion Ltd* (1989)). Also at common law shareholders who knowingly received, or ought to have known that they had received, an unlawful dividend payment were required to repay the money received or to indemnify the directors for payments they might have already been required to have made (*Moxham* v *Grant* (1900)). Section 847 of the Companies Act 2006 restates the common law rule providing that shareholders, who either know or have reasonable grounds for knowing that any dividend was paid from capital, shall be liable to repay any such money received to the company.

In addition, the company can recover the distribution from:

- any director, unless he can show he exercised reasonable care in relying on properly prepared accounts

- the auditors, if the dividend was paid in reliance on erroneous accounts.

59 CAPITAL

Key answer tips

This is a straightforward question deals with the concept of capital maintenance in part (a) and then how a company can reduce its capital in part (b). In part (b) candidates should explain the difference in procedure for private and public companies.

(a) As shareholders in limited companies, by definition, have the significant protection of limited liability the courts have always seen it as the duty of the law to ensure that this privilege is not abused at the expense of the company's creditors. To that end they developed the doctrine of capital maintenance, the specific rules of which are now given expression in the Companies Act (CA) 2006. The rules, such as that stated in CA 2006 s.580 against shares being issued at a discount, ensure that companies receive at least the full nominal value of their share capital. The rules relating to the doctrine of capital maintenance operate in conjunction to those rules to ensure that the capital can only be used in limited ways. Whilst this may be seen essentially as a means of protecting the company's creditors, it also protects the shareholders themselves from the depredation of the company's capital.

There are two key aspects of the doctrine of capital maintenance: firstly that creditors have a right to see that the capital is not dissipated unlawfully; and secondly that the members must not have the capital returned to them surreptitiously. There are a number of specific controls over how companies can use their capital, but perhaps the two most important are the rules relating to capital reduction and company distributions.

(b) The procedures through which a company can reduce its capital are laid down by ss.641–653 Companies Act 2006.

Section 641 states that, subject to any provision in the articles to the contrary, a company may reduce its capital in any wayby passing a special resolution to that effect. In the case of a public company any such resolution must be confirmed by thecourt. In the case of a private company, however, it is also possible to reduce capital without court approval as long as thedirectors issue a statement as to the company's present and continued solvency for the following 12 months (ss.642 &

643). The special resolution, a copy of the solvency statement, a statement of compliance by the directors confirming that thesolvency statement was made not more than 15 days before the date on which the resolution was passed, and a statementof capital must be delivered to the registrar within 15 days of the date of passing the special resolution.

Section 641 sets out three particular ways in which the capital can be reduced by:

(a)   removing or reducing liability for any capital remaining as yet unpaid. In effect the company is deciding that it will not need to call on that unpaid capital in the future.

(b)   cancelling any paid up capital which has been lost through trading or is unrepresented by in the current assets. Thiseffectively brings the balance sheet into balance at a lower level by reducing the capital liabilities in recognition of a lossof assets.

(c)   repayment to members of some part of the paid-up value of their shares in excess of the company's requirements. Thismeans that the company actually returns some of its capital to its members on the basis that it does not actually needthat level of capitalisation to carry on its business.

It can be seen that procedure (a) reduces the potential creditor fund, for the company gives up the right to make future calls against its shares and procedure (c) reduces the actual creditor fund by returning some of its capital to the members. Inrecognition of this fact, creditors are given the right to object to any such reduction. However procedure (b) does not actually reduce the creditor fund, it merely recognises the fact that capital has been lost. Consequently creditors are not given the right to object to this type of alteration (ss.645 & 646).

Under s.648 the court may make an order confirming the reduction of capital on such terms as it thinks fit. In reaching its decision the court is required to consider the position of creditors of the company in cases (a) and (c) above and may do so in any other case. The court also takes into account the interests of the general public. In any case the court has a general discretion as to what should be done. If the company has more than one class of shares, the court will also consider whether the reduction is fair between classes. In this it will have regard to the rights of the different classes in a liquidation of the company since a reduction of capital is by its nature similar to a partial liquidation.

When a copy of the court order together with a statement of capital is delivered to the registrar of companies a certificate of registration is issued (s.649).

Examiner's Report

Part (a) required candidates to comment on their understanding of the doctrine of capital maintenance. A majority of candidates correctly identified that the capital should be maintained as a buffer for creditors and should not be used to pay dividends to shareholders. A number of candidates went on to explain that shares should not be issued below nominal value, the rules relating to the payment of dividends and that public companies are required to have £50,000 minimum share capital. A minority of candidates struggled to clearly explain the doctrine and as a result spent a lot of time discussing the different types of shares and debt (fixed and floating charges) for which no marks were awarded.

Part (b) required candidates to discuss when a company may want to reduce its capital and the procedure to be adopted by both public and private companies. A vast majority of candidates correctly identified when a reduction in capital would be appropriate, a few also

---

mentioned share buyback for which credit was given. With regard to the procedural aspects their appeared to be some confusion. A number correctly distinguished the procedure differences, however, many candidates went off tangent by either writing a substantial amount of text regarding share buyback or a combination of company law points, which were not directly related to the question.

Overall, this was very well attempted question. As in the previous question, it appears that candidates are gradually becoming more familiar with the technical aspects of the Companies Act 2006.

ACCA marking scheme			Marks
(a)		Thorough explanation of the doctrine of capital maintenance perhaps with some examples of its application.	3–4
		Some knowledge but lacking in detail.	0–2
(b)		Good to full consideration of the procedure for reducing capital. Reference must be made to the 2006 Act procedure and the difference between public and private companies should be mentioned specifically.	4–6
		Some general knowledge but lacking in detail as regards to the process or not mentioning the difference between the two company forms.	2–3
		Little or no understanding of the process.	0–1

60 CLASS RIGHTS

Key answer tips

This question in part (a) deals with shares and the different rights that can attach to a share. The most important distinction is that between a preference share and an ordinary share. In part (b) candidates are required to explain how class rights can be altered, and here candidates should make reference to s.630 of the Companies Act 2006.

(a)   A company may only issue one class of shares giving the holders the same rights. However, it is possible, and quite common, for companies to issue shares with different rights. Thus, preference shares may have priority rights over ordinary shares with respect to dividends or the repayment of capital. Shares may also carry different voting rights. Each of these is an example of class rights and the holders of shares which provide such rights constitute distinct classes within the generality of shareholders.

The nature of **specific class rights** can be clearly seen with regard to preference shares. Such shareholders are usually given priority over ordinary shareholders in relation to:

- payment of dividend
- return of capital on winding-up of the company.

Dividend

A preference share generally confers the right to receive a dividend up to a specified amount before any dividend is paid on the ordinary shares. The rights of preference shares depend essentially on what is expressly provided in their terms of issue. Preferential dividends are deemed to be cumulative unless expressly described as non-cumulative. This means that the preference shareholder will be entitled to any arrears of dividend if not paid out in one year before any payment can be made to the ordinary shareholders by way of dividend. The preference shareholder is only entitled to receive a dividend out of available profits out of which the dividend is declared payable. The right to a preference dividend is exhaustive. In other words, if the preference dividend is paid in full there is no further right to dividend unless, once again, there is an express right to the contrary.

Preference shares carrying the right to participate equally with ordinary shares after the ordinary shareholders have received a dividend of a specified amount are called *participating preference shares.*

If a company goes into liquidation with arrears outstanding on preference dividends, the right to receive arrears is lost unless the articles provide that the arrears shall be paid out of the assets available in winding up. They have no claim on any reserves which could have been applied in paying their dividends.

Capital

Unless expressly so provided, in a winding up (or return of capital on reduction) preference shares do not have any priority over ordinary shares in return of capital.

They then rank *pari passu* (equally) with ordinary shares in bearing their proportion of any deficiency of paid-up capital. However, in practice preference shares are usually given priority in any return of capital, but that priority right is exhaustive, i.e. they are entitled to be repaid capital as provided but not to participate in any surplus assets *(Re Saltdean Estates* (1968)).

It is usual for class rights to attach to particular shares and for those rights to be transferred with the shares to which they are attached. The specific rights may be set out in the memorandum of association, although it is more usual for such rights to be provided for in the articles of association. It is now recognised, however, that such class rights may be created by external agreements and may be conferred upon a person in the capacity of shareholder of a company, although not attached to any particular shares. Thus in *Cumbrian Newspapers Group Ltd v Cumbernauld & Westmorland Herald Newspaper & Printing Co Ltd* (1986), following a merger between the plaintiff and defendant companies, the defendent's articles were altered so as to give the plaintiff certain rights of pre-emption and also the right to appoint a director, so long as it held at least 10% of the defendant's ordinary shares. Scott J held that these rights were in the nature of class rights and could not be altered without going through the procedure for altering such rights.

As the *Cumbrian* case demonstrates, class rights become an issue when the company looks to alter them. As has been shown with regard to preference shares, class rights usually provide their holders with some distinct advantage or benefit not enjoyed by the holders of ordinary shares and that the class members are usually in a minority within the company. It can be appreciated, therefore, that the procedure for varying such rights requires some sensitivity towards the class members.

(b) **Alteration of class rights**

The procedure for altering class rights is set out in s.630 CA 2006. The precise procedure depends upon two matters, firstly, where the rights are set out and secondly, whether there is a pre-established procedure for altering the rights.

(i) Where the articles set out a procedure for varying class rights, then that procedure should be followed.

(ii) If there is no specified procedure within the Articles of Association then, under s.630 CA 2006, variation needs a special resolution or written consent from the holders of 75% in nominal value of the shares of that class.

Any alteration of class rights is subject to challenge in the courts. To raise such a challenge any objectors must:

- hold no less than 15% of the issued shares in the class in question (s.633(2));

- not have voted in favour of the alteration; and

- apply to the court within 21 days of the consent being given to the alteration (s. 633(4)).

The court has the power to either confirm the alteration or to cancel it as unfairly prejudicial.

In *Greenhalgh v Arderne Cinemas* (1946) it was held that the subdivision of 50 pence shares which had previously carried one vote each, into five 10 pence shares which each carried one vote, did not vary the rights of another class of shares. Note that, although strictly speaking such an alteration did not affect the rights held by the other shares, it did alter their real voting power. Also in *House of Fraser plc v ACGE Investments Ltd* (1987) it was held that the return of all the capital held in the form of preference shares amounted to a total extinction of their rights. It could not therefore be seen as a variation of those rights and the procedure now contained in s.630 CA 2006 did not have to be followed.

61 JUDDER LTD *Walk in the footsteps of a top tutor*

Key answer tips

This question requires candidates to consider the procedure involved in companies altering their share capital, specifically reducing it. However, in order to explain the procedure, some attention should be given to the idea of capital maintenance as a means of explaining the requirements. The highlighted words are key phrases that markers are looking for.

Reduction of capital

This procedure is a rigorous one, for the reason that it amounts to an actual reduction, or a recognition of the reduction, of the capital fund against which creditors can claim.

Under s.641, a company can reduce its share capital provided that any reduction does not result in only redeemable shares being left in issue. The section sets out three particular ways in which the capital can be reduced by:

(i) removing or reducing liability for any capital remaining as yet unpaid. In effect the company is deciding that it will not need to call on that unpaid capital in the future;

(ii) cancelling any paid capital which has been lost through trading or is unrepresented by the current assets. This effectively brings the balance sheet into balance at a lower level by reducing the capital liabilities in recognition of a loss of assets;

(iii) repayment to members of some part of the paid-up value of their shares in excess of the company's requirements. This means that the company actually returns some of its capital to its members on the basis that it does not actually need that level of capitalisation to carry on its business.

For private companies, such as Judder Ltd, a special resolution must be passed. This must be supported by a solvency statement made not more than 15 days before the date on which the resolution is passed.

A solvency statement is a statement by each of the directors that the company will be able to meet its debts within the following year. A solvency statement made without reasonable grounds is an offence punishable by fine and/or imprisonment of up to two years.

Copies of the resolution, solvency statement and a statement of capital must be filed with the Registrar within 15 days.

(Note that as Judder Ltd is a private company, the reduction does not require court approval).

62   FIN

Key answer tips

This scenario question deals with the issue of a shareholder's liability with regard to paid-up and unpaid capital as well as shares being issued at less than nominal value. Candidates should be clear in their treatment of each scenario in order to score a reasonable mark and not try to answer both requirements at the same time.

(a) The proportion of the nominal value of the issued capital actually paid by the shareholder is called the 'paid-up' capital. It may be the full nominal value, in which case it fulfils the shareholder's responsibility to outsiders; or it can be a mere part payment, in which case the company has an outstanding claim against the shareholder. It is possible for a company to pass a resolution that it will not make a call on any unpaid capital. However, even in this situation, the unpaid element can be called upon if the company cannot pay its debts from existing assets in the event of its liquidation.

Applying this to Fin's case, it can be seen that he has a maximum potential liability in relation to his shares in Gulp Ltd. of 50 pence per share. The exact amount of his liability will depend on the extent of the company's debts but it may amount to £10,000.

(b) In relation to Heave Ltd., Fin bought shares of a nominal value of £1. Although the company agreed to treat the shares as fully paid up, Fin was only required to pay 50 pence for each share. This issue concerns the rules preventing companies from issuing shares at a discount. It is a long established rule that companies are not permitted to issue shares for a consideration that is less than the nominal value of the shares together with any premium due. The strictness of this rule may be seen in *Ooregum Gold Mining Co of India v Roper* (1892). In that case the shares in the company, although nominally £1, were trading at 12.5p. In an honest attempt to refinance the company, new £1 preference shares were issued and credited with 75p already paid (note the purchasers of the shares were actually paying twice the market value of the ordinary shares). When, however, the company subsequently went into insolvent liquidation, the holders of the new shares were required to pay a further 75p.

The common law rule that shares cannot be issued at a discount to their nominal value is now given statutory effect in s.580 CA 2006 and is supported by s.582 which states that shares are only treated as paid up to the extent that the company has received money or money's worth. Anyone who takes shares without paying the full value, plus any premium due, is liable to pay the amount of the discount as unpaid share capital, together with interest at the appropriate rate (s.580(2) CA 2006). Also, any subsequent holder of such a share who was aware of the original underpayment will be liable to make good the shortfall (s.588 CA 2006). The reason for such rigour in relation to preventing the issue of shares at a discount is the protection of the company's creditors. Shareholders were seen to enjoy the benefit of limited liability, but that privilege was only extended to them on the basis that they fully subscribed to the company's capital, the capital being seen as a creditor fund against which they could claim in the event of dispute.

Applying the foregoing to Fin's situation in relation to Heave Ltd., it follows that he cannot avoid having to make a further payment on the shares to pay off the company's creditors. The extent of his payment will depend on the actual debts owed, but cannot exceed the nominal value of the shares. Ignoring potential interest payments, his maximum liability in relation to the shares will be 50 pence per share, a total of £10,000.

MANAGEMENT, ADMINISTRATION AND REGULATION OF COMPANIES

63 DIRECTORS' DUTIES

Key answer tips

This question requires candidates to explain the duty of directors to promote the success of the company and to whom such a duty is owed. The question requires specific to s172 of the Companies Act 2006 and not a general description of all the duties of a director.

By virtue of s.172 Companies Act 2006 a director of a company must act in the way he considers would be most likely to promote the success of the company for the benefit of its members as a whole.

Specifically the director must consider the following:

– the likely consequences of any decision in the long term;

– the interests of the company's employees;

– the need to foster the company's business relationships with suppliers, customers and others;

– the impact of the company's operations on the community and the environment;

- the desirability of the company maintaining a reputation for high standards of business conduct; and

- the need to act fairly as between members of the company.

The above list is not exhaustive, and merely highlights areas of particular importance for the directors to focus on. The actual decision as to what will promote the success of the company has to be taken in good faith by the directors. This ensures that business decisions on, for example, strategy and tactics are for the directors, and not subject to decision by the courts.

Sub-section 172(2) provides that where, or to the extent that, the purposes of the company consist of, or include, purposes other than the benefit of its members, then the reference to promoting the success of the company for the benefit of its members in subsection (1) is to be read as referring to achieving those other purposes. This subsection is aimed at, essentially, but not exclusively, charitable companies and community interest companies. Consequently where the purpose of the company is other than the benefit of its members, the directors must act in the way they consider, in good faith, would be most likely to achieve that purpose. Where the company is partially for the benefit of its members and partly for other purposes, the extent to which those other purposes apply in place of the benefit of the members is a matter for directors to determine, once again, in good faith.

Sub-section 172(3) provides that the general duty is subject to any specific enactment or rule of law requiring directors to consider or act in the interests of creditors of the company. This formally recognises that the duty to the shareholders is displaced when the company is insolvent or is heading towards insolvency. For example, s.214 of the Insolvency Act 1986 provides a mechanism under which the liquidator can require the directors to contribute towards the funds available to creditors in an insolvent winding up, where they ought to have recognised that the company had no reasonable prospect of avoiding insolvent liquidation and then failed to take all reasonable steps to minimise the loss to creditors.

As directors owe their duties to the company (see *Percival v Wright* (1902)) it is apparent that many of the duties set out in

s.172 (1) are not capable of being enforced if the company itself, or members of the company, does not wish to enforce those duties.

Examiner's Report

This question required candidates to explain the duty of directors to promote the success of the company and to whom such a duty is owed. This question required specific reference to section 172 of the Companies Act 2006, but only a small minority of candidates appeared to be aware of that Act let alone the detail of section 172. Very few produced satisfactory answers to this question. They were clearly up to speed on the Companies Act 2006 and exhibited a sound knowledge and understanding of directors' duties and, specifically, the duty to promote the success of the company. The others either used the out of date 1985 Act or relied on a general description of directors' duties.

ACCA Marking Scheme	
	Marks
Weak answer, not fully explaining the law or issues involved.	0–3
A good answer but perhaps unfocused or lacking in detail as to the specific duties applied under s.172.	4–7
A very good answer revealing a thorough to complete understanding of both elements of the question.	8–10

64 TYPES OF DIRECTORS

Key answer tips

This question requires candidates to explain three types of directors. It should be noted that candidates are not asked to draw comparisons between the different types of directors.

(a) Executive directors usually work on a full-time basis for the company and may be employees of the company with specific contracts of employment. Section 227 of the Companies Act 2006 defines a director's service contract as a contract under which a director of the company undertakes personally to perform services (as director or otherwise) for the company. Section 228 requires a copy of every director's service contract to be kept available for inspection and under s.229 company members have the right to inspect and request a copy of such contracts.

Additionally s.188 of the Companies Act 2006, relating to directors' long-term service contracts, requires that no such contract may be longer than two years, unless it has been approved by resolution of the members of the company.

In fact the Combined Code on Corporate Governance recommends that the maximum period for directors' employment contracts should be one year.

(b) Non-executive directors do not usually have a full-time relationship with the company; they are not employees and only receive directors' fees. The role of the non-executive directors, at least in theory, is to bring outside experience and expertise to the board of directors. They are also expected to exert a measure of control over the executive directors to ensure that the latter do not run the company in their, rather than the company's, best interests.

It is important to note that there is no distinction in law between executive and non-executive directors and the latter are subject to the same controls and potential liabilities as are the former.

(c) Shadow director Section 250 of the Companies Act 2006, defines a director as including 'any person occupying the position of a director, by whatever name called.' The point of such a tautological definition is to emphasise the fact that it is the person's function rather than their title that defines them as a director and makes them subject to all the rules of company law that apply to directors.

It is possible that someone who in reality exercises control over a company's decision making might seek to evade their responsibilities and potential liabilities as a director. For example they could attempt to do this by appointing some other people as nominal directors without themselves being formally appointed to the board of directors. They would, nonetheless, exercise control over the business. It was in order to regulate such potential activity by those who exercise control over companies from behind the scenes that the concept of the shadow director was introduced. Thus s.251 of the Companies Act 2006 provides that a shadow director in relation to a company, means a person in accordance with whose directions or instructions the directors of the company are accustomed to act. However it should be noted that a person is not to be regarded as a shadow director simply for the reason that the directors act on advice given by him in a professional capacity. Thus neither accountants nor lawyers are made liable on the simple basis that they provide advice which the board of directors may act on.

Examiner's Report

The question required candidates to demonstrate an understanding of the difference in role between executive and non-executive directors (NED) and an awareness of the legal responsibility placed on those who the law considers to be shadow directors.

Most candidates made a reasonable attempt at explaining the role of the executive directors and gave comprehensive explanations about the role they play in the day-to-day management of the company. There was also a reasonable effort shown in tackling part (b) of the question about the role of the NED. Many made good reference to the importance of corporate governance and the need for some sort of "check" on the powers of the executive directors.

Part (c) of the question on shadow directors was however inadequately answered. Most candidates obviously had little idea what the term meant. Many guessed that such directors were advisers to the other directors; some did say that they were in the background, but most did not explain correctly what this meant. Overall because of the amount of marks candidates were able to earn in the first two parts of the questions there was generally reasonable marks gained for this question.

ACCA marking scheme	
	Marks
Little if any knowledge of the topic or very unbalanced in its treatment of the question.	0–2
Some, but limited knowledge of the nature of the three elements, or unbalanced in dealing with only one or two aspects of the question.	3–4
Lacking in detail in some or all elements of the topic. Unbalanced answer that only focuses on two of the elements.	5–7
Full understanding and explanation of all three elements of the question.	8–10

65   COMPANY SECRETARIES

Key answer tips

This question focuses on the important role played by the company secretary in a public company. Although presented in one sentence, the question is divided into three distinct sections, each of which should be addressed.

Appointment

Every public company must have a company secretary. Section 273 CA2006 requires that the directors of public companies must ensure that the company secretary has the requisite knowledge and experience to discharge their functions. Section 273(2) sets out a list of alternative specific minimum qualifications which a secretary to a public limited company must have. Any of the following qualifications are suitable:

(i)   they must have held office as a company secretary in a public company for three of the five years preceding their appointment to their new position;

(ii)   they must be a member of one of a list of recognised professional accountancy bodies;

(iii)   they must be a solicitor or barrister or advocate within the UK; or

(iv)   they must have held some other position, or be a member of such other body, as appears to the directors of the company to make them capable of acting as company secretary.

Duties

The duties of company secretaries are set by the board of directors and therefore vary from company to company, but as an officer of the company they will be responsible for ensuring that the company complies with its statutory obligations. The following are some of the most important duties undertaken by company secretaries. Main matters calling for the attention of the secretary:

- to ensure that the necessary registers required to be kept by the Companies Acts are established and properly maintained;

- to ensure that all returns required to be lodged with the Companies Registry are prepared and filed within the appropriate time limits;

- to organise and attend meetings of the shareholders and directors;

- to ensure that the company's books of account are kept in accordance with the Companies Acts and that the annual accounts and reports are prepared in the form and at the time required by the Acts;

- to be aware of all the statutory requirements placed on the company's activities and to ensure that the company complies with them; and

- to sign such documents as require their signature under the Companies Acts.

Powers

Although old authorities such as *Houghton & Co* v *Northard Lowe & Wills* (1928) suggest that company secretaries have extremely limited authority to bind their company, later cases have recognised the reality of the contemporary situation and have extended to company secretaries potentially extensive powers to bind their companies. As an example consider *Panorama Developments Ltd* v *Fidelis Furnishing Fabrics Ltd* (1971). In this case the

Court of Appeal held that a company secretary was entitled 'to sign contracts connected with the administrative side of a company's affairs, such as employing staff and ordering cars and so forth. All such matters now come within the ostensible authority of a company's secretary.'

66 APPOINTING AND REMOVING DIRECTORS

This is a fairly straightforward question requiring candidates to explain the rules on how a director can be appointed and consequently removed. It should be noted that there are three marks for the first part of the requirement and seven marks for the latter. Candidates should ensure their answer reflect this weighting.

(a) **Appointment of directors**

All companies are required to have directors. In the case of public companies there must be at least two directors, whilst in the case of private companies the requirement is for at least one director. **The first directors** are usually named in the application for registration.

Subsequent directors are appointed under the procedure stated in the articles. The usual procedure is for the company to elect the directors by an ordinary resolution. However, **casual vacancies** are usually filled by the board of directors co-opting someone to act as director. That person then serves until the next general meeting when they must stand for election in the usual manner.

(b) **Removal of directors**

There are a number of ways in which a person may be obliged to give up their position as a director:

Rotation

The model articles for public companies provide that one-third of the directors shall retire at each AGM, being those with longest service. They are, however, open to re-election and, in practice, are usually re-elected.

Removal

A director can be removed at any time by the passing of an ordinary resolution of the company (s.168 CA06). The company must be given special notice (28 days) of the intention to propose such a resolution.

The power to remove a director under s.168 cannot be removed or restricted by any provision in the company's documents or any external contract. It is possible, however, for the effect of the section to be avoided in private companies by the use of weighted voting rights *(Bushell* v *Faith* (1969)). As regards private/quasi-partnership companies, it has been held, in *Re Bird Precision Bellows Ltd* (1984), that exclusion from the right to participate in management provides a ground for an action for a court order to remedy unfairly prejudicial conduct under s.994 CA06

Disqualification

The articles of association usually provide for the disqualification of directors on the occurrence of certain circumstances: bankruptcy; mental illness; or prolonged absence from board meetings. In addition, individuals can be disqualified from acting as directors up to a maximum period of 15 years under the Company Directors Disqualification Act 1986.

Grounds for disqualification include:

(i)   persistent breach of the companies legislation;

(ii)   committing offences in relation to companies;

(iii)   fraudulent trading; and

(iv)   general unfitness.

67   DISQUALIFICATION

Key answer tips

This is a very specific question asking candidates to explain the various circumstances in which a director can be disqualified under the Company Directors Disqualification Act 1986.

The Company Directors Disqualification Act (CDDA) 1986 was introduced to control individuals who persistently abused the various privileges that accompany incorporation, most particularly the privilege of limited liability. The Act applies to more than just directors and the court may make an order preventing any person (without leave of the court) from being:

(i)   a director of a company;

(ii)   a liquidator or administrator of a company;

(iii)   a receiver or manager of a company's property; or

(iv)   in any way, whether directly or indirectly, concerned with or taking part in the promotion, formation or management of acompany.

The CDDA 1986 identifies three distinct categories of conduct, which may, and in some circumstances must, lead the court todisqualify certain persons from being involved in the management of companies.

(a)   General misconduct in connection with companies

This first category involves the following:

(i)   A conviction for an indictable offence in connection with the promotion, formation, management or liquidation of acompany or with the receivership or management of a company's property (s.2 of the CDDA 1986). The maximumperiod for disqualification under s.2 is five years where the order is made by a court of summary jurisdiction, and 15years in any other case.

(ii)   Persistent breaches of companies legislation in relation to provisions which require any return, account or otherdocument to be filed with, or notice of any matter to be given to, the registrar (s.3 of the CDDA 1986). Section 3 providesthat a person is conclusively proved to be persistently in default where it is shown that, in the five years ending with the date of the application, he has been adjudged guilty of three or more defaults (s.3(2) of the CDDA 1986). This is without prejudice to proof of persistent default in any other manner. The maximum period of disqualification under this sectionis five years.

(iii) Fraud in connection with winding up (s.4 of the CDDA 1986). A court may make a disqualification order if, in the courseof the winding up of a company, it appears that a person:

(1) has been guilty of an offence for which he is liable under s.993 of the CA 2006, that is, that he has knowinglybeen a party to the carrying on of the business of the company either with the intention of defrauding thecompany's creditors or any other person or for any other fraudulent purpose; or

(2) has otherwise been guilty, while an officer or liquidator of the company or receiver or manager of the property ofthe company, of any fraud in relation to the company or of any breach of his duty as such officer, liquidator, receiveror manager (s.4(1)(b) of the CDDA 1986).

The maximum period of disqualification under this category is 15 years.

(b) *Disqualification for unfitness*

The second category covers:

(i) Disqualification of directors of companies which have become insolvent, who are found by the court to be unfit to be directors (s.6 of the CDDA 1986). Under s. 6, the minimum period of disqualification is two years, up to a maximum of 15 years;

(ii) disqualification after investigation of a company under Pt XIV of the CA 1985 (*it should be noted that this part of the previous Act still sets out the procedures for company investigations*) (s.8 of the CDDA 1986). Once again, themaximum period of disqualification is 15 years.

Schedule 1 to the CDDA 1986 sets out certain particulars to which the court is to have regard in deciding whether a person'sconduct as a director makes them unfit to be concerned in the management of a company. In addition, the courts have givenindications as to what sort of behaviour will render a person liable to be considered unfit to act as a company director. Thus, in *Re Lo-Line Electric Motors Ltd* (1988), it was stated that:

'Ordinary commercial misjudgment is in itself not sufficient to justify disqualification. In the normal case, the conductcomplained of must display a lack of commercial probity, although . . . in an extreme case of gross negligence or total incompetence, disqualification could be appropriate.'

(c) *Other cases for disqualification*

This third category relates to:

(i) participation in fraudulent or wrongful trading under s.213 of the Insolvency Act (IA)1986 (s.10 of the CDDA 1986);

(ii) undischarged bankrupts acting as directors (s.11 of the CDDA 1986); and

(iii) failure to pay under a county court administration order (s.12 of the CDDA 1986).

For the purposes of most of the CDDA 1986, the court has discretion to make a disqualification order. Where, however, aperson has been found to be an unfit director of an insolvent company, the court has a duty to make a disqualification order (s.6 of the CDDA 1986). Anyone who acts in contravention of a disqualification order is liable:

(i)   to imprisonment for up to two years and/or a fine, on conviction on indictment; or

(ii)   to imprisonment for up to six months and/or a fine not exceeding the statutory maximum, on conviction summarily (s.13 of the CDDA 1986).

Examiner's Report

This question required candidates to explain the operation of the Company Directors Disqualification Act 1986. Performance in relation to the question was patchy, with some candidates providing thorough, answers, but a large number mistaking the whole import of the question and delivering an answer, either on directors' duties, or the removal of directors, or a mixture of both. Unfortunately these issues overlapped and even then marks had to be awarded generously. Not only did this confusion not allow candidates to do well in this particular question but it indicated an overall confusion about the nature of directors' duties and their control. In the final analysis, if the candidate cannot refer to the appropriate legislation they are not going to get many marks.

ACCA Marking Scheme	
	Marks
Thorough to complete answers, showing a detailed understanding of the legislation.	8–10
A clear understanding of the topic, but perhaps lacking in detail. Alternatively an unbalanced answer showing good understanding of one part but less in the other.	5–7
Some knowledge, although perhaps not clearly expressed, or very limited in its knowledge and understanding of the topic.	2–4
Little or no knowledge of the topic.	0–1

68   ROLE OF COMPANY AUDITORS

Key answer tips

This question requires candidates to consider the crucially important role of the auditor in relation to companies and the precise way in which this relationship is regulated by company law.

Auditors are appointed to ensure that the interests of the shareholders in a company are being met. Their key function is to produce reports confirming, or otherwise, that the accountancy information provided to shareholders is reliable.

Qualifications

The essential requirement for any person to act as a company auditor is that he or she is eligible under the rules and a member of a recognised supervisory body. This in turn requires him/her to hold a professional accountancy qualification. 'Supervisory bodies' in the UK control the eligibility of potential company auditors and the quality of their operation. The recognised supervisory bodies are:

(i)   the Institute of Chartered Accountants in England and Wales;

(ii)   the Institute of Chartered Accountants of Scotland;

(iii)   the Institute of Chartered Accountants in Ireland;

(iv)   the Chartered Association of Certified Accountants; and

(v)   the Association of Authorised Public Accountants.

The first four bodies in the above list are also recognised as 'qualifying bodies', meaning that accountancy qualifications awarded by them are recognised professional qualifications for auditing purposes. There still is the small possibility of unqualified but appropriately experienced individuals acting as auditors in relation to what used to be known as 'exempt private companies'.

A person is ineligible for appointment as auditor if he/she is either:

(i)   an officer or employee of the company being audited (the auditor being specifically declared not to be an officer or employee), and/or

(ii)   a partner or employee of a person in (i) above, or is in a partnership of which such a person is also a partner.

It is a criminal offence to act whilst ineligible.

Appointment and removal

The auditors should generally be appointed by the shareholders by ordinary resolution. However, the directors can appoint the company's first auditor and fill casual vacancies.

An auditor may be **removed** at any time by ordinary resolution of the company (s.510). This does, however, require special notice. Any auditor who is to be removed or not re-appointed is entitled to make written representations and require these to be circulated or have them read out at the meeting (s.511 CA2006).

An auditor may **resign** at any time (s.516 CA 2006). Notice of resignation must be accompanied either by a statement of any circumstances that the auditor believes ought to be brought to the attention of members and creditors, or alternatively by a statement that there are no such circumstances (s.529 CA 2006). The company is required to file a copy of the notice with the Registrar of Companies within 14 days (s.517 CA 2006). Where the auditor's resignation statement states that there are circumstances that should be brought to the attention of members, then he may require the company to call a meeting to allow an explanation of those circumstances to the members of the company (s.518 CA 2006).

Rights and duties

The auditors have the right of access at all times to the company's books and accounts, and officers and employees of the company are required to provide such information and explanations as the auditors consider necessary (s.499 CA 2006). It is a criminal offence to make false or reckless statements to auditors or to fail to provide the information or explanations required (s.501 CA 2006). Auditors are entitled to receive notices and other documents in connection with all general meetings, to attend such meetings and to speak when the business affects their role as auditors (s.502 CA 2006). They are also entitled to receive copies of any written resolutions sent to the members.

Under s.495 CA 2006, the auditors are specifically required to report on:

(i)   whether the accounts have been properly prepared in accordance with the Act and the relevant financial reporting framework;

(ii)   whether the individual company accounts and the group accounts show a true and fair view of the profit or loss and state of affairs of the company and of the group, so far as concerns the members of the company.

The auditor is also required to report on whether the information in the directors' report is consistent with the accounts presented: s.460.

Under s.498 CA 2006 auditors are required to investigate:

(i) whether the company has kept adequate accounting records and obtained adequate accounting returns from branches; and

(ii) whether the accounts are in agreement with the records; and

(iii) whether they have obtained all the information and explanations that they considered necessary.

The Companies Act places further duties on auditors, relating to such issues as:

(i) the valuation of any non-cash consideration for shares allotted by a public company or a company converting to a public company (s.93 CA 2006); and

(ii) the purchase of its own shares by a company by payment out of capital (s.714 CA 2006).

69 AUTHORITY OF DIRECTORS

Key answer tips

This question requires candidates to explain the various forms of authority. Candidates should provide an explanation of the principal/agent relationship as an introduction to their answer.

An agent is a person who is empowered to represent another legal party, called the principal, and to bring the principal into a legal relationship with a third party. Any contract entered into is between the principal and the third party, each of whom may enforce it. In the normal course of events the agent has no personal rights or liabilities in relation to the contract.

The principal/agent relationship can be created in a number of ways. It may arise as the outcome of a distinct contract, which may be made either orally or in writing, or it may be established purely gratuitously, where some person simply agrees to act for another.

In establishing a relationship of principal/agent however, the principal does not give the agent unlimited power to enter into any contract whatsoever but is likely to place strict limits on the nature of the contracts that the agent can enter into on his behalf. In other words the authority of the agent is limited and in order to bind a principal any contract entered into must be within the limits of the authority extended to the agent. The authority of an agent can take a number of distinct forms.

(a) **Express authority**

In this instance, when the principal/agency relationship is established, the agent is instructed as to what particular tasks are required to be performed and is informed of the precise powers given in order to fulfill those tasks. If the agent subsequently contracts outside of the ambit of their express authority then they will be liable to the principal and to the third party for breach of warrant of authority. The consequences for the relationship between the principal and third party depends on whether the third party knew that the agent was acting outside the scope of their authority.

For example, an individual director of a company may be given the express power by the board of directors to enter into a specific contract on behalf of the company. In such circumstances the company would be bound by the subsequent contract but the director would have no power to bind the company in other contracts.

(b) **Implied authority**

This refers to the way in which the scope of express authority may be increased. Third parties are entitled to assume that agents holding a particular position have all the powers that are usually provided to such an agent. Without actual knowledge to the contrary they may safely assume that the agent has the usual authority that goes with their position.

In *Watteau* v *Fenwick* (1893) the new owners of a hotel continued to employ the previous owner as its manager. They expressly forbade him to buy certain articles including cigars. The manager, however, bought cigars from a third party, who later sued the owners for payment as the manager's principal. It was held that the purchase of cigars was within the usual authority of a manager of such an establishment and that for a limitation on such usual authority to be effective it must be communicated to any third party.

Directors of companies can also bind their companies on the basis of implied authority. In *Hely-Hutchinson* v *Brayhead Ltd* (1968) although the chairman and chief-executive of a company acted as its *de facto* managing director he had never been formally appointed to that position. Nevertheless, he purported to bind the company to a particular transaction. When the other party to the agreement sought to enforce it, the company claimed that the chairman had no authority to bind it. It was held that although the director derived no authority from his position as chairman of the board he did acquire such authority from his position as chief executive and thus the company was bound by the contract he had entered into on its behalf, as it was within the implied authority of a person holding such a position.

(c) **Apparent/ostensible authority**

This type of authority, which is an aspect of agency by estoppel, can arise in two distinct ways:

(i) Where a person makes a representation to third parties that a particular person has the authority to act as their agent without actually appointing them as their agent. In such a case the person making the representation is bound by the actions of the ostensible/apparent agent. The principal is also liable for the actions of the agent where they are aware that the agent claims to be their agent and yet does nothing to correct that impression.

In *Freeman & Lockyer* v *Buckhurst Park Properties (Mangal) Ltd* (1964), although a particular director had never been appointed as managing director, he acted as such with the clear knowledge of the other directors and entered into a contract with the plaintiffs on behalf of the company. When the plaintiffs sought to recover fees due to them under that contract it was held that the company was liable: a properly appointed managing director would have been able to enter into such a contract and the third party was entitled to rely on the representation of the other directors that the person in question had been properly appointed to that position.

(ii) Where a principal has previously represented to a third party that an agent has the authority to act on their behalf. Even if the principal has subsequently revoked the agent's authority they may still be liable for the actions of the former agent unless they have informed third parties who had previously dealt with the agent about the new situation (*Willis Faber & Co Ltd v Joyce* (1911)). Thus companies should inform their previous clients where a director has had his authority, either express or implied, removed or reduced.

70 FRAN, GILL AND HARRY

Key answer tips

This scenario question is based on how a director can be removed and whether a provision in the articles of association constitutes a contract. Candidates should refer to the relevant sections of the Companies Act 2006 as well as case law to support their answer.

(a) Directors can be removed at any time by a simple majority vote of the members under s.168 CA06. This right cannot be removed, although it can be restricted where the company has introduced weighted voting rights on such votes (*Bushell v Faith* (1969)). Those proposing to remove the director must give the company 28 days' notice of the resolution and the director in question must receive a copy of the resolution and is entitled to speak on the resolution at the meeting at which it is considered (s.169 CA06). Gill and Harry can, therefore, use their majority voting power to remove Fran from her role as company director. Even if the removal of the person from the board of directors leads to a breach of their contract of service, the company cannot be prevented from doing so (*Southern Foundries Ltd v Shirlaw* (1940)).

Directors in quasi-partnership private companies may have a legitimate expectation to act as a director and could make a claim under s.260 CA06 that the company's business is being conducted in a manner that is unfairly prejudicial to them (*Re Bird Precision Bellows Ltd* (1984)) but as the usual remedy offered would be a sale of shares at fair value this would not further Fran's cause.

(b) Under s33 CA 2006, the articles of association constitute a contract between the members and the company, and vice versa, as well as a contract between the members. The essential point to bear in mind, however, is that the contract between the members and the company only applies to membership rights and the articles cannot form a contract between the company and either, a non-member, or between the company and a member acting in some capacity other than that of a member (*Eley v Positive Government Security Life Assurance Co* (1876)).

In this situation, Fran is claiming that the articles create a contract between her and the company for her to act as the company's solicitor. However, acting as a solicitor is clearly not a membership right, so she would not normally be able to rely on the articles as the basis of the contract. It is possible for the courts to imply a contract of service from the behaviour of the parties and rely on the articles to provide the actual terms of the contract (*Re New British Iron Co ex parte Beckwith* (1898)), in which case Fran would be able to claim recompense on a 'quantum meruit' basis.

71   GLAD LTD

Key answer tips

This question requires candidates to examine the law relating to the power of companies to change their articles of association. Candidates must ensure that they do not misinterpret the question as relating to directors' duties. They must explain the test for deciding whether the alteration could be challenged in court i.e. that it must be 'bona fide in the interest of the company as a whole'.

Section 21 of the Companies Act 2006 provides for the alteration of articles of association on the passing of a special resolution. However, at common law any such alteration has to be made *'bona fide* in the interest of the company as a whole'. This test involves a subjective element in that those deciding the alteration must actually believe they are acting in the interest of the company. There is additionally, however, an objective element requiring that any alteration has to be in the interest of the 'individual hypothetical member' (*Greenhalgh v Arderne Cinemas Ltd* (1951)). Whether any alteration meets this requirement depends on the facts of the particular case, but in *Brown v British Abrasive Wheel Co Ltd* (1919) an alteration to a company's articles to allow the 98% majority to buy out the 2% minority shareholders was held to be invalid as not being in the interest of the company as a whole. This was in spite of the fact that the company needed additional capital and the majority shareholder was willing to provide that capital if they could gain total control of the company.

In *Dafen Tinplate Co Ltd v Llanelly Steel Co* (1907) a minority shareholder was acting to the detriment of the company. Nonetheless, an alteration to the articles, to allow for the compulsory purchase of any member's shares on request so to do, was also held to be too wide to be in the interest of the company as a whole.

However, in *Sidebottom v Kershaw Leese & Co* (1920) an alteration to the articles to give the directors the power to require any shareholder, who entered into competition with the company, to sell their shares to nominees of the directors at a fair price was held to be valid.

Applying the law to the facts in the problem scenario, it might seem that, as Fred is in direct competition with Glad Ltd, the alteration would be valid in line with the *Sidebottom v Kershaw Leese & Co* case, but it should be noted that the actual alteration to the articles goes much wider than is necessary to cover Fred's situation as it extends to all members, whether or not they are in competition with the company. Consequently it is unlikely that the alteration would be validated by the court as being in the interest of the company as a whole on the basis of *Dafen Tinplate Co Ltd v Llanelly Steel Co* (1907).

Examiner's Report

This question required candidates to examine the law relating to the power of companies to change their articles of association. As the substantive law, either in the statute or case law relating to this area has not been changed this question allowed even those candidates who were unaware of the Companies Act 2006 an opportunity to do well. Unfortunately it was an opportunity not taken by many candidates, as the question tended to be done inadequately. As has already been stated in the introduction above, a number of candidates wilfully misinterpreted the question as relating to directors' duties and wasted a lot of time and effort in pursuing that path. The majority of candidates recognised that the issue was about the alteration of articles, and recognised that it required the passing of a special resolution with a 75% majority. However very few were able to explain the tests for deciding whether the alteration could be challenged in court. Even those who were aware of the bona fide *'interest of the company as whole'* test tended not to gone to explain it further, with only a small number considering the situation of the *'hypothetical individual'* member.

As a result although many concluded that the alteration could be challenged in the courts, no legal principle or authority was cited to support that conclusion, or irrelevant law relating to directors or indeed partnerships was cited. The final point to mention is that candidates were credited with marks, even if they reached a different conclusion from that suggested in the model answer, just as long as they used the appropriate legal authorities to support their decision.

ACCA Marking Scheme	Marks
Very weak answers which might recognise what the question is about but show no ability to analyse or answer the problem as set out.	0–2
Identification of some of the central issues in the question and an attempt to apply the appropriate law. Towards the bottom of this range of marks there will be major shortcomings in analysis or application of law.	3–4
Candidates will exhibit a sound knowledge of the relevant law together with the ability to recognise the issues contained in the question. Knowledge may be less detailed or analysis less focused.	5–7
Candidates will exhibit a thorough knowledge of the relevant law together with the ability to analyse the problems contained in the question.	8–10

72   KING LTD

Key answer tips

This question requires candidates to consider the authority of company directors to enter into binding contracts on behalf of their companies.   Candidates should discuss the three forms of authority and refer to relevant case law to score a reasonable mark.

Lex

The model articles of association provide that the directors of a company may exercise all the powers of the company. It is important to note that this power is given to the board as a whole and not to individual directors and, consequently, individual directors cannot bind the company without their being authorised in some way so to do. There are three ways in which the power of the board of directors may be extended to individual directors.

(i)   The individual director may be given **express authority** to enter into a particular transaction on the company's behalf. To this end, the model articles allow for the delegation of the board's powers to one or more directors. Where such express delegation has been made then the company is bound by any contract entered into by the person to whom the power was delegated. However, in the present situation it does not appear that Lex has been expressly given the power to enter into the contract with Nat, and so the company cannot be made liable on this basis.

(ii) A second type of authority that may empower an individual director to bind his company is **implied authority**. In this situation, the person's authority flows from their position. The model articles provide for the board of directors to appoint a **managing director** and also allow them to delegate to any managing director such powers as they consider desirable to be exercised by that person. Thus the board of directors may expressly confer any of their powers on the managing director as they see fit. The mere fact of appointment, however, will mean that the person so appointed will have the implied authority to bind the company in the same way as the board, whose delegate he or she is. Outsiders, therefore, can safely assume that a person appointed as managing director has all the powers usually exercised by a person acting as a managing director.

Implied actual authority to bind a company may also arise as a consequence of the appointment of an individual to a **position other than that of managing director**. In *Hely-Hutchinson* v *Brayhead Ltd.* (1968), although the chairman and chief executive of a company acted as its *de facto* managing director, he had never been formally appointed to that position. Nevertheless, he purported to bind the company to a particular transaction. When the other party to the agreement sought to enforce it, the company claimed that the director had no authority to bind it. It was held that, although the director derived no authority from his position as chairman of the board, he did acquire such authority from his position as chief executive and thus the company was bound by the contract he had entered into on its behalf.

Once again, however, it would appear that Nat cannot make use of this method of fixing King Ltd with liability for his contract as Lex has not been appointed to any executive office in the company.

(iii) The third way in which an individual director may possess the power to bind his company is through the operation of **ostensible authority**, which is alternatively described as **apparent authority** or **agency by estoppel**.

This arises where an individual director has neither express nor implied authority. Nonetheless, the director is held out by the other members of the board of directors as having the authority to bind the company. If a third party acts on such a representation, then the company will be estopped from denying its truth. In *Freeman and Lockyer* v *Buckhurst Park Properties (Mangal) Ltd.*(1964), although a particular director had never been appointed as managing director, he acted as such with the clear knowledge of the other directors and entered into a contract with the plaintiffs on behalf of the company. When the plaintiffs sought to recover fees due to them under that contract, it was held that the company was liable: a properly appointed managing director would have been able to enter into such a contract and the third party was entitled to rely on the representation of the other directors that the person in question had been properly appointed to that position.

The situation in the question is very similar to that in *Freeman and Lockyer* v *Buckhurst Park Properties (Mangal) Ltd*. The board of King Ltd. has permitted Lex to act as its managing director and he has even used that title. The board has therefore acquiesced in his representation of himself as their managing director and consequently they and King Ltd. are bound by any contracts he might make within the scope of a managing director's implied authority. As entering into a contract to draw up plans would clearly come within that authority, King Ltd. will be liable to pay Nat or face an action for breach of contract.

73   CLEAN LTD

Key answer tips

This is a specific question relating to statutory directors' duties, in particular the duty to avoid conflicts of interest under s175 of the Companies Act 2006.

This question requires an analysis of the doctrine of corporate opportunity and the rules relating to directors' duties. Section 178 of the Companies Act (CA) 2006 places directors' duties on a statutory basis, and although s.170 provides that the new statement of duties replaces the old common law rules and equitable principles, it nonetheless expressly provides that the duties now stated in the Act are to be interpreted and applied in the same way as those rules and principles were. Section 178 specifically preserves the existing civil consequences of breach of any of the general duties, so the remedies for breach of the newly stated general duties will be exactly the same as those that were available following a breach of the equitable principles and common law rules that the general duties replace. Section 178(2) specifically provides that the directors' duties are enforceable in the same way as any other fiduciary duty owed to a company by its directors and remedies available may include:

(i)   damages or compensation where the company has suffered loss;

(ii)   restoration of the company's property;

(iii)   an account of profits made by the director; and

(iv)   rescission of a contract where the director failed to disclose an interest.

It should be noted that the foregoing does not apply to the duty to exercise reasonable care, skill and diligence under s.174, which is not considered to be a fiduciary duty.

Section 175 of the Act specifically deals with the duty to avoid conflicts of interest and replaces the previous no-conflict rule. Under the previous rule, certain consequences followed if directors placed themselves in a position where their personal interests cameinto conflict with their duties to the company, unless the company knew about the conflict and specifically consented to it. Section 175 continues that procedure in an amended form, which allows the other independent directors to authorise the conflict. Anyconflicted directors must not count in the quorum for the meeting or vote. The section makes clear that a conflict of interest may, in particular, arise when a director makes personal use of information, property or opportunities belonging to the company or specifically under ss.177 and 182 where the duties to declare interests in transactions are set out, when a director enters into acontract with his company. This is the case whether or not the company itself could have taken advantage of the property, information or opportunity, so once again the previous common law and equitable rules are maintained. As well as allowing thedirectors to approve a conflict under s.175, s.180 preserves the ability of the members of a company to authorise conflicts thatwould otherwise be a breach of this duty.

Applying the preceding rules to the facts of the problem scenario it can be seen that Des has beached his statutory duty under CA2006 s.175 by allowing a conflict of interest to arise without declaring it to the board and getting the approval of the other directorsor indeed the members.

The operation of the previous fiduciary duty not to make an undisclosed benefit from the position as directors and not to profit personally from what is a corporate opportunity even survived after the director in question has left the company (*IDC* v *Cooley* (1972)). As the CA 2006 continues the previous equitable principles and specifically states that the duty to avoid conflicts of interest applies to former directors, Des will still be liable for his action.

It is also now clear that the rules against allowing a conflict of interest to arise apply even if the company cannot itself takeadvantage of the opportunity wrongly misappropriated, which continues the previous very strict application of principle (*Regal (Hastings)* v *Gulliver* (1942)). However the duty is not infringed if the situation cannot reasonably be regarded as likely to give rise to a conflict of interest: s.175(4)(a).

Applying this to the facts of the problem it would appear that Des has acted in breach of his statutory duty and will be held liableto account to the company for any profits he made on the transaction.

He will not be allowed to hide his personal profit behind the separate personality of Flush Ltd as the courts will simply lift the veil of incorporation as in *Gilford Motor Co* v *Horne* (1933).

Examiner's Report

This question required an analysis of the doctrine of corporate opportunity and the rules relating to directors' duties. It has to be said it was the least popular question on the paper and was not attempted by a considerable minority of candidates, and those who did tackle it, did not do particularly well in it. There were essentially two core issues in the question, relating to conflict of interest, corporate opportunities and the much less essential corporate personality issue.

The majority of candidates recognised that the question related to directors' duties in some way, but apart from citing those generally, could get no further than that. Very few candidates even considered the corporate opportunities issue, preferring to go down the road of patent law, which is not even part of the syllabus of this paper.

As for the corporate personality issue, although not central to the question a number of candidates saw it as the key issue and spent all their time dealing with that –perhaps it would not be too cynical to suggest that this was in response to their lack of knowledge relating to any other aspect of the question.

ACCA marking scheme	
	Marks
Thorough to complete answers, showing a detailed understanding of the rules relating to conflict of interest.	8–10
A clear understanding of the topic but perhaps lacking in detail or application.	5–7
Some knowledge, although perhaps not clearly expressed, or very limited in its application.	2–4
Little or no knowledge of the topic.	0–1

74 CALLING AND VOTING

Key answer tips

This question specifically deals with general meetings and therefore candidates must ensure this is the only meeting they refer to in their answer.

(a) General meetings may be convened in a number of ways by various people as follows:

(i) Meetings are usually called by the board of directors. Directors may call a general meeting whenever they consider it necessary. However, by virtue of s.336 CA 2006, public companies are required to hold an annual general meeting (AGM) once a year within the six months following the accounting reference date.

(ii) Apart from their usual power, directors of public limited companies are required, under s.656 CA 2006, to call meeting where there has been a serious loss of capital. This is defined as the assets falling to half or less than the nominal value of the called up share capital.

(iii) The members (shareholders) of the company may call a general meeting. A meeting may be called by those members who hold at least 10% of the paid up voting capital or, in the case of a private company, 5% of the paid up voting capital, if more than 12 months has elapsed since the last general meeting (s.303 CA 2006). If the directors then fail to convene a meeting as required within 21 days of the deposit of the requisition, (and to hold it within 28 days of the notice calling the meeting) then the requisitionists may themselves convene a meeting and recover any expenses from the company: s.305 CA 2006.

(iv) The resigning auditor of a company may require the directors to convene a general meeting of the members. This power is provided so that, where there is cause for concern, the auditor can explain the reason for his resignation to the members generally and put them on notice: s.518 CA 2006.

(v) The court may order a meeting under s.306 CA 2006 where it is impracticable otherwise to call a meeting, for example to break deadlock. The court's power under s.306 is extremely wide and any such meeting is to be called, held and conducted in any manner the court thinks fit. In *Re El Sombrero Ltd.* (1958) the applicant held 900 of the company's 1,000 shares although he was not a director of the company. The only two directors held 50 shares each. When the majority shareholder sought to exercise his power to remove the two existing directors under s.168 CA 2006, they refused to call an annual general meeting and made it clear that they would not attend any meeting called. As the articles of association set the quorum for a general meeting at two, their refusal to attend prevented the applicant from taking any action. Under such circumstances, the court used its power under s.306 to order the holding of a general meeting at which the quorum was set at one person only. Thus the applicant could remove the other two members from the board of directors.

(b)   There are two methods of deciding votes at general meetings: by a show of hands or by a poll vote.

A resolution is decided upon initially by a show of hands unless a poll is demanded. On a show of hands every member has one vote. In a poll it is usual for each share to carry a vote and thus for the outcome of the poll to reflect concentration of interest in the company. A poll may be demanded by members holding at least 10% of the total voting rights (or by not less than 5 members having the right to vote on the resolution). A poll means one vote per share. The result of a poll replaces the result of the previous show of hands.

The use of voting by poll is sometimes used to overcome the decisions of activist shareholders who attend general meetings in order to pursue particular causes. As very few shareholders attend meetings it is possible for a small group of activists to win a vote by a show of hands, even against the wishes of the board of directors. However, when a poll vote is taken the directors are by and large able to win the vote through the deployment of the proxy votes of the non-attending members. Non-attending members usually authorise the chairman to cast their votes on their behalf, and so the proxy votes are usually controlled by the board.

75   RESOLUTIONS

Key answer tips

This question invites candidates to examine the types of reolutions that can be passed by companies. Resolutions are the way in which companies take decisions. It should be noted that it is the shareholders that pass a resolution **not** directors.   Whereas an ordinary resolution requires a simple majority, a special resolution requires three-quarters of the votes.

Under the provisions of the Companies Act (CA) 2006 there are three types of resolutions: ordinary resolutions, special resolutions and written resolutions.

(a)   Section 282 CA 2006 defines an ordinary resolution of the members generally, or a class of members, of a company, as a resolution that is passed by a simple majority.

If the resolution is to be voted on a show of hands, the majority is determined on the basis of those who vote in person or as duly appointed proxies. Where a poll vote is called, the majority is determined in relation to the total voting rights of members who vote in person or by proxy.

A special resolution of the members (or of a class of members) of a company means a resolution passed by a majority of not less than 75% determined in the same way as for an ordinary resolution (s.283). If a resolution is proposed as a special resolution, it must be indicated as such, either in the written resolution text or in the meeting notice. Where a resolution is proposed as a special resolution, it can only be passed as such although anything that may be done as an ordinary resolution may be passed as a special resolution (s.282(5)). There is no longer a requirement for 21 days' notice where a special resolution is to be passed at a meeting.

Where a provision of the Companies Acts requires a resolution, but does not specify what kind of resolution is required, the default provision is for an ordinary resolution.

However, the company's articles may require a higher majority, or indeed may require a unanimous vote to pass the resolution. The articles cannot alter the requisite majority where the Companies Acts actually state the required majority, so if the Act provides for an ordinary resolution the articles cannot require a higher majority.

(b) **Written resolutions**

Private limited companies are no longer required to hold meetings and can take decisions by way of written resolutions (s.281 CA 2006). The Companies Act 2006 no longer requires unanimity to pass a written resolution. It merely requires the appropriate majority of total voting rights, a simple majority for an ordinary resolution (s.282(2)) and a 75% majority of the total voting rights for a special resolution (s.283(2)).

By virtue of s.288 (5) CA 2006 anything which in the case of a private company might be done by resolution in a general meeting, or by a meeting of a class of members of the company, may be done by written resolution with only two exceptions:

– the removal of a director; and

– the removal of an auditor both of which still require the calling of a general meeting of shareholders.

A written resolution may be proposed by the directors or the members of the private company (s.288 (3)). Under s.291 in the case of a written resolution proposed by the directors, the company must send or submit a copy of the resolution to every eligible member. This may be done as follows:

– either by sending copies to all eligible members in hard copy form, in electronic form or by means of a website;

– by submitting the same copy to each eligible member in turn or different copies to each of a number of eligible members in turn;

– by a mixture of the above processes.

The copy of the resolution must be accompanied by a statement informing the members both how to signify agreement to the resolution and the date by which the resolution must be passed if it is not to lapse (s.291(4)). It is a criminal offence not to comply with the above procedure, although the validity of any resolution passed is not affected.

The members of a private company may require the company to circulate a resolution if they control 5% of the voting rights (or a lower percentage if specified in the company's articles). They can also require a statement of not more than 1,000 words to be circulated with the resolution (s.292). However, the members requiring the circulation of the resolution will be required to pay any expenses involved, unless the company resolves otherwise.

Agreement to a proposed written resolution occurs when the company receives an authenticated document, in either hard copy form or in electronic form, identifying the resolution and indicating agreement to it. Once submitted, agreement cannot be revoked.

The resolution and accompanying documents must be sent to all members who would be entitled to vote on the circulation date of the resolution. The company's auditor should also receive such documentation (s.502 CA 2006).

Examiner's Report

This question required candidates to explain the meaning of and procedure for the passing of (a) an ordinary and a special resolution and (b) a written resolution. Once again although the terms were continued from the previous companies Act, the 2006 Act made significant changes to them.

As a whole, candidates performed well on part (a) with the majority of candidates identifying that resolutionswere decisions by members, usually held by a poll or a show of hands at a meeting (either AGM or GM) and that a simple majority is required for the passing of the ordinary resolution and 75% for a special resolution. Some candidates went further and provided examples of when the two types of resolutions would be used. It has to be noted, however, that a number of candidates thought that such decisions were taken by directors rather than members.

Part (b) relating to written resolutions was inadequately answered. Most candidates worked out from the question that this procedure applied only to private companies, but only a few went on to develop their answers. While some candidates were aware that these resolutions were available when such companies did not hold general meetings, some insisted that they were passed at general meetings. As has been said very few candidates wereaware of the changes introduced by the 2006 Companies Act.

	ACCA Marking Scheme	
		Marks
(a)	Some awareness of the area but lacking in detailed knowledge.	0–2
	A good explanation of the difference between the two types of resolution.	3–5
(b)	Unbalanced, or may not deal with all of the required aspects of the topic. Alternatively the answer will demonstrate very little understanding of what is actually meant by a written resolution.	0–2
	Candidates must not only show an understanding of what is meant by a written resolution but also the rules relating to them.	3–5

76 TYPES OF MEETING *Walk in the footsteps of a top tutor*

Key answer tips

This question requires consideration of the three types of meetings as well as requiring candidates to distinguish between them. Candidates should explain the purpose of each meeting first and then draw comparisons between them. The highlighted words are key phrases that markers are looking for.

In theory, the ultimate control over a company's business lies with the members in a general meeting. One would obviously conclude that a meeting involved more than one person; and indeed there is authority to that effect in *Sharp* v *Dawes* (1876) in which a meeting between a lone member and the company secretary was held not to be validly constituted. It is possible, however, for a meeting of only one person to take place in the following circumstances:

(i)   in the case of a meeting of a particular class of shareholders and all the shares of that class are owned by the one member; and

(ii)   by virtue of s.306 of the Companies Act 2006 the court may order the holding of a general meeting at which the quorum is to be one member.

Types of meetings

There are three types of meeting:

(a)   **Annual general meeting**. By virtue of s.336 CA06, every public company is required to hold an annual general meeting (AGM) once a year, within the six months following the accounting reference date. (Private companies are no longer required to hold an AGM).

If a company fails to hold an AGM then every officer in default may be fined.

S.307 CA06 states that 21 days' notice is normally required unless 95% of those members entitled to attend and vote agree to a shorter period. The usual business of an AGM includes consideration of the accounts, appointment of the auditors, election of the directors and the declaration of dividends.

Members can force the inclusion of a resolution on the agenda if they hold 5% of the voting rights or 100 members each hold an average of £100 of the paid up share capital: s.338 CA06.

(b)   A **general meeting** can be held whenever required. At least 14 days' notice must be given and the person who requisitions the meeting may set the agenda.

In the case of a public limited company, a general meeting must be held if a serious loss of capital has occurred: s656 CA06. This is defined as the assets falling to half or less than the nominal value of the called up share capital.

(c)   A **class meeting** is one held by a class of shareholders or debenture holders, usually to consider a variation of their class rights. A quorum for a class meeting is two persons holding, or representing by proxy, at least one-third in nominal value of the issued shares of the class in question: s.334 CA06.

Meetings may be convened in a number of ways by various people:

(i)   by the directors of the company;

(ii)   by the members using the power to requisition a meeting under s.303 CA 2006;

(iii) by the auditor of a company under s.518, which provides for a resigning auditor to require the directors to convene a meeting in order to explain the reason for the auditor's resignation; and

(iv)   the court may order a meeting under s.306 where it is impracticable otherwise to call a meeting.

LEGAL IMPLICATIONS RELATING TO COMPANIES IN DIFFICULTY OR IN CRISIS

77 WINDING UP *Walk in the footsteps of a top tutor*

Key answer tips

This question requires candidates to explain that a company being an artificial person must be liquidated before its 'life' can be terminated. The second part of the question requires the candidates to explain the difference between the two types of winding up and to provide relevant illustrations. The highlighted words are key phrases that markers are looking for.

(a) One of the many consequences of incorporation is that a registered company becomes a legal entity in its own right having existence apart from its member shareholders. One of the attributes of this legal personality is that the company has not only separate but perpetual existence, in that it continues irrespective of changes in its membership. Indeed the company can continue to exist where it has no members at all. Winding up, otherwise called liquidation, is the process whereby the life of the company is brought to an end and its assets realised and distributed to its members and/or creditors. The rules governing winding up are detailed in the provisions of the Insolvency Act 1986 (IA) and the exact nature of procedure depends on the type of winding up involved and depends upon the solvency of the company when liquidation commences.

(b) There are two different types of liquidation. It may be voluntary or compulsory. As the name suggest, a voluntary liquidation is initiated by the shareholders of the company. S.84 IA provides that the company may be voluntarily wound up and gives reasons for such liquidation. The first reason is if any period that has been fixed for the duration of the company by the articles or any event occurs which shall, according to the articles, lead to its dissolution. Under such circumstances the winding up has to be approved by an ordinary resolution. The company may also be wound up for any other reason whatsoever by passing of special resolutions. If the company's liabilities indicate that it is insolvent, an extraordinary resolution is required.

If the winding up is initiated by the shareholders it will be called members' voluntary winding up. This take place when the directors of the company are of the opinion that the company is solvent and is capable of paying off its creditors but nevertheless they wish to terminate the life of the company. The directors are required to make a formal declaration to the effect that they have investigated the affairs of the company and that in their opinion it will be able to pay its debts within 12 months of the start of liquidation. It is a criminal offence for directors to make a false declaration without having reasonable grounds for believing that the statement is true. On appointment, by an ordinary resolution of the company, the job of the liquidator is to wind up the affairs of the company, to realise the assets and distribute the proceeds to its creditors. On completion of this task the liquidator must present a report of the process to a final meeting of the shareholders. The liquidator then informs the registrar of the holding of the final meeting and submits a copy of his report to him. The registrar formally registers these reports and the company is deemed to be dissolved three months after that registration.

Creditors' voluntary winding up takes place where no declaration of solvency has been made. This means that the company is insolvent. Creditors play an active part in the process of overseeing the liquidation of the company. Firstly, a meeting of the creditors must be called within 14 days of the resolution to liquidate the company at which directors must submit a statement of company's affairs. The creditors have the final say in who should be appointed as the liquidator and may, if they elect, appoint a liquidation committee to work with the liquidator. On completion of the winding up, the liquidator calls and submits his report to meetings of the members and creditors. The liquidator then informs the companies' registry of the holding of these final meetings and submits a copy of his report to it. The registrar formally registers these reports and the company is deemed to be dissolved three months after that registration

78 GROUNDS FOR WINDING UP

Key answer tips

This is a fairly straightforward question which requires candidates to state the seven grounds under which a company can be wound up under the Insolvency Act 1986.

The seven grounds under which a registered company may be wound up by the court under the Insolvency Act 1986 (IA), are as follows:

(i)   the company has passed a special resolution that it be wound up by the court;

(ii)   it is a public company which has not within a year since its registration obtained a certificate of compliance with the share capital requirements;

(iii)   it is an 'old public company' which has failed to re-register;

(iv)   it has not commenced business within a year from its incorporation or has suspended its business for a whole year;

(v)   (except in the case of a private company limited by shares or by guarantee) the number of members is reduced below two;

(vi)   the company is unable to pay its debts;

(vii) the court is of the opinion that it is just and equitable that the company should be wound up.

The most common of these grounds are (i) (vi) (vii).

If for any reason the members of the company no longer wish to continue the business they will use (i).

Outsiders may apply to have a company wound up under (vi). Section 123 (IA) provides that, if a company with a debt exceeding £750, fails to pay it within three weeks of receiving a written demand, then it is deemed unable to pay its debts.

Procedure (vii) may be used in private companies where there is deadlock in management (*Re Yenidje Tobacco Co Ltd* (1916)).

79   ADMINISTRATION

Key answer tips

The law on administration was changed by the Enterprise Act 2002, which amended the Insolvency Act 1986. In the context of company insolvency, the Enterprise Act introduced changes designed to make administration arrangements more common and administrative receivership less common. It also removed the preferential creditor status of debts owed to the government for money owing to Her Majesty's Revenue and Customs (HMRC) and social security contributions.

Administration is a procedure for dealing with the affairs of an insolvent company, as an alternative to liquidation (winding up) and administrative receivership. It was first introduced in the Insolvency Act 1986, but the terms of this Act were amended by the Enterprise Act 2002, with the intention of making administration a more commonly-used procedure as an alternative to administrative receivership.

Administration involves the appointment of a suitably-qualified individual, known as an administrator, to manage the affairs, business and property of the company. An administrator may be appointed in one of three ways: by order of the court in response to a petition (e.g. from a creditor or creditors of the company), by the holder of a 'qualifying' floating charge over the company's assets, or by the company or its directors (provided that winding up procedures have not already begun, or an administrative receiver has not already been appointed). Significantly, with the exception of appointment by court order, an administrator may be appointed without involvement of the court. The court will only agree to appoint an administrator if it is satisfied that the company is or is likely to become unable to pay its debts, and the administration order is likely to achieve the purpose of administration.

An administrator should not agree to act for a company unless he/she believes that administration is likely to achieve its objective.

The objective of administration should be:

(a)   rescuing the company as a going concern, or

(b)   achieving a better result for the company's creditors as a whole than would be likely if the company were would up (without first being in administration), or

(c)   realising property in order to make a payment to one or more secured or preferential creditors.

The administrator should perform his functions in the interests of the company's creditors as a whole, and as quickly and efficiently as is reasonably practical. The initial period of appointment is for one year, although the term of the appointment can be extended.

The effect of appointing an administrator is to dismiss any petition that might have been submitted to the court for the winding up of the company. While the administration continues:

(a)   no resolution may be passed or order made for the winding up of the company;

(b)   no other steps may be taken to enforce any security over the company's assets, or to repossess goods in the company's possession under a hire purchase agreement, except with the consent of the administrator or permission of the court.

As soon as possible after his appointment, the administrator should be supplied with a statement of the company's affairs from a relevant person, and he should then formulate proposals on how the objectives of the administration may be achieved, for submission to the creditors and members of the company, and the registrar of companies.

GOVERNANCE AND ETHICAL ISSUES RELATING TO BUSINESS

80   TELA & CO

Key answer tips

This is a scenario question based on the Combined Code and whether in this scenario the principles laid down in the Combined Code are being adhered to. Candidates should state the reasons as to how SGCC is **not** complying with the Combined Code rather than how it is.

SGCC plc does not comply with the Combined Code of Corporate Governance for the following reasons:

Chief Executive Officer (CEO) and Chairman

Mr Sheppard is both CEO and chairman of SGCC plc. Corporate governance indicates that the person responsible for running the company (the CEO) and the person responsible for controlling the board (the chairman) should be different people. This is to ensure that no one individual has unrestricted powers of decision.

Composition of board

The current board ratio of executive to non-executive directors is 5:2. This means that the executive directors can dominate the board proceedings. Corporate governance codes suggest that there should be a balance of executive and non-executive directors so this cannot happen. A minimum of three non-executive directors are also normally recommended, although reports such as Cadbury note this may be difficult to achieve.

Director appointment

At present, Mr Sheppard appoints directors to the board, giving him absolute authority over who is appointed. This makes the appointment procedure and qualities directors are being appointed against difficult to determine. Corporate governance suggests that appointment procedures should be transparent so that the suitability of directors for board positions can be clearly seen.

Review of board performance

It is correct that the performance of senior managers is reviewed, but this principle should also be applied to the board. While Mr Sheppard may undertake some review, this is not transparent and it is not clear what targets the board either met or did not meet.

Board pay

At present, board members' pay is set by Mr Sheppard. This process breaches principles of good governance because the remuneration structure is not transparent and Mr Sheppard sets his own pay. Mr Sheppard could easily be setting remuneration levels based on his own judgements without any objective criteria.

Internal control

The system of internal control in SGCC plc does not appear to be reviewed correctly. While external auditors will review the control system, this review is based on their audit requirement and cannot be relied on to test the overall effectiveness of the system. The system may therefore still contain weaknesses and errors.

Internal audit

SGCC plc does not have an internal audit department. Given the lack of formal review of internal control in the company, this is surprising. Good corporate governance implies that the control system is monitored and that an internal audit department is established to carry out this task.

Financial statements

There appears to be acceptable disclosure in the financial statements regarding the past results of the company However, the board should also provide an indication of how the company will perform in the future, by a forecast review of operations or similar statement. This is partly to enable investors to assess the value of their investment in the company.

Audit committee

There is no mention in the report of an audit committee. Good corporate governance implies that there is some formal method of monitoring external auditors as well as checking that the reports from the external auditors are given appropriate attention in the company.

81 STANDARDS

Key answer tips

This question requires candidates to focus on two particular items: the Higgs Review and the Combined Code. The candidates should list the recommendations that have been made and then briefly evaluate whether those are likely to be effective.

The Higgs Committee was established as a direct result of the collapse of the US company Enron. The insolvency of Enron came as a surprise to everyone as there were no prior warnings that the company might have been in financial difficulties. This highlighted the fact that the existence of non-executive directors and the auditors does not by itself ensure full accountability and proper control procedures within big companies.

Attention has been focused on the issue of independence of non-executive directors and auditors and the way the independence is determined. The report was produced in December 2003 and its recommendations are published on the Internet. The report was specifically focused on the issue of non-executive directors and the meaning of the word independence. Its main recommendations were the establishment of the procedures and the composition of the board of directors. The board should consist of executive and non-executive directors, but the number of non-executives should equal at least half of the total number of directors, excluding the chairman. The committee re-emphasised the recommendation of the Cadbury Committee that the role of the chairman and the managing director should not be combined. In terms of the procedures, the non-executive directors should have a meeting at least once a year to discuss the 'health' of the company without the presence of executive directors to ensure freedom of discussion and judgment. The annual report should contain a statement saying whether they have done so or not.

They should also identify an independent leader as a senior independent director who should participate in the discussions and also be a point of contact for shareholders. The review also described the role of the non-executive directors with regards to strategy, risk, performance and people. Non executive directors should positively challenge the executive directors to explain and analyse the strategy they have adopted and evaluated its appropriateness. They should make regular reviews of the performance of the directors and they should monitor how performance is reported. They should be satisfied that all reported information is accurate and fair and that the risk is assessed and communicated to shareholders on a regular basis. They should also be responsible for the appointments of and setting the levels of remuneration for executive directors. However, the most important aspect of the Higgs Review was the provision of a description of what is meant by independence. 'A non executive director is considered independent when the board determines that the director is independent in character and judgement and there are no relationships or circumstances which could affect, or appear to affect, the director's judgment. Such relationships and circumstances cannot arise where the director:

- is a former employee of the company or group until five years after employment (or any other material connection) has ended;

- has, or has had within the last three years, a material business relationship with the company either directly, or as a partner, shareholder, director or senior employee of a body that has such a relationship with the company;

- has received or receives additional remuneration from the company apart from a director's fee, participates in the company's share option or a performance-related pay scheme, or is a member of the company's pension scheme;

- has close family ties with any of the company's advisers, directors or senior employees;

- holds cross-directorships or has significant links with other directors through involvement in other companies or bodies;

- represents a significant shareholder; or

- has served on the board for more than ten years.

The board should make a declaration in the annual report stating which of their directors are independent and should state their reasons for such determination.

The Higgs recommendations caused quite a substantial unease within public listed companies, but they have been either written into the Combined Code or included in the best practice guidelines that accompanied the Code.

It is difficult, as yet, to measure the effectiveness of the Higgs Review. The definition of independence should make substantial improvements as it has necessitated changes in the composition of the board for many publicly listed companies and made the appointment process more transparent. However, its success will depend on whether it is properly complied with.

82   COMBINED CODE

Key answer tips

This straightforward question requires candidates to discuss the structure and content of the Combined Code. Candidates should explain the meaning of 'principles based approach' as opposed to 'rule based approach'.

The Combined Code on Corporate Governance was first issued in 1998 as a result of the recommendation of three independent Committees: Cadbury, Greenbury and Hampel. The recommendations of all those committees included a suggestion that the best practices and methods of corporate governance should be incorporated into a single code to ensure practicality and ease of use. Since the original publications the Code has been revised twice: firstly in 2003 and then most recently in November 2006. The latest revision has not, however, introduced substantial changes.

Both Combined Codes (2003 and 2006) start with a preamble which describes the function of the Code. It specifies that the Code contains main and supporting principles and provisions. The drafters expected that the Code would be complied with by the vast majority of companies in nearly all circumstances; however, it was recognised that sometimes it may be justified not to adhere to the principles. Before the company chooses not to comply with the provisions, it must carefully review each provision and provide detailed explanations as to why it felt unable or unwilling to comply.

The Code is divided into two sections. The first one deals with companies and is further divided into four parts: directors; remuneration; accountability and audit; and relations with shareholders. The second section focuses on the companies' relationships with institutional shareholders and is directed at the shareholders. The code is supplemented by three schedules. Schedule A prescribes provisions on the design of performance-related remuneration; Schedule B deals with guidance on liability of non-executive directors: care, skills and diligence; and Schedule C regulates disclosure of corporate governance arrangements. In addition to the Schedules the Code has annexed two previous reports: The Turnbull Guidance on internal controls and The Smith Guidance on audit committees as well as some suggestions adopted from the Higgs report.

In section one, the Code makes it imperative that the company should have an effective board and the board should collectively be responsible for the success and performance of the company. The effectiveness should be achieved by the directors taking decisions objectively, strictly adhering to the fiduciary duty of acting only in the company's interest. The board should devise a coherent strategy for the future of the company and should ensure that all relevant resources, whether human or physical, are in place. The board should provide effective leadership in an entrepreneurial spirit, but with clear and transparent control mechanisms. The control mechanisms should include a provision that no single person should have unlimited power to make and enforce decisions within the company and there should be clear division of responsibility. Non-executive directors should play an important and meaningful role. They should not be a mere figurehead but should actively participate in the decision-making process, challenge the executive directors and constructively question the suitability and effectiveness of the company's strategy. The non-executives should be independent and their judgment should not be in any way fettered by the executive directors. The performance and effectiveness of the board should be regularly evaluated. Performance reviews should be done collectively for the board as a whole and for each director individually at regular intervals and this should be coupled with a regular rotation of directors. The levels of remuneration should be adequate to attract high quality candidates; however, the company should not pay more than is necessary.

With regards to accountability and audit; the Code requires each company to have a coherent system of internal controls and the board should regularly review and present a balanced and clear assessment of the company's position and prospects. They should have an open and regular dialogue with shareholders and stakeholders to ensure that they are fully aware of the circumstances of the company and that they accept the strategy and future plans. All companies should make it a priority to engage shareholders and positively encourage their participation in the decision-making process.

Section two refers to institutional shareholders and attempts to encourage them to actively participate in the corporate governance regime. They should actively consider how they vote and they should regularly evaluate the company's governance arrangements, especially those which relate to board structure and composition.

The Code does not prescribe comprehensive rules which must always be followed. It operates on principles and recommendations and it is up to the company to decide how those principles are to be implemented. In other words, the Code prescribes the end outcomes that the companies must strive to achieve but leaves the method of achieving those outcomes to the companies themselves. Such an approach has substantial advantages. In the first place, it prevents the development of a 'tick-box' mentality where form becomes more important than the substance. It also allows for regular reviews of its effectiveness and changes can be implemented quickly. There are also some disadvantages in the way that the code is very general and directors will interpret it according to their own experience and abilities. This in turn will result in substantial variation in the standards of corporate governance. However, it is submitted that the advantages outweigh the disadvantages and accordingly, the principle based approach should continue.

83   FRAUDULENT TRADING

Key answer tips

This question requires candidates to explain the distinction between the criminal offence of fraudulent trading and its civil counterpart.

S.993 of the Companies Act 2006 establishes the criminal offence of fraudulent trading, which applies whether or not the company has been or is in the course of being wound up. A party found guilty of fraudulent trading is liable on indictment to seven years' imprisonment and/ or an unlimited fine; or on summary conviction to six months' imprisonment and/or a fine of up to the statutory maximum. S.993 does not just apply to fraudulent trading in relation to creditors, and as was held in *R v Kemp* (1988) if a company is used for any kind of fraud, those liable may be convicted under s.993. In *R. v Grantham* (1984) the Court of Appeal held that a jury had not been misdirected that dishonesty and an intention to defraud might be present if they determined that a defendant charged under what is now s.993 obtained or helped to obtain credit, knowing that there was no good reason for thinking funds would be available to pay the debt when it fell due or shortly afterwards. It was not necessary for the prosecution to prove that the defendant knew that there was no reasonable prospect that the creditor would ever be paid. In *R v Lockwood* (1986) the Court of Appeal required the same standard of dishonesty applied in other criminal cases to be applied to fraudulent trading – there was not to be one standard for criminal cases in general and a separate, more restricted, one for cases involving commercial fraud.

Under s.213 of the Insolvency Act 1986, if in the course of a winding up it appears that any business of the company has been carried on with intent to defraud creditors or for any fraudulent purpose, the court may on application of the liquidator order any persons who were knowingly parties to the carrying on of the business to make such contributions, if any, to the company's assets as the court think proper.

In *Re William C Leith Brothers Ltd* (1932) the controlling director of a company ordered goods at a time when he knew that the company could not pay its debts. The court held that if a company continued to carry on business and to incur debts at a time when there was, to the directors' knowledge, no reasonable prospect of the creditors receiving any payment of debts it may be inferred that the company is carrying on business with intent to defraud, and the directors may be held liable for fraudulent trading.

However, fraudulent trading under s.213 of the Insolvency Act 1986, and its predecessors, has been notoriously difficult to establish because of the high burden of proof involved in demonstrating dishonesty. In order to establish liability for fraudulent trading under s.213, the prosecution must actually demonstrate an intention to defraud which must be proved by showing that the person had the requisite knowledge. The difficulty in establishing such an intention led to the introduction of s.214 of the Insolvency Act 1986, which relates to the lesser category of wrongful trading.

84 WRONGFUL TRADING

Key answer tips

This is a fairly straightforward question requiring candidates to explain wrongful trading. Good knowledge of s.214 of the Insolvency Act 1986 is required to score a reasonable mark.

Wrongful trading was introduced by s. 214 of the Insolvency Act 1986. Prior to the introduction of this provision directors could only be made liable for the debts of their insolvent companies where they had been guilty of fraudulent trading. The difficulty of proving the necessary mental element (*mens rea*) to substantiate a charge of fraud meant that the provision was hardly ever used.

The purpose for introducing the new heading of wrongful trading was to protect creditors of limited companies by placing additional duties on directors which may make them responsible to contribute to the assets of the company in the event of its going into insolvent liquidation. Directors no longer can rely on separate personality and limited liability where their wrongful actions have been responsible for their company's insolvency.

A person may be liable for wrongful trading under s.214 where:

(a)   the company has gone into insolvent liquidation;

(b)   at some time before the commencement of the winding up of the company that person knew, or ought to have known, that there was no reasonable prospect that the company would avoid going into insolvent liquidation; and

(c)   that person was a director of the company at that time.

The court may then, on the application of the liquidator, declare that the person is to be liable to make such contribution (if any) to the company's assets as the court thinks proper.

Directors may escape liability, however, where they can show that, after the time when they knew, or ought to have known, that there was no reasonable chance of the company avoiding insolvent liquidation, they took every step with a view to minimising the potential loss to the company's creditors. In deciding what a director ought to have done the courts adopt a partly objective standard by considering what would have been done by a reasonably diligent person having the general knowledge, skill and experience that may reasonably be expected of a person carrying out the same functions of the director in question. There is an additional subjective test which may increase the individual's liability depending on the actual knowledge, skill and experience that the director involved has.

The extent of liability is determined by reference to the losses incurred by the company from the date when the defendants ought to have realised that the company could not avoid going into insolvent liquidation (*Re Produce Marketing Consortium Ltd* (1989)).

85 HUGE PLC

Key answer tips

This question requires candidates to recognise and explain the law relating to two criminal offences: insider dealing under part V of the Criminal Justice Act 1993 in part (a) and monely laundering under the Proceeds of Crime Act 2002 in part (b)

(a)   Insider dealing is dealing in shares, on the basis of access to unpublished price sensitive information. Such activity is unlawfuland is governed by part V of the Criminal Justice Act 1993 (CJA). Money laundering refers to the attempt to disguise theorigin of money acquired through criminal activity in order to make it appear legitimate. The aim of the process is to disguisethe source of the property, in order to allow the holder to enjoy it free from suspicion as to its source.

Such activity is regulated by the Proceeds of Crime Act 2002 (PCA) together with the specifically anti-terrorist legislation, theTerrorism Act 2000 and the Anti-terrorism Crime and Security Act 2001 and the Prevention of Terrorism Act 2005.

Under s.52 of the Criminal Justice Act (CJA) 1993 an individual is guilty of insider dealing if they have information as aninsider and deal in price-affected securities on the basis of that information.

Section 54 specifically includes shares amongst those securities and dealing is defined in s.55, amongst other things, asacquiring or disposing of securities, whether as a principal or agent, or agreeing to acquire securities.

Section 56 defines 'inside information' as:

(i)   relating to particular securities;

(ii)   being specific or precise;

(iii)   not having been made public; and

(iv)   being likely to have a significant effect on the price of the securities.

Section 57 states that a person has information as an insider only if they know it is inside information and they have it froman inside source and covers those who get the inside information directly through either:

(i)   being a director, employee or shareholder of an issuer of securities; or

(ii)   having access to the information by virtue of their employment, office or profession.

On summary conviction, an individual found guilty of insider dealing is liable to a fine not exceeding the statutory maximumand/or maximum of six months imprisonment. On indictment the penalty is an unlimited fine and/or a maximum of sevenyears imprisonment. It is quite clear from the facts of the problem scenario that Greg has engaged in insider dealing underthe CJA 1993.

(b)   Although he has tried to disguise his criminal activity, that has merely involved him in further criminal activity; money laundering.

Under s.327 of the Proceeds of Crime Act 2002 it is an offence to conceal, disguise, convert, transfer or remove criminalproperty from England and Wales, Scotland or Northern Ireland. Concealing or disguising criminal property is widely definedto include concealing or disguising its nature, source, location, disposition, movement or ownership or any rights connectedwith it. These offences are punishable on conviction by a maximum of 14 years' imprisonment and/or a fine.

Applying the general law to the problem scenario, one can conclude that Greg is an 'insider' as he receives inside informationas a result of his position as a director of Huge plc. The information fulfils the requirements for 'inside information' as it: relatesto particular securities, the shares in Kop plc; is specific, in that it relates to the company's take-over plans; has not been made public; and is likely to have a significant effect on the price of the securities. On that basis Greg is clearly guilty of anoffence under s.52 of the CJA when he arranges for Jet Ltd to buy the shares in Kop plc.

It is equally apparent that Greg has attempted to disguise the source of his profit from the illegal activity of insider dealing by pretending that it is the result of legitimate work that he has carried out for his company Imp Ltd. As a consequence he would also be liable for prosecution under s.327 of the Proceeds of Crime Act 2002.

Examiner's Report

This question required candidates to explain the meaning and regulation of the two criminal offences of insider dealing and money laundering and apply that law to a problem scenario.

This question tended to be sufficiently well done.

The money laundering aspect of the problem was particularly well done, with candidates explaining in very full terms what was involved in the process and the details of its legal regulation. However, there was some concern as to the insider dealing part of the problem, which raised some concerns and which suggest that a full question on that area would have met with much less success. The essential problem was that candidates seemed to think that insider dealing was just using or revealing information gained from inside a company. That, of course, is completely incorrect and it is not insider dealing unless the purchase or sale of securities is involved. This concern, as to the general understanding of insider dealing, is confirmed by the number of candidates who claimed that Des, in question 9, was liable to be charged with that particular offence.

ACCA Marking Scheme	
	Marks
Clear analysis of the problem scenario – recognition of both the criminal law issues raised and a convincing application of the legal principles to the facts.	8–10
Sound analysis of the problem – recognition of the major principles involved and a fair attempt at applying them. Perhaps sound in knowledge but lacking in analysis and application.	6–7
Unbalanced answer perhaps showing some appropriate knowledge but weak in analysis or application.	3–5
Very weak answer showing little analysis, appropriate knowledge or application.	0–2

86 MONEY LAUNDERING *Walk in the footsteps of a top tutor*

Key answer tips

This is a fairly straightforward question requiring candidates to explain money laundering in part (a) and explain how the Proceeds of Crime Act 2002 seeks to control money laundering in part (a). In part (a) candidates should explain the three distinct phases of money laundering and in part (b) they should state the three categories of criminal offences. The highlighted words are key phrases that markers are looking for.

(a) Money laundering is the process by which the proceeds of crime, either money or other property, are converted into assets, which appear to have a legitimate rather than an illegal origin. The aim of the process is to disguise the source of the property, in order to allow the holder to enjoy it free from suspicion as to its source.

The process usually involves three distinct phases:

- 'placement' is the initial disposal of the proceeds of criminal activity into apparently legitimate business activity or property;

- 'layering' involves the transfer of money from business to business, or place to place in order to conceal its initial source; and

- 'integration' is the culmination of the previous procedures through which the money takes on the appearance of coming from a legitimate source.

Money laundering was first made a criminal offence in the United Kingdom under the Drug Trafficking Offences Act 1986 and is now regulated by the Proceeds of Crime Act 2002 together with the specifically anti-terrorist legislation, the Terrorism Act 2000 and the Anti-terrorism, Crime and Security Act 2001.

(b) The Proceeds of Crime Act 2002 seeks to control money laundering by creating three categories of criminal offences in relation to the activity.

- **Laundering**

The first category of principal money laundering offences relates to laundering the proceeds of crime, or assisting in that process and is contained in ss.327 – 329.

Under s.327, it is an offence to conceal, disguise, convert, transfer or remove criminal property from England and Wales, Scotland or Northern Ireland. Concealing or disguising criminal property is widely defined to include concealing or disguising its nature, source, location, disposition, movement or ownership or any rights connected with it. These offences are punishable on conviction by a maximum of 14 years' imprisonment and/or a fine.

- **Failure to report**

    The second category of offence relates to failing to report a knowledge or suspicion of money laundering and is contained in ss.330 – 332.

    Under s.330 it is an offence for a person who knows or suspects that another person is engaged in money laundering not to report the fact to the appropriate authority. However, the offence only relates to individuals, such as accountants who are acting in the course of business in the regulated sector. The offences set out in these sections are punishable on conviction by a maximum of five years' imprisonment and/or a fine.

- **Tipping off**

    The third category of offence relates to tipping off and is contained in s.333, which makes it an offence to make a disclosure, which is likely to prejudice any investigation under the Act. The offences set out in these sections are punishable on conviction by a maximum of five years' imprisonment and/or a fine.

87   KEN *Walk in the footsteps of a top tutor*

Key answer tips

This scenario question requires a general explanation of the meaning of money laundering together with a consideration of the way in which the Proceeds of Crime Act 2002 seeks to control it. The highlighted words are key phrases that markers are looking for.

Money laundering is the process by which the proceeds of crime, either money or other property, are converted into assets, which appear to have a legitimate rather than an illegal origin. The aim of the process is to disguise the source of the property, in order to allow the holder to enjoy it free from suspicion as to its source.

The process usually involves three distinct phases:

- placement is the initial disposal of the proceeds of criminal activity into apparently legitimate business activity or property.

- layering involves the transfer of money from business to business, or place to place in order to conceal its initial source.

- integration is the culmination of the previous procedures through which the money takes on the appearance of coming from a legitimate source.

Money laundering was first made a criminal offence in the United Kingdom under the Drug Trafficking Offences Act 1986 and is now regulated by the Proceeds of Crime Act 2002 together with the specifically enacted anti-terrorist legislation, the Terrorism Act 2000 and the Anti-terrorism, Crime and Security Act 2001.

The Proceeds of Crime Act 2002 seeks to control money laundering by creating three categories of criminal offences in relation to the activity:

Laundering

The first category of principal money laundering offences relates to laundering the proceeds of crime or assisting in that process and is contained in ss.327–329. Under s.327, it is an offence to conceal, disguise, convert, transfer or remove criminal property from England and Wales, Scotland or Northern Ireland. Concealing or disguising criminal property is widely defined to include concealing or disguising its nature, source, location, disposition, movement or ownership or any rights connected with it. These offences are punishable on conviction by a maximum of 14 years' imprisonment and/or a fine.

Failure to report

The second category of offence relates to failing to report a knowledge or suspicion of money laundering and is contained in ss.330–332. Under s.330 it is an offence for a person who knows or suspects that another person is engaged in money laundering not to report the fact to the appropriate authority. However, the offence only relates to individuals, such as accountants, who are acting in the course of business in the regulated sector. The offences set out in these sections are punishable on conviction by a maximum of five years' imprisonment and/or a fine.

Tipping off

The third category of offence relates to tipping off and is contained in s.333, which makes it an offence to make a disclosure which is likely to prejudice any investigation under the Act. The offences set out in these sections are punishable on conviction by a maximum of five years' imprisonment and/or a fine.

It is apparent from the scenario that the various people involved in the scenario are liable to control and prosecution under the Proceeds of Crime Act 2002 as they are involved in money laundering. If the original money to purchase the bookshop was the product of crime, then that transaction itself was an instance of money laundering. However, even if that was not the case and the bookshop was bought with legitimate money, it is nonetheless the case that it is being used to conceal the fact that the source of much of Ken's money is criminal activity. Ken would therefore be guilty on the primary offence of money laundering under s.327 of the Proceeds of Crime Act as explained in the section above.

Los is also guilty of an offence in relation to the Proceeds of Crime Act as he is clearly assisting Ken in his money laundering procedure. His activity is covered both by s.327, as he is actively concealing and disguising criminal property, and s.328 as his arrangement with Ken 'facilitates the retention of criminal property'.

Mel is equally guilty under the same provisions as Los, in that he is actively engaged in the money laundering process, by producing false accounts. Had he not been an active party to the process, he might nonetheless have been liable, under s.330, for failing to disclose any suspiciously high profits from the bookshop business.

88   SID AND VIC

Key answer tips

This is a fairly straightforward scenario question that requires application of the rules on insider dealing under the Criminal Justice Act 1993. In order to achieve a reasonable mark, candidates should go into detail on the three distinct phases of insider dealing.

(a)   Insider dealing is a crime under part V of the Criminal Justice Act 1993 (CJA). Section 52 of the CJA sets out the three distinct offences of insider dealing:

(i)   an individual is guilty of insider dealing if they have information as an insider and deal in price-affected securities on the basis of that information.

(ii)   an individual who has information as an insider will also be guilty of insider dealing if they encourage another person to deal in price-affected securities in relation to that information.

(iii)   an individual who has information as an insider will also be guilty of insider dealing if they disclose it to anyone other than in the proper performance of their employment, office or profession.

The CJA goes on to explain the meaning of some of the above terms. Thus s.54 defines what securities are covered by the legislation and these are set out in the second Schedule to the Act and specifically include shares and debentures.

Dealing is defined in s.55, amongst other things, as acquiring or disposing of securities, whether as a principal or agent, or agreeing to acquire securities.

Section 56 defines 'inside information' as:

(i)   relating to particular securities,

(ii)   being specific or precise,

(iii)   not having been made public and

(iv)   being likely to have a significant effect on the price of the securities.

Section 57 states that a person has information as an insider only if they know it is inside information and they have it from an inside source. The section then goes on to consider what might be described as primary and secondary insiders. The first category of primary insiders covers those who get the inside information directly through either:

(i)   being a director, employee or shareholder of an issuer of securities; or

(ii)   having access to the information by virtue of their employment, office or profession.

On summary conviction an individual found guilty of insider dealing is liable to a fine not exceeding the statutory maximum and/or maximum of six months imprisonment. On indictment the penalty is an unlimited find and/or a maximum of seven years imprisonment.

Applying the general law to the problem scenario, one can conclude as follows:

Sid is an 'insider' as he receives inside information from his position as a director in both Trend plc and Umber plc. The information fulfils the requirements for 'inside information' as it relates to particular securities, the shares in both companies; is specific, in that it relates to the level of their profits; has not been made public; and is likely to have a significant effect on the price of their securities. On that basis Sid is clearly guilty of an offence under s.52 in selling his shares in Trend plc to avoid a loss and buying shares in Umber plc to make a profit.

He is also guilty of a further offence when he advised his brother to buy shares in Umber plc. However, his brother has not committed any offence as he did not receive any specific information from Sid.

(b)   There is little that Vic can do in relation to Sid's insider dealing. There was no relationship between the two and in any case Vic sold his shares voluntarily on the stock market and consequently can take no action against Sid or his brother. However, the companies may take action against Sid for breaching his fiduciary duty.

Examiner's Report

This question required candidates to consider the criminal offence of insider dealing and to apply the appropriate law to the facts contained in the problem. Considering the number of times this topic has been examined in the past it is not a little surprising that it was attempted by a significant number of candidates, and not done well by most of those who did attempt it.

There seemed to be a general lack of detailed knowledge about the meaning of insider dealing and contents of the Criminal Justice Act 1993 and those who did have such knowledge tended not to apply it properly. There was a general misunderstanding that insider dealing was simply having 'secret' information without explaining the specific, price-sensitive, nature of that information and the need to deal in shares on the basis of that information.

There was also some confusion as to Vic, in part (b) of the question with a number of candidates clearly not reading the question with sufficient care and incorrectly assuming that Vic was in fact Sid's brother.

ACCA marking scheme	
	Marks
Little if any understanding of what the question is about.	0-2
Some, but limited, knowledge of what the question is about, or a recognition of what it is about but lacking in any analysis.	3-4
Good but limited analysis or perhaps unbalanced in not dealing equally well with the application of the law.	5-7
A thorough understanding of the legislation together with an accurate application of it to the individuals in the question is to be expected for the very highest marks.	8-10

Section 3

DECEMBER 2009 EXAM QUESTIONS

ALL TEN questions are compulsory and MUST be attempted

1   APPROACHES TO INTERPRETATION

In relation to the courts' powers to interpret legislation, explain and differentiate between:

(a)   the literal approach, including the golden rule; and   **(5 marks)**

(b)   the purposive approach, including the mischief rule.   **(5 marks)**

(Total: 10 marks)

2   LAW OF CONTRACT

In relation to the law of contract, explain:

(a)   the postal rule;   **(5 marks)**

(b)   the doctrine of privity.   **(5 marks)**

(Total: 10 marks)

3   BREACH OF CONRACT

In relation to remedies for breach of contract, explain:

(a)   the difference between liquidated damages and penalty clauses;   **(5 marks)**

(b)   the duty to mitigate losses.   **(5 marks)**

(Total: 10 marks)

4   DUTY OF CARE

In relation to the law of negligence, explain the extent of a company auditor's duty of care and to whom any such duty is owed.   **(Total: 10 marks)**

5   LIMITED LIABILITY

In relation to company law:

(a)   explain the meaning of limited liability.   **(3 marks)**

(b)   Explain and distinguish between:

(i)   unlimited companies;   **(2 marks)**

(ii)   companies limited by guarantee;   **(2 marks)**

(iii)   companies limited by shares.   **(3 marks)**

(Total: 10 marks)

6 WINDING UP/ADMINISTRATION

In the context of companies in financial difficulty, distinguish between and explain the operation of:

(a) compulsory winding up; **(4 marks)**

(b) administration. **(6 marks)**

(Total: 10 marks)

7 EMPLOYEE/EMPLOYER COMMON LAW DUTIES

In the context of contracts of employment, explain the common law duties imposed on:

(a) employers; **(6 marks)**

(b) employees. **(4 marks)**

(Total: 10 marks)

8 BASH LTD

Whilst at work Andy always parked his car in a car park operated by Bash Ltd. On the entry to the car park just in front of the payment machine there is a large sign in fluorescent red paint which states:

'These premises are not staffed by our employees and may be dangerous. Clients use these facilities strictly at their own risk and Bash Ltd accept no liability whatsoever for any damage or injury sustained by either those using this facility or their vehicles or property, no matter how caused.'

Andy was aware of the sign, but had never paid much attention to it. However, one day he returned to his car to find that it had been badly damaged by a towing vehicle driven by an employee of Bash Ltd. Whilst on his way to the car park office to complain he was hit by the same towing vehicle, which was clearly being driven dangerously by one of Bash Ltd's employees. As a result, not only was his car severely damaged, but he suffered a broken leg and was off work for eight weeks.

Bash Ltd has accepted that its employee was negligent on both counts but denies any liability, relying on the exclusion clause.

Required:

On the understanding that the clause excluding Bash Ltd's liability was incorporated into its contract with Andy, advise Andy whether there is any action he can take against Bash Ltd.

(Total: 10 marks)

9   DULL PLC

Caz is a director of Dull plc, but she also carries out her own business as a wholesale supplier of specialist metals under the name of Era Ltd.

Last year Dull plc entered into a contract to buy a large consignment of metal from Era Ltd. Caz attended the board meeting that approved the contract and voted in favour of it, without revealing any link with Era Ltd.

Required:

Analyse the situation explaining any potential liability that Caz may have in relation to the sale of the metal to Dull plc by Era Ltd.   **(Total: 10 marks)**

10   IRE LTD

Fran, Gram and Hen registered a private limited company Ire Ltd in January 2005 with a share capital of £300, which was equally divided between them, with each of them becoming a director of the company.

Although the company did manage to make a small profit in its first year of trading, it was never a great success and in its second year of trading it made a loss of £10,000.

At that time Fran said he thought the company should cease trading and be wound up. Gram and Hen, however, were insistent that the company would be profitable in the long-term so they agreed to carry on the business, with Fran taking less of a part in the day-to-day management of the business, although retaining his position as a company director.

In the course of the next three years Gram and Hen falsified Ire Ltd's accounts to disguise the fact that the company had continued to suffer losses, until it became obvious that they could no longer hide the company's debts and that it would have to go into insolvent liquidation, with debts of £100,000.

Required:

Advise Fran, Gram and Hen as to any potential liability they might face as regards:

(a)   fraudulent trading, under both criminal and civil law;   **(5 marks)**

(b)   wrongful trading under s.214 of the Insolvency Act 1986.   **(5 marks)**

(Total: 10 marks)

Section 4

ANSWERS TO DECEMBER 2009 EXAM QUESTIONS

1   APPROACHES TO INTERPRETATION

Tutorial note

In order to apply any piece of legislation, judges have to determine its meaning. In other words they are required to interpret the statute before them in order to give it meaning. The difficulty, however, is that the words in statutes do not speak for themselves and interpretation is an active process, and at least potentially a subjective one depending on the situation of the person who is doing the interpreting.

Judges have considerable power in deciding the actual meaning of statutes, especially when they are able to deploy a number of competing, not to say contradictory, mechanisms for deciding the meaning of the statute before them. There are, essentially, two contrasting views as to how judges should go about determining the meaning of a statute – the restrictive, literal approach and the more permissive, purposive approach.

(a)   **The literal approach**

The literal approach is dominant in the English legal system, although it is not without critics, and devices do exist for circumventing it when it is seen as too restrictive. This view of judicial interpretation holds that the judge should look primarily to the words of the legislation in order to construe its meaning and, except in the very limited circumstances considered below, should not look outside of, or behind, the legislation in an attempt to find its meaning.

Within the context of the literal approach there are two distinct rules:

(i)   *The literal rule*

Under this rule, the judge is required to consider what the legislation actually says rather than considering what it might mean. In order to achieve this end, the judge should give words in legislation their literal meaning, that is, their plain, ordinary, everyday meaning, even if the effect of this is to produce what might be considered an otherwise unjust or undesirable outcome (*Fisher v Bell* (1961)) in which the court chose to follow the contract law literal interpretation of the meaning of offer in the Act in question and declined to consider the usual non-legal literal interpretation of the word (offer).

(ii)   *The golden rule*

This rule is applied in circumstances where the application of the literal rule is likely to result in what appears to the court to be an obviously absurd result. It should be emphasised, however, that the court is not at liberty to ignore, or replace, legislative provisions simply on the basis that it considers them absurd; it must find genuine difficulties before it declines to use the literal rule in favour of the golden one. As examples, there may be two apparently contradictory meanings to a particular word used in the statute, or the provision may simply be ambiguous in its effect. In such situations, the golden rule operates to ensure that preference is given to the meaning that does not result in the provision being an absurdity. Thus in *Adler v George* (1964) the defendant was found guilty, under the Official Secrets Act 1920, with obstruction 'in the vicinity' of a prohibited area, although she had actually carried out the obstruction 'inside' the area.

(b)   **The purposive approach**

The purposive approach rejects the limitation of the judges' search for meaning to a literal construction of the words of legislation itself. It suggests that the interpretative role of the judge should include, where necessary, the power to look beyond the words of statute in pursuit of the reason for its enactment, and that meaning should be construed in the light of that purpose and so as to give it effect. This purposive approach is typical of civil law systems. In these jurisdictions, legislation tends to set out general principles and leaves the fine details to be filled in later by the judges who are expected to make decisions in the furtherance of those general principles.

European Community (EC) legislation tends to be drafted in the continental manner. Its detailed effect, therefore, can only be determined on the basis of a purposive approach to its interpretation. This requirement, however, runs counter to the literal approach that is the dominant approach in the English system. The need to interpret such legislation, however, has forced a change in that approach in relation to Community legislation and even with respect to domestic legislation designed to implement Community legislation. Thus, in *Pickstone v Freemans plc* (1988), the House of Lords held that it was permissible, and indeed necessary, for the court to read words into inadequate domestic legislation in order to give effect to Community law in relation to provisions relating to equal pay for work of equal value. (For a similar approach, see also the House of Lords' decision in *Litster v Forth Dry Dock* (1989) and the decision in *Three Rivers DC v Bank of England* (No 2) (1996).) However, it has to recognise that the purposive rule is not particularly modern and has its precursor in a long established rule of statutory interpretation, namely the mischief rule.

The mischief rule

This rule permits the court to go behind the actual wording of a statute in order to consider the problem that the statute is supposed to remedy.

In its traditional expression it is limited by being restricted to using previous common law rules in order to decide the operation of contemporary legislation. Thus in *Heydon's case* (1584) it was stated that in making use of the mischief rule the court should consider what the mischief in the law was which the common law did not adequately deal with and which statute law had intervened to remedy. Use of the mischief rule may be seen in *Corkery v Carpenter* (1950), in which a man was found guilty of being drunk in charge of a carriage although he was in fact only in charge of a bicycle.

ACCA marking scheme	
	Marks
This question requires candidates to consider the powers of judges to interpret legislation and the rules they apply in exercising such interpretative powers. Although the question requires answers to focus on the two main general approaches, it also requires an explanation of the various traditional rules of statutory interpretation employed by the courts.	
(a) Requires a consideration of the literal approach, including the golden rule.	
Full detailed explanation with supporting cases or examples.	3–5
Limited knowledge of the topic; perhaps lacking detail or cases/examples.	1–2
No knowledge of the topic under consideration.	0
(b) Requires a consideration of the purposive approach, including the mischief rule.	
Full detailed explanation with supporting cases or examples.	3–5
Limited knowledge of the topic; perhaps lacking detail or cases/examples.	1–2
No knowledge of the topic under consideration.	0
Candidates may simply produce a global answer considering the traditional rules and will be marked according to the content provided.	

2 LAW OF CONTRACT

(a) The effect of the postal rule is such that where acceptance of a contractual offer is through the postal service, acceptance is complete as soon as the letter, properly addressed and stamped, is posted. The contract is concluded, even if the letter subsequently fails to reach the offeror. Thus in *Adams v Lindsell* (1818), the defendant made an offer to the plaintiff on 2 September. Due to misdirection, the letter was delayed. It arrived on 5 September and Adams immediately posted an acceptance. On 8 September, Lindsell sold the merchandise to a third party. On 9 September, the letter of acceptance from Adams arrived. It was held that a valid acceptance took place when Adams posted the letter. Lindsell was, therefore, liable for breach of contract.

The postal rule applies equally to telegrams (*Byrne v Van Tienhoven* (1880)), but it does not apply when means of instantaneous communication are used (*Entores v Far East Corp* (1955)). Also the postal rule will apply only where it is in the contemplation of the parties that post will be used as the means of acceptance. If the parties have negotiated either face-to-face, for example in a shop, or over the telephone, then it might not be reasonable for the offeree to use the post as a means of communicating their acceptance and they would not gain the benefit of the postal rule.

Where acceptance is by e-mail, it has been argued that this situation should be treated as a 'face-to-face' situation where receipt only occurs when the recipient reads the e-mail (*Brinkibon Ltd v Stahag Stahl und Stahlwarenhandelsgesellshaft mbH* (1983)). Where the agreement is conducted on the Internet, regulation 11 of the Electronic Commerce (EC Directive) Regulations 2002 indicates that the contract is concluded when the service provider's acknowledgment of receipt of acceptance is received by electronic means.

(b) **Privity of contract**

The doctrine of privity in contract law provides that a contract can only impose rights or obligations on persons who are parties to it. Its operation may be seen in *Dunlop v*

Selfridge (1915). Dunlop sold tyres to a distributor, Dew and Co, on terms that the distributor would not sell them at less than the manufacturer's list price, and that they would extract a similar undertaking from anyone they supplied with tyres. Dew and Co resold the tyres to Selfridge who agreed to abide by the restrictions and to pay Dunlop £5 for each tyre they sold in breach of them. When Selfridge sold tyres at below Dunlop's list price, Dunlop sought to recover the promised £5 per tyre sold. It was held that Dunlop could not recover damages on the basis of the contract between Dew and Selfridge to which they were not a party.

There are a number of ways in which consequences of the application of strict rule of privity may be avoided to allow a third party to enforce a contract. These occur at both common law and under statute.

(i)   *Common law:*

   •   The beneficiary sues in some other capacity.

        A person who was not originally a party to a particular contract may, nonetheless, acquire the power to enforce the contract where they are legally appointed to administer the affairs of one of the original parties. An example of this can be seen in *Beswick v Beswick* (1967) where a coal merchant sold his business to his nephew in return for a consultancy fee of £6 10 shillings (in pre-decimal currency) during his lifetime, and thereafter an annuity of £5 per week payable to his widow. After the uncle died, the nephew stopped paying the widow. When she became administratrix of her husband's estate, she sued the nephew for specific performance of the agreement in that capacity as well as in her personal capacity. It was held that, although she was not a party to the contract and therefore could not be granted specific performance in her personal capacity, such an order could be awarded to her as the administratrix of the deceased person's estate.

   •   The situation involves a collateral contract.

        A collateral contract arises where one party promises something to another party if that other party enters into a contract with a third party, for example, A promises to give B something if B enters into a contract with C. In such a situation, the second party can enforce the original promise, that is, B can insist on A complying with the original promise. In *Shanklin Pier v Detel Products Ltd* (1951), the plaintiffs contracted to have their pier repainted. On the basis of promises as to its quality, the defendants persuaded the pier company to insist that a particular paint produced by Detel be used. The painters used the paint but it proved unsatisfactory. The plaintiffs sued for breach of the original promise as to the suitability of the paint. The defendants countered that the only contract they had entered into was between them and the painters to whom they had sold the paint, and that as the pier company were not a party to that contract they had no right of action against Detel. The pier company were successful. It was held that, in addition to the contract for the sale of paint, there was a second collateral contract between the plaintiffs and the defendants by which the latter guaranteed the suitability of the paint in return for the pier company specifying that the painters used it.

- There is a valid assignment of the benefit of the contract.

  A party to a contract can transfer the benefit of that contract to a third party through the formal process of assignment. The assignment must be in writing, and the assignee receives no better rights under the contract than the assignor possessed. The burden of a contract cannot be assigned without the consent of the other party to the contract.

- Where it is foreseeable that damage caused by any breach of contract will cause a loss to a third party.

  In *Linden Gardens Trust Ltd v Lenesta Sludge Disposals Ltd* (1994), the original parties had entered into a contract for work to be carried out on property with the likelihood that it would subsequently be transferred to a third party. The defendant's poor work, amounting to a breach of contract, only became apparent after the property had been transferred. There had been no assignment of the original contract and, normally, under the doctrine of privity, the new owners would have no contractual rights against the defendants and the original owners of the property would have suffered only a nominal breach as they had sold it at no loss to themselves. Nonetheless, the House of Lords held that, under such circumstances, and within a commercial context, the original promisee should be able to claim full damages on behalf of the third party for the breach of contract.

- One of the parties has entered the contract as a trustee for a third party.

  There exists the possibility that a party to a contract can create a contract specifically for the benefit of a third party. In such limited circumstances, the promisee is considered as a trustee of the contractual promise for the benefit of the third party. In order to enforce the contract, the third party must act through the promisee by making them a party to any action. For a consideration of this possibility, see *Les Affreteurs Reunis SA v Leopold Walford (London) Ltd* (1919).

  The other main exception to the privity rule at common law is agency, where the agent brings about contractual relations between two other parties even where the existence of the agency has not been disclosed.

(ii) *Statute*

The first area in which statute has intervened in relation to the doctrine of privity is in relation to motor insurance where third parties claim directly against the insurers of the party against whom they have a claim.

The most significant alteration of the operation of the doctrine of privity however, has been made by the *Contracts (Rights of Third Parties) Act 1999* which sets out the circumstances in which third parties can enforce terms of contracts. In order for the third party to gain rights of enforcement, the contract in question must, either, expressly confer such a right on them or, alternatively, it must have been clearly made for their benefit (s.1). The contractual agreement must actually identify the third party, either by name, or as a member of a class of persons, or answering a particular description. The third person need not be in existence when the contract was made, so it is possible for parties to make contracts for the benefit of as yet unborn children. This provision should also reduce the difficulties relating to pre-incorporation contracts in relation to registered companies. The third party may exercise the right to any remedy which would have been available had they been a party to the contract. Such rights are, however, subject to the terms and conditions contained in the contract and they can get no better right than the original promisee.

Section 2 of the Act provides that, where a third party has rights by virtue of the Act, the original parties to the contract cannot agree to rescind it or vary its terms without the consent of the third party; unless the original contract contained an express term to that effect.

Section 3 allows the promisor to make use of any defences or rights of set-off they might have against the promisee in any action by the third party. Additionally, the promisor can also rely on any such rights against the third party.

Section 5 removes the possibility of the promisor suffering from double liability in relation to the promisor and the third party. It provides, therefore, that any damages awarded to a third party for a breach of the contract be reduced by the amount recovered by the original promisee in any previous action relating to the contract.

The Act does not alter the existing law relating to negotiable instruments, contracts of employment, or contracts for the carriage of goods or the statutory contracts constituted by to companies' constitutional documents.

ACCA marking scheme		
		Marks
This question is divided into two parts relating to distinct aspects of the law of contract.		
(a)	A good to excellent understanding of the postal rule demonstrated by references to cases or examples.	4–5
	Some, but limited, understanding of the topic, or clear understanding of only one aspect.	2–3
	Little or no knowledge of the topic	0
(b)	A good to excellent understanding of privity demonstrated by references to cases or examples.	4–5
	Some, but limited, understanding of the topic, or clear understanding of only one aspect.	2–3
	Little or no knowledge of the topic	0

3 BREACH OF CONRACT

This question requires an explanation of two aspects the law relating to damages for breach of contract. Every failure to perform a primary obligation is a breach of contract. The secondary obligation on the part of the contract-breaker, by implication of the common law, is to pay monetary compensation to the other party for the loss sustained by him in consequence of the breach (*Photo Productions Ltd v Securicor Transport Ltd* (1980)). Such monetary compensation for breach of contract is damages. There are, however, two distinct aspects to this general concept that have to be considered.

(a) *Liquidated damages and penalty clauses*

It is possible, and common in business contracts, for the parties to an agreement to make provisions for possible breach by stating in advance the amount of damages that will have to be paid in the event of any breach occurring. Damages under such a provision are known as liquidated damages. They will only be recognised by the court if they represent a genuine pre-estimate of loss, and are not intended to operate as a penalty against the party in breach. If the court considers the provision to be a penalty, it will not give it effect, but will award damages in the normal way.

In *Dunlop v New Garage and Motor Co (1915),* the plaintiffs supplied the defendants with tyres, under a contract designed to achieve resale price maintenance. The contract provided that the defendants had to pay Dunlop £5 for every tyre they sold in breach of the resale price agreement. When the garage sold tyres at less than the agreed minimum price, they resisted Dunlop's claim for £5 per tyre, on the grounds that it represented a penalty clause. On the facts of the situation, the court decided that the provision was a genuine attempt to fix damages, and was not a penalty. It was, therefore, enforceable.

In deciding the legality of such clauses, the courts will consider the effect, rather than the form, of the clause as is seen in *Cellulose Acetate Silk Co Ltd v Widnes Foundry (1925) Ltd (1933).* In that case, the contract expressly stated that damages for late payment would be paid by way of penalty at the rate of £20 per week. In fact, the sum of £20 was in no way excessive and represented a reasonable estimate of the likely loss. On that basis, the House of Lords enforced the clause in spite of its actual wording.

(b)   *The duty to mitigate losses*

This rule relates to the rule that the injured party in the situation of a breach of contract is under a duty to take all reasonable steps to minimise their loss. The operation of the rule means that the buyer of goods that are not delivered, as required under the terms of a contract, has to buy the replacements as cheaply as possible. Correspondingly, the seller of goods that are not accepted in line with a contractual agreement has to try to get as good a price as they can when they sell them.

In *Payzu v Saunders* (1919), the parties entered into a contract for the sale of fabric, which was to be delivered and paid for in instalments. When the purchaser, Payzu, failed to pay for the first instalment on time, Saunders refused to make any further deliveries unless Payzu agreed to pay cash on delivery. The plaintiff refused to accept this and sued for breach of contract. The court decided that the delay in payment had not given the defendant the right to repudiate the contract. As a consequence, he had breached the contract by refusing further delivery. The buyer, however, should have mitigated his loss by accepting the offer of cash on delivery terms. His damages were restricted, therefore, to what he would have lost under those terms, namely, interest over the repayment period.

In W*estern Web Offset Printers Ltd v Independent Media Ltd* (1995), the parties had entered into a contract under which the plaintiff was to publish 48 issues of a weekly newspaper for the defendant. In the action, which followed the defendant's repudiation of the contract, the only issue in question was the extent of damages to be awarded. The Court of Appeal decided that as the claimant had been unable to replace the work due to the recession in the economy and, therefore, had not been able to mitigate the loss, it was entitled to receive the full amount that would have been due in order to allow it to defray the expenses it would have had to pay during the period the contract should have lasted.

However, in relation to anticipatory breach of contract the injured party can wait until the actual time for performance before taking action against the party in breach. In such a situation, they are entitled to make preparations for performance, and claim the agreed contract price, even though this apparently conflicts with the duty to mitigate losses (*White and Carter (Councils) v McGregor* (1961)).

ACCA marking scheme	
	Marks
This question requires an explanation of two aspects the law relating to damages for breach of contract. It is split into two parts with 7 marks being available for part (a) and 3 marks for part (b).	
(a) A good explanation of the difference between liquidated damages and penalty clauses with perhaps some examples or cases.	5–7
Some, but limited, understanding of the topic, or clear understanding of only one aspect.	3–4
Little knowledge of either element of the question or unbalanced in only dealing with one of the elements.	0–2
(b) A thorough explanation of the duty the duty to mitigate losses with examples or cases.	2–3
Some, if little, knowledge of the duty but not clear or lacking in detail.	0–1

4 DUTY OF CARE

Whilst there is a contractual relationship between an auditor and his client the company as a legal entity, on which the client company can sue, the contentious legal area arises in respect of other people who may rely on reports made or advice given in a non-contractual capacity. Indeed, in many situations, the potential plaintiff may be unknown to the accountant. Although it is apparent that the law of negligence allows individuals in non-contractual relationships to sue for damages sustained as result of the negligent behaviour of another party, the success of any such action in relation to company auditors appears to depend upon the purpose for which reports are made or accounts prepared and on establishing a duty of care between the auditor and the person making the claim in negligence. The applicable law may derived from a number of important cases.

In *JEB Fasteners v Marks, Bloom and Co* (1983), the defendants, a firm of accountants, negligently overstated the value of stock in preparing audited accounts for their client. At the time of preparation, the accountants were aware that their client was in financial difficulties and actively seeking financial assistance. After seeing the accounts, the plaintiffs decided to take over the company. They then discovered the true financial position and sued the accountants for negligent misstatement. It was held that a duty of care was owed by the accountants as it was foreseeable that someone contemplating a takeover might rely on the accuracy of the accounts, but that they were not liable as their negligence had not caused the loss to the plaintiffs. The evidence revealed that, when they took over the company, they were not interested in the value of the stock but in acquiring the expertise of the directors, so, although they relied on the accounts, the accounts were not the cause of the loss as they would have taken over the company in any respect.

The case of *Caparo Industries plc v Dickman* (1990) served to limit the potential liability of auditors in auditing company accounts. Accounts were audited in accordance with the Companies Act 1985. The respondents, who already owned shares in the company, after seeing the accounts, decided to purchase more shares and take over the company. They then incurred a loss which they blamed on the inaccurate and negligently audited accounts. It was held that when the accounts were prepared, a duty of care was owed collectively to members of the company, that is, the shareholders, but only so far as to allow them to exercise proper control over the company; enabling the shareholders collectively to question the past management of the company, vote for or against the appointment of directors and take other decisions affecting the company. This duty did not extend to members as individuals, even when they used the accounts as the basis for purchasing more shares in the company, and it certainly did not extend to potential outside purchasers of shares. The onus was clearly on the appellants in these circumstances to make their own independent enquiries as it was unreasonable to rely on the auditors.

However, in *Morgan Crucible Co plc v Hill Samuel Bank Ltd* (1991), it was held that, where express representations are made about the accounts and the financial state of the company by directors or financial advisers of that company, with the intention that the person interested in the takeover will rely on them, then a duty of care is owed, and the auditor will be responsible for consequential losses. This was also the situation in *ADT v BDO Binder Hamilton* (1995) where a partner in the defendant accountancy firm told the plaintiff company that he stood by the audited accounts of BSG, the company that the ADT were in the process of taking over. This was taken as an assumption of responsibility and as the accounts had been prepared negligently, Binder Hamilton were held libel to repay the amount that ADT had overpaid for BSG a total of £65 million.

Following *Caparo Industries plc v Dickman* (1990) it can be stated that a company's auditors certainly do owe a duty of care to shareholders collectively as a body to allow them to exercise proper control over the management of the company.

As regards members individually, then again following Caparo, normally the auditors do not owe them a duty of care, even when they use the information supplied to purchase more shares in the company.

Following from the foregoing it can be seen that auditors owe no duty of care to non-members unless they actually assume responsibility for the accuracy of information they supply (*Morgan Crucible Co plc v Hill Samuel Bank Ltd* (1991) and *ADT v BDO Binder Hamilton* (1995)).

ACCA marking scheme	
	Marks
This question requires candidates to explain the extent of a company auditor's duty of care and to whom such a duty is owed.	
A thorough understanding of how professional negligence applies to auditors demonstrated by references to cases or examples.	8–10
A clear understanding of the topic, perhaps lacking in detail.	
Alternatively an unbalanced answer showing good understanding of one part but less in the others.	5–7
Some, but limited, understanding of the topic, or clear understanding of only one aspect.	2–4
Little or no knowledge of the topic	0–1

5   LIMITED LIABILITY

This question requires candidates to explain the concept of limited liability and to consider three alternative categories of companies; the first unlimited in nature, whilst the second and third are limited in different ways.

(a)   In this context, liability refers to the extent to which shareholders in companies are responsible for the debts of their companies and limited liability indicates that a limit has been placed on such liability. The point is that the limitation on liability is enjoyed by the member shareholders rather than the company. One of the major advantages of forming a company is that the members of the company may achieve limited liability. The great majority of registered companies are limited liability companies. This means that the maximum liability of shareholders is fixed and cannot be increased without their agreement. As will be seen below there are two ways of establishing limited liability.

(b) Section 3 of the Companies Act (CA) 2006 sets out the various types of companies that can be registered in term of different liabilities.

(i) Companies can be formed without limited liability. These, by virtue of s.3(4) CA 2006, are referred to as unlimited companies. Such companies are incorporated under the Companies Acts and receive all the benefits that flow from incorporation except limited liability. Consequently the shareholders in such unlimited companies remain liable to the full extent of their personal wealth for any unpaid debt of the company. It should be noted that, in line with the doctrine of separate personality, even in the case of unlimited companies any subsequent debt is owed to the company and not directly to the creditors of the company. The compensating benefit enjoyed by such companies is that they do not have to submit their accounts and make them available for public inspection.

(ii) The company limited by guarantee (s.3(3) CA 2006) is usually restricted to non-trading enterprises such as charities and professional and educational bodies. It limits the shareholders' liability to an agreed amount which is only called on if the company cannot pay its debts on being wound up. In reality, the sum guaranteed is usually a nominal sum, so no real risk is involved on the part of the guarantor.

(iii) The more common procedure is to limit liability by reference to shares (s.33(2)). The effect of this is to limit liability to the amount remaining unpaid on shares held (Insolvency Act 1986 s.74(2)(d)). If the shareholder has paid the full nominal value of the shares to the company, then that is the end of responsibility with regard to company debts. Consequently, if the company should subsequently go into insolvent liquidation the shareholders cannot be required to contribute to its assets in order to pay off its outstanding debts.

ACCA marking scheme			
			Marks
This question is likely to be answered in a global way and marks will be awarded in line with points made.			
(a)	Up to 3 marks for a general explanation of limited liability.		3
(b)	(i)	Up to 2 marks for an explanation of unlimited liability and why it might be used.	2
	(ii)	Up to 2 marks for knowledge of companies limited by guarantee. What they are, where they are used and the nature of liability.	2
	(iii)	Up to 3 marks for a thorough explanation of liability limited by reference to the amount unpaid on shares and how it operates.	3

6 WINDING UP/ADMINISTRATION

This question requires candidates to explain the meaning of the terms 'compulsory winding up' and 'administration'.

(a) Winding up, or liquidation, is the process whereby the life of the company is terminated. It is the formal and strictly regulated procedure whereby the business is brought to an end and the company's assets are realised and distributed to its creditors and members. The procedure is governed by the Insolvency Act (IA)1986 and may be divided into three distinct categories:

Member's voluntary winding up,

Creditors' voluntary winding up,

Compulsory winding up.

This question requires attention to be focused on the last of these three. A compulsory winding up is a winding up ordered by the court under s.122 of the IA 1986. Although there are seven distinct grounds for such a winding up, the most common reason for the winding up of a company is its inability to pay its debts. Section 123 provides that, if a company with a debt exceeding £750 fails to pay it within three weeks of receiving a written demand, then it is deemed unable to pay its debts.

On the presentation of a petition to wind a company up compulsorily, the court will normally appoint the Official Receiver to be the company's provisional liquidator. The Official Receiver will require the present or past officers, or indeed employees of the company to prepare a statement of the company's affairs. This statement must reveal:

- particulars of the company's assets and liabilities;
- names and addresses of its creditors;
- any securities held by the creditors (fixed or floating charges) and the dates on which they were granted;
- any other information which the Official Receiver may require.

After his appointment, the Official Receiver calls meetings of the company's members and creditors in order to select a liquidator to replace him and to select a liquidation committee if required. Once again, in the event of disagreement, the choice of the creditors prevails.

Section 142 of the IA 1986 states that the functions of the liquidator are 'to secure that the assets of the company are got in, realised and distributed to the company's creditors and, if there is a surplus, to the persons entitled to it'. Once the liquidator has performed these functions, he must call a final meeting of the creditors, at which he gives an account of the liquidation and secures his release from the creditors. Notice of the final meeting has to be submitted to the registrar of companies and, three months after that date, the company is deemed to be dissolved.

(b)   Administration, on the other hand is a means of safeguarding the continued existence of business enterprises in financial difficulties, rather than merely ensuring the payment of creditors. Administration was first introduced in the Insolvency Act 1986. The aim of the administration order is to save the company, or at least the business, as a going concern by taking control of the company out of the hands of its directors and placing it in the hands of an administrator. Alternatively, the procedure is aimed at maximising the realised value of the business assets.

Once an administration order has been issued, it is no longer possible to commence winding up proceedings against the company or enforce charges, retention of title clauses or even hire-purchase agreements against the company. This major advantage was in no small way undermined by the fact that, under the previous regime, an administration order could not be made after a company has begun the liquidation process. Since companies are required to inform any person who is entitled to appoint a receiver of the fact that the company is applying for an administration order, it was open to any secured creditor to enforce their rights and to forestall the administration procedure. This would cause the secured creditor no harm, since their debt would more than likely be covered by the security, but it could well lead to the end of the company as a going concern.

The Enterprise Act 2002 introduced a new scheme, which limited the powers of floating charge holders to appoint administrative receivers, whose function had been essentially to secure the interest of the floating charge holder who had appointed them, rather than the interests of the general creditors. By virtue of the Enterprise Act 2002, which amends the previous provisions of the Insolvency Act 1986, floating charge holders no longer have the right to appoint administrative receivers, but must now make use of the administration procedure as provided in that Act. As compensation for this loss of power the holders of floating charges are given the right to appoint the administrator of their choice.

The function of the administrator is to:

- Rescue the company as a going concern, or
- Achieve a better result for the company's creditors as *a whole* than would be likely if the company were to be wound up, or
- Realise the value of the property in order to make a distribution to the secured or preferential creditors.

The administrator is only permitted to pursue the third option where:

- He thinks it is not reasonably practicable to rescue the company as a going concern, and
- Where he thinks that he cannot achieve a better result for the creditors as a whole than would be likely if the company were to be wound up, and
- If he does not unnecessarily harm the interests of the creditors of the company as a whole.

An application to the court for an administration order may be made by a company, the directors of a company, or any of its creditors, but in addition the Enterprise Act allows the appointment of an administrator without the need to apply to the court for approval. Such 'out of court' applications can be made by the company or its directors, but may also be made by any floating charge holder.

During the administration process the administrator has the powers to:

- do anything necessary for the management of the company
- remove or appoint directors
- pay out monies to secured or preferential creditors *without the need to seek the approval of the court*
- pay out monies to unsecured creditors *with the approval of the court*
- take custody of all property belonging to the company
- dispose of company property. This power includes property which is subject to both fixed and floating charges, which may be disposed of without the consent of the charge holder, although they retain first call against any money realised by such a sale.

The administration period is usually 12 months, although this may be extended by six months with the approval of the creditors, or longer with the approval of the court. When the administrator concludes that the purpose of their appointment has been achieved, a notice to this effect is sent to the creditors, the court and the companies registry. Such a notice terminates the administrator's appointment. If the administrator forms the opinion that none of the purposes of the administration can be achieved, the court should be informed and it will consider ending the appointment. Creditors can always challenge the actions of the administrator through the courts.

ACCA marking scheme	
	Marks
This question, in two parts, carrying 4 marks for part (a) and 6 marks for part (b), requires candidates to explain the meaning of the terms 'compulsory winding up' and 'administration'.	
(a) A good explanation of the meaning and effect of winding up generally and compulsory winding up in particular.	3–4
Some, if little knowledge of winding up, or perhaps too general or unbalanced in not dealing specifically with compulsory winding up.	0–2
(b) A good explanation of the meaning and effect of administration generally and contrasting its purpose with that of compulsory winding up.	4–6
Some, if little, explanation of administration, but perhaps too general or lacking in detail.	2–3
Little or no knowledge of the topic.	0–1

7   EMPLOYEE/EMPLOYER COMMON LAW DUTIES

(a)   Although a contract of employment need not be in writing, the employer must provide the employee with particulars of the main terms of the contract in writing as required by the Employment Rights Act 1996. Such express terms are agreed upon by the employer and employee on entering into the contract of employment. However, in the absence of stated terms the law will impose duties on both employer and employee. Such implied terms have to be read subject to any express terms to the contrary. Although where the implied term is necessary to give efficacy to the contract, the implied term will take precedence over the express term (*Johnstone v Bloomsbury Health Authority* (1991)).

Duties of the employer

(i)   *To provide work*

The employer normally will be expected to provide work for the employee and where the employee is skilled and needs practice to maintain those skills, there may be an obligation to provide a reasonable amount of work *Langston v Amalgamated Union of Engineering Workers* (1974). No breach of this implied duty will occur so long as the employee continues to be paid even though there may be no work available.

(ii)   *To pay wages*

Normally the rate of pay is expressly stated in the contract of employment. However, in the absence of an express provision, the law will impose the duty to pay a reasonable remuneration for the work done. Following from (i) above, an employer must pay employees their wages even if there is no work available, although an express term to the contrary may be included in the contract of employment. Where workers, in the pursuit of an industrial dispute, offer only part performance by working to rule or adopting a 'go-slow' policy, the employer can refuse to accept such part performance and can refuse to make any payment for work done.

(iii)   *To indemnify the employee*

Where the employee in the course of his or her employment incurs any legal liability or necessary expenses on behalf of the employer, the employee is entitled to be indemnified or reimbursed.

(iv)   *Mutual respect*

The employment relationship is assumed to be based on mutuality of respect, trust and confidence and the employer must not act in a way calculated to damage such mutuality. As will be seen this is a reciprocal relationship, but it is clear that employers cannot treat their employees in an abusive manner (*Isle of Wight Tourist Board v Coombes* (1976)) and must be prepared to address any grievances they might have (*WA Goold (Pearmak) Ltd v McConnell & Another* (1995)).

(v)   *To provide a safe system of work*

At common law the employer is required to take reasonable care for the health and safety of his employees. Failure to comply will render the employer liable for an action in negligence. The duty extends to the provision of competent fellow employees, safe plant and equipment, a safe place of work and a safe system of work. If the employer has taken all reasonable steps to comply with the duty of care then they will not be liable for any injury sustained (*Latimer v AEC Ltd* (1953)).

(b)   There are a number of implied duties imposed on employees, which may all be understood as deriving from their relationship of trust and confidence with their employer and the consequential duty of loyalty and faithful service that derives from that relationship. The specific duties may be cited as:

(i)   *to act faithfully*

This is the fundamental duty and it covers such aspects of confidentially, i.e. not passing on information derived from one's employment to outsiders and not competing with the employer either directly or indirectly.

The courts are reluctant to accept that what workers do in their spare time should be of any concern to their employer (*Nova Plastics Ltd v Froggett* (1982)). However, sometimes an employer's interests may be harmed by an employee's spare-time work if this involved direct competition with the employer's business (*Hivac Ltd v Park Royal Scientific Instruments Ltd* (1946)).

An employee may not do anything while still employed, which is in breach of the duty to act faithfully. However, it is perfectly lawful for ex-employees to canvass customers of their former employer after leaving service. Moreover, they are entitled to make use of any knowledge and skills acquired while in the former employer's business, apart from such information which can be classified as a trade secret. In this sense the implied duty of confidentiality for ex-employees is narrower than in the case of an existing employee (*Faccenda Chicken Ltd v Fowler* (1986)).

(ii)   *to obey reasonable orders*

Employees must obey any reasonable and lawful instruction given to them by their employer. Whether any instruction fulfils these criteria is a matter of fact in each instance. The classic case in this area is *Pepper v Webb* (1969) in which a gardener not only indicated that he was not willing to follow an instruction but actually swore at his employer. In a subsequent action it was held that as the order was both lawful and reasonable the gardener had breached his implied duty.

(iii) *to use skill and care*

Should an employee not exercise the level of skill and care that may reasonably be expected, then they will not only be liable to dismissal, but they may also lose the protection of the employer's duty to indemnify them for losses (see part (a) above), and be made personally liable for claims for compensation. The classic case in this instance is *Lister v Romford Ice and Cold Storage Ltd* (1957) in which an employee lorry driver, rather than his employer, was held liable to compensate a fellow worker, due to his gross negligence in driving his lorry, which was held to breach his implied duty of skill and care.

(iv) *not to take bribes or make a secret profit*

This duty almost goes without saying, as an example of the general duty of good faith, but it covers the situation where an employee has received money or gifts from customers or clients. In this instance the classic case is *Boston Deep Sea Fishing Ice Co v Ansell* (1888) in which a managing director of a company was held to have been properly dismissed for having taken money as commission from the company's suppliers for orders he placed with them.

ACCA marking scheme		
		Marks
This question requires an explanation of the common law duties owed by both employers and employees.		
(a)	Good awareness of the implied duties imposed on employers. Examples used to highlight answers.	5–6
	Sound understanding but perhaps no examples.	3–4
	Limited knowledge only about the topic.	0–2
(b)	Good awareness of the implied duties imposed on employees.	3–4
	Limited knowledge about the topic.	0–2

8 BASH LTD

Given that the question scenario clearly states that the exclusion clause was incorporated into the contract between Andy and Bash Ltd (and there can be no doubt that it is), it is only necessary to consider the effect of the clause. On the basis of the clear wording, it would appear that the wording of the exclusion clause is sufficiently clear and specific to cover Bash Ltd's negligence. As a consequence, it only remains to consider how the legislation governing exclusion clauses would be likely to deal with this particular clause in the context of the question.

The Unfair Contract Terms Act 1977 (UCTA) is the original statutory attempt to control exclusion clauses. The original Unfair Terms in Consumer Contracts Regulations (UTCCR) were enacted in 1994 to implement the European Unfair Contract Terms Directive and were subsequently replaced by the current regulations in 1999.

Section 2(1) of UCTA provides an absolute prohibition on exemption clauses in relation to liability in negligence resulting in death or injury. It is therefore apparent that Bash Ltd cannot avoid responsibility for the injury sustained by Andy and will be liable for the injuries and the consequential loss he suffered.

Section 2 also provides that any exemption clauses relating to liability for other damage caused by negligence will only be enforced to the extent that they satisfy the 'requirement of reasonableness'; and s.11 provides that the requirement of reasonableness means 'fair and reasonable ... having regard to the circumstances ...'.

In looking at the circumstances of the case the court will take into account matters relating to the relative strength of bargaining power: inducements to accept the restrictions: whether the customer knew or ought to have known of the exclusion: whether the goods involved were specially made or adapted. The final outcome, therefore, is dependent on judicial interpretation. The onus of showing reasonableness rests with the party relying on the clause (*St Alban's CDC v International Computers Ltd* (1994)). If one were to ask the question: 'Was it reasonable for Bash Ltd to deny responsibility for the consequence of their negligence in this case?' the answer is likely to be no. Consequently Bash Ltd is likely to be liable for all the damages consequent upon its vicarious negligence, and the exclusion clause to have no effect (see *George Mitchell (Chesterhall) Ltd v Finney Lock Seeds Ltd* (1983) and *Smith v Bush* (1989)).

Although the Unfair Terms in Consumer Contracts Regulations 1999 do not affect the outcome of the situation in any material way, it is worth mentioning them at this point. The regulations are potentially wider in scope than UCTA, in that they cover all terms and not just exclusion clauses. Regulation 3(1) states that it applies to 'any term in a contract concluded between a seller or supplier and a consumer where the term has not been individually negotiated'. Under regulation 4(i), a term is unfair 'if contrary to the requirements of good faith, it causes a significant imbalance in the parties' rights and obligations arising under the contract to the detriment of the consumer'. Consequently reg.5(1) provides that if a term is found to be unfair it will not be binding on the consumer, although the remainder of the contract will continue to operate if it can do so after the excision of the unfair term.

ACCA marking scheme	
	Marks
This question requires candidates to apply the law relating to exclusion clauses to a specific problem scenario. Marks will be awarded for both knowledge and application, but application is essential.	
The best candidates should provide a clear understanding of the legal control of exclusion clauses and be able to apply the law. Some detailed reference should be made to the provisions of the Unfair Contract Terms Act (UCTA) 1997 and the very best answers will at least mention the Unfair Terms in Consumer Contracts Regulations 1999. Cases or examples should be used to demonstrate points made.	8–10
Weaker candidates may show little detailed knowledge of the legislation but be able to consider the UCTA generally.	5–7
Some but limited knowledge of the appropriate law or lacking in application.	3–4
The poorest candidates will provide nothing but the briefest reference to the legislation.	0–2

9   DULL PLC

This question requires candidates to analyse a problem scenario and explain and apply the law relating to directors' contracts with their companies.

As a consequence of the position they hold, company directors owe fiduciary duties to their companies. One such duty is the duty not to permit a conflict of interest and duty to arise. This equitable rule is strictly applied by the courts and the effect of its operations may be seen in *Regal (Hastings) v Gulliver* (1942). In that case, the directors of a company owning one cinema provided money for the creation of a subsidiary company to purchase two other cinemas. After the parent and subsidiary companies had been sold at a later date, the directors were required to repay the profit they had made on the sale of their shares in the subsidiary company on the grounds that they had only been in the situation to make that profit because of their positions as directors of the parent company. It is not necessary to prove an actual conflict of interest, merely the possibility of such a conflict, and the rigorous nature of this principle may be seen in *Boardman v Phipps* (1967).

One obvious area where directors place themselves in a position involving a conflict of interest is where they have an interest in a contract with the company. The common law position was that in the event of any such situation arising, any contract involved was voidable at the instance of the company (*Aberdeen Rly Co v Blaikie* (1854)). However, s.182 of the Companies Act 2006 places a duty on directors to declare any interest, direct or indirect, in any contracts with their companies, and provides for a fine if they fail in this regard. A director's disclosure can take the form of a general declaration of interest in a particular company, which is considered sufficient to put the other directors on notice for the future. Any declaration of interest must be made at the board meeting that first considers the contract, or if the director becomes interested in the contract after that, at the first meeting thereafter. Failure to disclose any interest renders the contract voidable at the instance of the company and the director may be liable to account to the company for any profit made in relation to it.

Applying the above to the problem scenario, it appears that Caz did not declare her interest in either Era Ltd generally, or the particular contract in question. Dull plc could have avoided the contract had they found out earlier and acted sooner, but in any case Caz can be held liable to account to Dull plc for any profit she made on the deal. Caz will also be liable to prosecution and a fine under s.183 of the Companies Act 2006, which criminalises any failure to comply with the requirements of s.182.

ACCA marking scheme	
	Marks
This question requires candidates to analyse a problem scenario and explain and apply the law relating to directors' contracts with their companies.	
A good analysis of the scenario with a clear explanation of the law relating to contracts between directors and their companies, both at common law and under statute. Cases and/or references to the Companies Act will be provided.	8–10
Some understanding of the situation but perhaps lacking in detail or reference to the statute.	5–7
Weak answer lacking in knowledge or application, with little or no reference to the Companies Act.	3–4
Little if any knowledge of the appropriate legal principles.	0–2

10   IRE LTD

This question requires candidates to consider fraudulent trading both under s.993 of the Companies Act 2006 and s.213 of the Insolvency Act 1986, and wrongful trading under s.214 of the Insolvency Act 1986.

(a)   There has long been civil liability for any activity amounting to fraudulent trading. Thus, s.213 of the Insolvency Act (IA) 1986 governs situations where, in the course of a winding up, it appears that the business of a company has been carried on with intent to defraud creditors, or for any fraudulent purpose. In such cases, the court, on the application of the liquidator, may declare that any persons who were knowingly parties to such carrying on of the business are liable to make such contributions (if any) to the company's assets as the court thinks proper. There is a major problem in making use of s.213, however, and that lies in meeting the very high burden of proof involved in proving dishonesty on the part of the person against whom it is alleged. It should be noted that there is also a criminal offence of fraudulent trading under s.993 of the Companies Act 2006, which applies to anyone who has been party to the carrying on of the business of a company with intent to defraud creditors or any other person, or for any other fraudulent purpose.

Given that it is stated that Gram and Hen hid the fact that Ire Ltd was insolvent it is possible that they might be liable under the fraudulent trading provisions both civil and criminal. As a consequence they may well be liable for a maximum prison sentence of 10 years and may have to contribute to the assets of the company to cover any loss sustained by creditors as a result of their actions. There is no evidence to support either action against Fran.

(b) Wrongful trading does not involve dishonesty but, nonetheless, it still makes particular individuals potentially liable for the debts of their companies. Section 214 applies where a company is being wound up and it appears that, at some time before the start of the winding up, a director knew, or ought to have known, that there was no reasonable chance of the company avoiding insolvent liquidation. In such circumstances, then, unless the directors took every reasonable step to minimise the potential loss to the company's creditors, they may be liable to contribute such money to the assets of the company as the court thinks proper. In deciding what directors ought to have known, the court will apply an objective test, as well as a subjective one. As in common law, if the director is particularly well qualified, they will be expected to perform in line with those standards. Additionally, however, s.214 of the IA 1986 establishes a minimum standard by applying an objective test which requires directors to have the general knowledge, skill and experience, which may reasonably be expected of a person carrying out the same functions as are carried out by that director in relation to the company.

The manner in which incompetent directors will become liable to contribute to the assets of their companies was shown in Re *Produce Marketing Consortium Ltd* (1989), in which two directors were held liable to pay compensation from the time that they ought to have known that their company could not avoid insolvent liquidation, rather than the later time when they actually realised that fact. Interestingly, the common law approach to directors' duty of care has been extended to accommodate the requirements of s.214 (Re *D'Jan of London Ltd* (1993)).

It is clearly apparent that both Gram and Hen will be personally liable under s.214 for the increase in Ire Ltd's debts from £10,000 to £100,000. However, as a director of the company Fran will also be liable to contribute to the assets of the company under s.214.

ACCA marking scheme		
		Marks
This question requires candidates to consider fraudulent trading both under s.993 of the Companies act 2006 and s.213 of the Insolvency Act 1986, and wrongful trading under s.214 of the Insolvency Act 1986.		
(a)	Clear explanation of operation of the law relating to fraudulent trading, under both criminal and civil law, but with the emphasis on the Insolvency Act provisions.	4–5
	Some to good understanding but lacking detail.	2–3
	Little or no knowledge.	0–1
(b)	Clear explanation of the law relating to wrongful trading, probably, but not necessarily referring to case law.	4–5
	Some to fair understanding but lacking detail.	2–3
	Little if any knowledge.	0–1

Section 5

JUNE 2010 EXAM QUESTIONS

ALL TEN questions are compulsory and MUST be attempted

1 CIVIL COURTS

Describe the structure and functions of the main civil courts in the English legal system, including the Supreme Court. **(Total: 10 marks)**

2 OFFERS

In relation to the law of contract:

(a) define an offer; **(5 marks)**

(b) explain the specific meaning and effect of

   (i) a counter-offer; **(3 marks)**

   (ii) a unilateral offer. **(2 marks)**

(Total: 10 marks)

3 DUTY OF CARE

In relation to the tort of negligence, explain the meaning of 'duty of care'.

(Total: 10 marks)

4 REGISTERING A PLC

Explain the documents necessary, and the procedure to be followed, in registering a public limited company under the provisions of the Companies Act 2006. **(Total: 10 marks)**

5 DEBENTURES AND CHARGES

Explain the meaning of the following terms in company law:

(a) a debenture; **(3 marks)**

(b) a fixed charge; **(3 marks)**

(c) a floating charge. **(4 marks)**

(Total: 10 marks)

6   COMPANY SECRETARIES

In the context of corporate governance, explain the rules relating to the appointment, duties and powers of a company secretary in a public limited company.   **(Total: 10 marks)**

7   SELF EMPLOYED VS. EMPLOYED

In the context of employment law, state how the courts decide whether someone is self-employed or is an employee.   **(Total: 10 marks)**

8   BRY AND CIS

In January 2010 Ami took over an old warehouse with the intention of opening an art gallery. As the warehouse had to be converted, Ami entered into two contracts, one with Bry to do all the necessary plastering and one with Cis, who was to do all the necessary painting. Both Bry and Cis were to be paid £5,000. Both received initial payments of £1,000 and agreed to have the work completed on 31 March, as the art gallery had to be ready for its first exhibition on 1 May.

At the end of February, Bry told Ami that he would not complete the plastering in time unless she agreed to increase his payment by a further £1,000. Ami agreed to pay the increased sum in order to ensure that the job was done on time. She then thought it was only fair that she should increase the amount of money promised to Cis by the same amount.

However, on completion of the work on time Ami refused to make either of the additional payments to Bry or Cis, beyond the original contractual price.

Required:

Advise Bry and Cis whether they have any rights in law to enforce Ami's promise to pay them an extra £1,000.   **(Total: 10 marks)**

9   CHI, DI AND FI

Chi, Di and Fi formed an ordinary partnership to run an art gallery. Each of them paid £100,000 into the business. As Fi had no prospect of raising any more money it was agreed between them that her maximum liability for any partnership debts would be fixed at her original contribution of £100,000. The partnership agreement specifically restricted the scope of the partnership business to the sale of 'paintings, sculptures and other works of art.' In January 2010 Chi took £10,000 from the partnership's bank drawn on its overdraft facility. She had told the bank that the money was to finance a short-term partnership debt but in fact she used the money to pay for a holiday. In February Di entered into a £25,000 contract on behalf of the partnership to buy some books, which she hoped to sell in the gallery.

Required:

Advise Chi, Di and Fi as to their various rights and liabilities in relation to the operation of the business under partnership law.   **(Total: 10 marks)**

10   GILT LTD

Gilt Ltd is a small company with an issued share capital of 100,000 £1 shares held by 100 members.

Harry, the managing director of Gilt Ltd, has been approached by Itt plc in respect of its making a takeover bid for Gilt Ltd. Itt plc has given Harry what is described as a facility fee of £50,000 for ensuring that the takeover is successful.

At the next board meeting Harry convinces the other directors that the take-over bid is in the long-term interest of Gilt Ltd, but they are concerned that the holders of the majority of the issued share capital will not approve of the takeover.

In order to ensure the success of the takeover, the directors of Gilt Ltd agree that they should allot sufficient new shares to Itt plc to ensure that a new majority of members will support the takeover.

After the allocation of the shares to Itt plc a general meeting is called to consider the takeover and it is approved, with Itt plc voting in favour.

May, a substantial shareholder in Gilt Ltd has subsequently found out about the actions of Itt plc, Harry and the other directors.

Required:

Advise May as to the legality of the share allotment and as to what action can be taken against Harry.   **(Total: 10 marks)**

Section 6

ANSWERS TO JUNE 2010 EXAM QUESTIONS

CORPORATE AND BUSINESS LAW (ENGLISH)

1   CIVIL COURTS

The civil court structure in ascending order of authority is as follows:

Magistrates' courts

Magistrates' courts have a significant, if limited, civil jurisdiction. They hear family proceedings and in such cases the court is referred to as a 'family proceedings court'. More generally, magistrates' courts have powers of recovery in relation to the council tax arrears and charges for water, gas and electricity. They also hear appeals against refusal by local authorities to grant licences for selling liquor in their area. Importantly the magistrates' courts have no jurisdiction over claims in contract or tort.

County courts

The network of county courts was introduced in 1846 to provide for local adjudication of relatively small-scale litigation. There are currently 243 county courts. The county court jurisdiction extends to probate, property cases, tort, contract, bankruptcy, and insolvency.

Of particular importance with regard to the county court is the provision of a small claims procedure operated under its auspices. This procedure essentially allows for an arbitration hearing to be conducted by a district judge in most cases involving claims of no more than £5,000. This small claims procedure is designed to be quicker, less formal and less expensive than a county court hearing.

The High Court of Justice

The High Court has three administrative divisions: the Court of Chancery, the Queen's Bench Division and the Family Division.

The Queen's Bench Division

This is the main common law court and is the division with the largest workload. It has some criminal jurisdiction and appellate jurisdiction, but its main jurisdiction is civil concerning contract and tort cases.

The Queen's Bench Divisional Court

This court, as distinct from the Queen's Bench Division, exercises appellate jurisdiction on a point of law by way of case stated from magistrates' courts, tribunals and the Crown Court. It also exercises the power of judicial review of the decisions made by governmental and public authorities, inferior courts and tribunals.

The Chancery Division

The jurisdiction of the Chancery Division includes matters relating to: the sale or partition of land and the raising of charges on land; mortgages; trusts; the administration of the estates of the dead; contentious probate business, such as the validity and interpretation of wills; copyright, company law, partnership and revenue law; and insolvency.

Chancery Divisional Court

Comprising one or two Chancery judges, this appellate court hears appeals from the Commissioners of Inland Revenue on income tax cases, and from county courts on certain matters like bankruptcy.

The Family Division

The Family Division of the High Court deals with all matrimonial matters both first instance and on appeal. Amongst other matters, it deals with issues relating to minors, legitimacy, adoption, and proceedings involving domestic violence.

The Family Divisional Court

The Family Divisional Court, consisting of two High Court judges, hears appeals from decisions of magistrates' courts and county courts in family matters.

The Court of Appeal (Civil Division)

The Court of Appeal was established by the Judicature Act 1873. The court hears appeals from the three divisions of the High Court; the divisional courts; the county courts; the Employment Appeal Tribunal; the Lands Tribunal and the Transport Tribunal. The most senior judge is the Master of the Rolls. Usually, three judges will sit to hear an appeal although for very important cases five may sit.

The Supreme Court

The Supreme Court, which came into operation in the autumn of 2009, is the highest court within the English civil system. It replaces the House of Lords as the highest judicial forum and exercises all of that court's functions. It was felt that the previous location of the highest court in the land in the legislature was contrary to the separation of powers and consequently the members of the Supreme Court no longer sit in the House of Lords. It consists of 12 justices and hears appeals on the most important legal issues.

ACCA marking scheme	
	Marks
This question requires candidates to describe the structure and functions of the main civil courts in the English legal system.	
A thorough to complete description of the various civil courts with an explanation of their relationships and function. At this level it is required that answers make reference to the Supreme Court.	8–10
A less detailed treatment of the court structure but still covering the main courts. This represents the maximum mark that can be achieved without reference to the Supreme Court.	5–7
Weak answer, perhaps just providing a sketch of the court structure with no explanation of that structure.	3–4
Little or no understanding of the topic.	0–2

2   OFFERS

(a)   *Offer*

An offer sets out the terms upon which an individual is willing to enter into a binding contractual relationship with another person. It is a promise to be bound on particular terms, which is capable of acceptance. The essential factor to emphasise about an offer is that it may, through acceptance by the offeree, result in a legally enforceable contract. The person who makes the offer is the offeror; the person who receives the offer is the offeree.

Offers, once accepted, may be legally enforced but not all statements will amount to an offer. It is important, therefore, to be able to distinguish what the law will treat as an offer from other statements, which will not form the basis of an enforceable contract. An offer must be capable of acceptance. It must therefore not be too vague (*Scammel v Ouston* (1941)). In *Carlill v Carbolic Smoke Ball Co* (1893) it was held that an offer could be made to the whole world and could be accepted and made binding through the conduct of the offeree.

In addition an offer should be distinguished, from the following:

(i)   a mere statement of intention, which cannot form the basis of a contract even although the party to whom it was made acts on it (*Re Fickus* (1900)).

(ii)   a mere supply of information, as in *Harvey v Facey* (1893) where it was held that the defendant's telegram, in which he stated a minimum price he would accept for property, was simply a statement of information, and was not an offer capable of being accepted by the claimant.

(b)   (i)   *Counter-offer*

A counter-offer arises where the offeree tries to change the terms of the original offer that has been made rather than directly accepting it. The consequence of making a counter-offer is to bring the original offer to an end so it is no longer possible for that original offer to be accepted at a later time. For example, in *Hyde v Wrench* (1840), Wrench offered to sell his farm for £1,000. Hyde offered £950, which Wrench rejected. Hyde then informed Wrench that he accepted the original offer. It was held that there was no contract. Hyde's counter-offer had effectively ended the original offer and it was no longer open to him to accept it.

A counter-offer must not be confused with a request for information. Such a request does not end the offer, which can still be accepted after the new information has been elicited. See *Stevenson v McLean* (1880), where it was held that a request by the offeree as to the length of time the offeror would give for payment did not terminate the original offer, which he was entitled to accept prior to revocation.

(ii)   *Unilateral offer*

A unilateral offer is one where one party promises something in return for some action on the part of another party. In relation to unilateral offers, revocation is not permissible once the offeree has started performing the task requested. Reward cases are examples of such unilateral promises. There is no compulsion placed on the party undertaking the action but it would seem to be unfair if the promisor were entitled to revoke their offer just before the offeree was about to complete their part of the contract. An example of unilateral contracts may be seen in *Carlill v Carbolic Smoke Ball Co* (1993), where the company promised to pay £100 to anyone who caught influenza after using their product. No one was forced to buy the product but once they did and started using it, the company was bound by its promise. In *Errington v Errington* (1952), a father promised his son and daughter-in-law that he would convey a house to them when they had paid off the outstanding mortgage. After the father's death, his widow sought to revoke the promise. It was held that the promise could not be withdrawn as long as the mortgage payments continued to be met.

ACCA marking scheme			
			Marks
This question is divided into three parts and requires candidate to explain the meaning of three elements in contract law: offer, counter-offer and unilateral offer.			
(a)		A good to complete answer explaining the meaning of an offer.	3–5
		For some indication as to the meaning of offer.	1–2
(b)	(i)	Awarded for explanation of the meaning and effect of counter-offer depending on clarify of explanation.	2–3
		For some knowledge	1
	(ii)	For a good to complete explanation of the meaning and effect of a unilateral offer.	2
		Some idea about unilateral offers but lacking in detail.	1

3 DUTY OF CARE

An individual is not automatically liable for every negligent act that he or she commits and in order to sustain an action in negligence it must be shown that the party at fault owed a duty of care to the person injured as a result of their actions.

Consequently, the onus is on the claimant to establish that the respondent owed them a duty of care.

The test for establishing whether a duty of care exists was initially set out in *Donoghue v Stevenson* (1932), the snail in the ginger beer bottle case. In putting forward the test to establish a duty of care Lord Atkin stated that:

'You must take reasonable care to avoid acts and omissions which you could reasonably foresee would be likely to injure your neighbour. Who, then, in law is my neighbour? ... any person so closely and directly affected by my act that I ought reasonably to have them in contemplation as being so affected when I am directing my mind to the acts and omissions which are called in question.'

It can be seen that this neighbour test for deciding the existence of a duty of care is an objective, rather than a subjective one. It is not a matter of what the respondent actually considered, but what they ought to have considered. Nor does the test require the contemplation of the resultant effect on the specific individual injured, but merely requires that identity of a class of individuals who might be injured as a consequence of the respondent's lack of care.

The idea of the neighbour, or proximity, test was extended in *Hedley Byrne v Heller* (1964), which established the possibility of liability for negligent misrepresentation causing economic loss, where a party gave inaccurate advice or information to another party, within a special relationship, and that party subsequently and reasonably relied on it.

The test in *Donoghue v Stevenson* was extended further in *Anns v Merton LBC* (1978), Lord Wilberforce introducing a two stage test for establishing the existence of a duty, as follows:

- Is there a sufficient relationship of proximity or neighbourhood between the alleged wrongdoer and the person who has suffered damage such that, in the reasonable contemplation of the former, carelessness on his part may be likely to cause damage to the latter?

- If the first question is answered in the affirmative, are there then any considerations which ought to negate, reduce or limit the scope of the duty or the class of persons to whom it is owed or the damages to which a breach of duty may give rise?

The impact of *Anns* led to the expansion of negligence, as the policy reasons acted only to limit liability once a duty had been found to exist, as opposed to limiting the existence of the duty itself. However, there was gradual criticism of, and retreat from the approach taken by Lord Wilberforce. Thus in *Peabody Donation Fund v Sir Lindsay Parkinson & Co Ltd* (1984), it was stressed that the proximity test had to be satisfied before a duty of care could be found to exist.

The decision in *Anns* was eventually overruled by *Murphy v Brentwood DC* (1990).

In *Caparo Industries plc v Dickman* (1990), a three stage test for establishing a duty of care was recommended. This requires consideration of the following questions:

- Was the harm caused reasonably foreseeable?

- Was there a relationship of proximity between the defendant and the claimant?

- In all the circumstances, is it just, fair and reasonable to impose a duty of care?

As regards the final element above see *Marc Rich & Co v Bishop Rock Marine Co Ltd (The Nicholas H)* (1996), for a subsequent application of the *Caparo* approach. In that case the House of Lords relied on policy reasons for not imposing a duty of care.

The present position appears to be that in establishing the existence of a duty of care in negligence, an incremental approach must be taken. The claimant must show that the defendant foresaw that damage would occur to the claimant, that is, that there was sufficient proximity in time, space and relationship between the claimant and the defendant. In practical terms, foreseeability of damage will determine proximity in the majority of personal injury cases. The courts will then, where appropriate, consider whether it is just and reasonable to impose a duty and whether there are any policy reasons for denying or limiting the existence of a duty, for example, under the floodgates argument.

ACCA marking scheme	
	Marks
This question requires candidates to explain the meaning of the concept duty of care in the tort of negligence	
Thorough explanation of the meaning of duty of care with appropriate references to cases.	8–10
Reasonable on duty of care but perhaps lacking in detail or cases authority.	5–7
Unbalanced answer, lacking in detailed understanding.	3–4
Very unbalanced answer, demonstrating very little understanding.	0–2

4   REGISTERING A PLC

Section 7 Companies Act 2006 (CA) sets out the method for forming a company, which is that one or more persons must subscribe their name to *a memorandum of association* and comply with the requirements of the provisions of the Act as to registration. Under s.9, the *memorandum of association* must be submitted to the companies' registrar together with an *application for registration,* which in turn lists other documents that must be submitted. As a result the following documents are required to be submitted.

(a)   *The memorandum of association*

Although the 2006 Act retains the previous requirement for individuals wishing to form a company to subscribe their names to a memorandum of association it nonetheless significantly reduces the importance of the memorandum and as a consequence it is no longer possible to amend or update the memorandum of a company formed under the 2006 Act. Nonetheless the memorandum of association, which must be in the prescribed form, remains an important, document to the extent that, as required by s.8, it evidences the intention of the subscribers to the memorandum to form a company and become members of that company on formation. Also in relation to a company limited by shares, the memorandum also provides evidence of the members' agreement to take at least one share each in the company.

(b)   *Application for registration*

Although the 2006 Act only requires the memorandum and application for registration to be submitted, s.9 sets out other documents as well as the specific information that must be delivered to the registrar when an application for registration is made.

Section 9 provides that in all cases the application for registration must state:

- the company's proposed name;
- whether the company's registered office is to be situated in England and Wales (or Wales), in Scotland or in Northern Ireland;
- a statement of the intended address of the company's registered office (that is, its postal address as opposed to the
- preceding statement confirming the jurisdiction in which the company's registered office is to be situated);
- whether the liability of the company's members is to be limited and if so whether it is to be limited by shares or by guarantee;
- whether the company is to be a private or a public company.

(c)   *Statement of capital and initial shareholdings*

This document is required where the company is to have a share capital. Alternatively a statement of guarantee is required where that is not the case (CA 2006 ss.10 & 11 set out the detailed provisions in these regards).

(d)   *A statement of the company's proposed officers*

Section 12 explains that this requirement relates to:

- any person/persons who are to be the first director or directors of the company
- the person/s who is/are to be the first secretary.

(e)   *A copy of any proposed articles*

As the model articles apply by default this requirement operates to the extent that the company does not intend to use the model articles.

(f)   *A statement of compliance*

This requirement to the effect that the rules relating to registration have been followed is as set out in s.13. Such a statement does not need to be witnessed and may be made in either paper or electronic form. Under s.1068, the registrar is authorised to specify the rules relating to, and who may make, such a statement. Section 1112 makes it a criminal offence to make a false statement of compliance, as is the case in relation to all documents delivered to, or statements made to, the registrar.

The appropriate fee must accompany the foregoing documents and once the registrar is satisfied that the requirements of the Act have been met, he shall issue a certificate that the company is duly incorporated. As previously, once issued the certificate is conclusive evidence that the requirements of this Act as to registration have been complied with and that the company is duly registered under the Act.

ACCA marking scheme	
	Marks
This question requires candidates to list and explain the documents required to be submitted to the companies' registry in order to register a company	
Thorough explanation of the documents and procedure.	8–10
Reasonable treatment but perhaps lacking in detail.	5–7
Unbalanced answer, perhaps not dealing with all elements of the question or lacking in detailed knowledge of those elements.	3–4
Very weak answer demonstrating little understanding of the documents or procedure.	0–2

5   DEBENTURES AND CHARGES

Companies ordinarily raise the money they need to finance their operations through the issue of share capital, but it is equally common for companies to raise additional capital through borrowing.

(a)   **Debentures**

A debenture is a document, which acknowledges the fact that a company has borrowed money. The use of the term debenture, however, has been extended to cover the loan itself. A debenture may be issued to a single creditor or to a large number of people, in which case each of the creditors has a proportionate claim against the total 'debenture stock'.

As creditors of the company, debenture holders receive interest on their loans and are entitled to receive payment whether the company is profitable or not. As regards repayment, debts rank in order of creation, so earlier debentures have to be paid before those created later. Where debentures are issued as part of a series, it is usual for a pari passu clause to be included in the document creating the debt, with the effect that all of the loans made within the series rank equally with regard to repayment.

Debentures which have no security are referred to as 'unsecured loan stock'. It is usual, however, for debentures to provide security for the amount loaned. Security means that if the company is wound up, the secured creditor will have priority in terms of repayment over any unsecured creditor. There are two types of security for company loans: fixed charges and floating charges.

(b) **Fixed charge**

In this situation a specific asset of the company is made subject to a charge in order to secure a debt. Once the asset is subject to the fixed charge the company cannot dispose of it without the consent of the debenture holders. The asset most commonly subject to fixed charges is land, although any other long-term capital asset may also be charged. It would not be appropriate, however, to give a fixed charge against stock-in-trade, as the company would be prevented from freely dealing with it without the prior approval of the debenture holders. Such a situation would obviously prevent the company from carrying on its day-to-day business. If the company fails to honour the commitments set out in the document creating the debenture, such as meeting its interest payments, the debenture holders can appoint a receiver who will if necessary sell the asset charged to recover the money owed. If the value of the asset that is subject to the charge is greater than the debt against which it is charged then the excess goes to pay off the rest of the company's debts. If it is less than the value of the debt secured then the debenture holders will become unsecured creditors for the amount remaining outstanding.

(c) **Floating charge**

This category of charge is peculiar to companies and represents one of the advantages of the company over other business forms. The floating charge is most commonly made in relation to the 'undertaking and assets' of a company and does not attach to any specific property whilst the company is meeting its requirements as stated in the debenture document. The security is provided by all the property owned by the company, some of which may be continuously changing, such as stock-in-trade. Thus, in contrast to the fixed charge, the use of the floating charge permits the company to deal with its property without the need to seek the approval of the debenture holders. However, if the company commits some act of default, such as not meeting its interest payments, or going into liquidation, the floating charge is said to crystallise. The value of the assets subject to the charge may be realised in order to pay the debt owed to the floating charge holder, although the Enterprise Act 2002 introduced a new procedure to limit the powers of floating charge holders to appoint administrative receivers and requires them to make use of the general administration procedure.

All charges, including both fixed and floating, have to be registered with the Companies Registry within 21 days of their creation. Failure to register the charge as required has the effect of making the charge void, i.e. ineffective, against any other creditor, or the liquidator of the company. The charge, however, remains valid against the company, which means in effect that the holder of the charge loses their priority as against other company creditors. In addition to registration at the Companies Registry, companies are required to maintain a register of all charges on their property. Although a failure to comply with this requirement constitutes an offence, it does not invalidate the charge.

In relation to properly registered charges of the same type, they take priority according to their date of creation. However, as regards charges of different types, a fixed charge takes priority over a floating charge even though it was created after it.

ACCA marking scheme	
	Marks
This question requires candidates to consider how companies may raise loan capital and how they secure such loans against their assets. Marks will be allocated as indicated in the paper.	
A good to full answer providing a clear explanation of each of the elements of the question.	8–10
Sound understanding of the concepts but perhaps lacking detail or slightly unbalanced.	5–7
Weak answer lacking in detailed knowledge.	3–4
Very weak answer demonstrating little understanding of the topic.	0–2

6 COMPANY SECRETARIES

This question requires candidates to consider the important role of the company secretary in relation to the operation of companies. The corporate governance structure specifies the distribution of rights and responsibilities among different participants in the corporation, such as, the board, managers, shareholders and other stakeholders, and spells out the rules and procedures for making decisions on corporate affairs. The essence of corporate governance is to ensure that companies are properly run and that its officers are accountable and subject to control. Whilst it is usual to focus on directors when considering the idea of corporate governance, it should be remembered that company secretaries also have an important function to perform in relation to the proper conduct of company affairs.

Every public company is required to have a secretary, who is one of the company's officers for the purposes of the Companies Act 2006 and who, in addition, may, or may not, be a director of the company. Private companies are no longer required to appoint company secretaries, although they still can do so if they wish.

Appointment

Section 1173 Companies Act (CA) 2006 includes the company secretary amongst the officers of a company. Every public company must have a company secretary and s.273 of the CA requires that the directors of a public company must ensure that the company secretary has the requisite knowledge and experience to discharge their functions. Section 273(2) & (3) sets out the following list of alternative specific minimum qualifications, which a secretary to a public limited company must have:

- they must have held office as a company secretary in a public company for three of the five years preceding their appointment to their new position;

- they must be a member of one of a list of recognised professional accountancy bodies, including ACCA;

- they must be a solicitor or barrister or advocate within the UK;

- they must have held some other position, or be a member of such other body, as appears to the directors of the company to make them capable of acting as company secretary.

Duties

The duties of company secretaries are set by the board of directors and therefore vary from company to company, but as an officer of the company, they will be responsible for ensuring that the company complies with its statutory obligations. The following are some of the most important duties undertaken by company secretaries:

- to ensure that the necessary registers required to be kept by the Companies Acts are established and properly maintained;

- to ensure that all returns required to be lodged with the Companies Registry are prepared and filed within the appropriate time limits;

- to organise and attend meetings of the shareholders and directors;

- to ensure that the company's books of accounts are kept in accordance with the Companies Acts and that the annual accounts and reports are prepared in the form and at the time required by the Acts;

- to be aware of all the statutory requirements placed on the company's activities and to ensure that the company complies with them;

- to sign such documents as require their signature under the Companies Acts.

With specific regard to the Combined Code on Corporate Governance company secretaries are required:

- to ensure the flow of necessary information within the board of directors and its committees;

- to ensure that new board members are properly inducted into their positions;

- to ensure the professional development of company directors;

- to provide advice and guidance to the board and its chair on all matters relating to corporate governance.

Powers

Although old authorities, such as *Houghton & Co v Northard Lowe & Wills* (1928) suggest that company secretaries have extremely limited authority to bind their company, later cases have recognised the reality of the contemporary situation and have extended to company secretaries potentially extensive powers to bind their companies. As an example consider *Panorama Developments Ltd v Fidelis Furnishing Fabrics Ltd* (1971). In this case the Court of Appeal held that a company secretary was entitled 'to sign contracts connected with the administrative side of a company's affairs, such as employing staff and ordering cars and so forth. All such matters now come within the ostensible authority of a company's secretary.'

ACCA marking scheme	
	Marks
This question requires candidates to consider the company secretary in the context of the idea of corporate governance.	
Thorough treatment of all three aspects of the question including at least some consideration of corporate governance itself.	8–10
Thorough treatment of some aspects of the question or a reasonable, but less than full, treatment of some aspects.	5–7
Unbalanced answer, merely dealing with a limited number of aspects of the question.	3–4
Demonstrating little or no understanding of the nature of the question.	0–2

7   SELF EMPLOYED VS. EMPLOYED

Employees are people working under a contract of service. Those who work under a contract for services are independent contractors. They are not employees, but are self-employed. It is essential to distinguish the two categories clearly, because important legal consequences follow from the placing of a person in one or other of the categories. For example, although employees are protected by various common law and statutory rights in relation to their employment, no such wide-scale protection is offered to the self-employed.

Given the importance of the distinction the courts have developed a variety of test for distinguishing the employee from the self-employed.

(i)   *The control test*

The first test to be applied by the courts was known as the control test and depended upon the degree to which the person who is using the other's services actually controls; not only what they do, but how they do it (in *Walker v Crystal Palace Football Club* (1910) a professional football player was held to be an employee of his club). The main shortcoming in the control test was its lack of subtlety. Highly skilled professionals, such as surgeons, by necessity have a high level of control over how they perform their day-to-day work, which meant that, under the control test, they were deemed to be self-employed rather than employees. Consequently, they were personally liable for any negligence in their performance, rather than the Health Authority, which used their services.

(ii)   *The integration test*

The integration test shifted the emphasis from the degree of control exercised of an individual to the extent to which the individual was integrated into the business of their employer (in *Whittaker v Minister of Pensions & National Insurance* (1967) a circus trapeze artist who was required to do other general tasks in relation to the operation of the circus was held to be an employee). However, even the integration test was not without problems, with some employers attempting to give the impression of using a self-employed work-force whilst effectively still controlling what that work-force did.

(iii) The multiple, or economic reality test

The economic reality test was first established in *Ready Mixed Concrete (South East) Ltd v Minister of Pensions and National Insurance* (1968). In that case, rather than relying on one single factor the court held that there were three conditions supporting the existence of a contract of employment:

*   the employee agrees to provide his own work and skill in return for a wage,

*   the employees agrees, either expressly or impliedly, that they will be subject to a degree of control, exercisable by the employer,

*   the other provisions of the contract are consistent with its being a contract of employment.

In deciding whether or not there is contract of employment the courts tend to focus on such issues as whether wages are paid regularly or by way of a single lump sum; whether the person receives holiday pay; and on who pays the due national insurance and income tax. However, there can be no definitive list of tests as the whole point of the multiple test is that it examines all aspects of the situation in order to reach a determination. For example in N*ethermore (St Neots) v Gardiner & Taverna* (1984), a group of home workers, i.e. people who carried out paid work in their own homes, were held to be employees on the grounds that they were subject to an irreducible minimum obligation to work for their employer.

ACCA marking scheme	
	Marks
This question asks candidates to explain the common law rules used to distinguish contracts of service from contracts for services.	
A thorough treatment of all of the rules, perhaps placing them in their historical context but certainly providing case support.	8–10
Good analysis and case support, although perhaps limited in appreciation.	5–7
Recognition of the areas covered by the question, but lacking in detailed analysis.	3–4
Little or no analysis or knowledge of the subject of the question.	0–2

8   BRY AND CIS

The provision of some form of consideration is an essential requirement in the establishment of contractual relationships. This question requires candidates to examine the operation of the rules relating to whether or not the performance of existing contractual duties can provide consideration for some new promise.

Bry and Cis entered into a contract with Ami to carry out the work for an agreed price. However, before the completion of the contracts Ami promised each of them a further payment, although she is now refusing to pay more than the original agreed sum of £5,000. The question is whether Bry and Cis can enforce Ami's promise to pay them the additional sums.

In order to require Ami to make payment at the new level, those claiming it must show that they provided legally 'sufficient' consideration for her promise. The question, therefore, is whether the performance of existing contractual duties can ever provide consideration for a new promise. The long-established rule of contract was that the mere performance of a contractual duty already owed to the promisor could not be consideration for a new promise. Thus in *Stilk v Myrick* (1809) when members of a ship's crew deserted, the captain promised the remaining members of the crew that they would share the deserter's wages if they completed the voyage. Subsequently, however, when the owners refused to make the promised payment it was held that the captain's promise could not be legally enforced as the sailors had only done what they were already obliged to do by their contracts of employment. Where, however, the promisee did more than they were already contractually bound to do then the performance of the additional task does constitute valid consideration for a new promise (*Hartley v Ponsonby* (1857)).

The more contemporary case of *Williams v Roffey Bros* (1991) expanded the category of consideration. In that case the Court of Appeal held that Roffey Bros had enjoyed practical benefits as a result of their promise to increase Williams' previously agreed payment for work under an existing contract, although Williams did no more than they were contractually bound to do. The benefits enjoyed were that the work would be completed on time, they would not have to pay any penalty; and they would not suffer the bother and expense of getting someone else to complete the work.

As a result it would now seem that the performance of an existing contractual duty can amount to consideration for a new promise in circumstances where there is no question of fraud or duress, and where practical benefits accrue to the promisor.

It remains to apply the preceding legal principles to the case in point. First of all as regards Bry, he had a contract with Ami to do the plastering, but insisted that Ami increase his money before he would complete the work. Bry might try to argue that his situation falls within the ambit of *Williams v Roffey Bros*, and that therefore he can enforce the promise. He would point out that Ami did enjoy practical benefits in that the gallery was finished on time thus allowing her to open her exhibition. It is clear, however, that this situation is significantly different in that whereas in *Williams v Roffey Bros* the plaintiff did not exert any undue pressure on the defendants to induce them to make their promise of additional money, in this situation Bry has clearly exerted a form of economic duress on Ami to force her to increase the contract price: Ami was left with no real choice but to agree to Bry's terms or else she would have suffered a potentially substantial loss. Such unfair pressure would take the case outside of *Williams v Roffey Bros*, and the old rule as stated in *Stilk v Myrick* would apply, and Bry would be unable to enforce the promise for the additional £1,000.

As regards Cis, it would appear that he did no more than he was required to do under his contract with Ami. Consequently he would be subject to the operation of *Stilk v Myrick* and could not enforce the promise for the additional £1,000.

ACCA marking scheme	
	Marks
Marks for this question will be awarded on the basis of a general knowledge of the law together with an ability to analyse the problem scenario and apply the general legal principles to the particular situation of the problem. In particular marks will be given for explanations of consideration, the law relating to existing duties and how those rules may be avoided. Knowledge of specific cases is not a requirement.	
Accurate analysis of the situation together with a detailed knowledge of the general legal principles involved linked to a sound application of those principles.	8–10
Sound knowledge of the law but perhaps lacking in application or alternatively not showing a sufficiently clear understanding of the legal principles involved.	5–7
Weak or unbalanced answer. Perhaps aware of the nature of the problem but lacking in clear knowledge of the principles or deficient in relation to how those principles should be applied.	3–4
Very weak answer. Perhaps mentioning some of the issues involved in the question but failing to consider them in any detail or merely recounting the facts of some of the cases with no attempt to derive principles or apply them.	0–2

9 CHI, DI AND FI

This question can be divided into three distinct sections.

The first element of this question requires a consideration of Fi's situation with respect to her potential liability. Partnerships do not normally provide their members with limited liability, unless the partnership has been registered as a limited partnership under the Limited Partnerships Act 1907 or registered as a limited liability partnership under the Limited Liability Partnerships Act 2000.

The situation in the problem scenario indicates that the partners have not gone through the appropriate procedure for the establishment of a limited partnership or a limited liability partnership. As a result, as far as outsiders are concerned, Fi is fully liable for any debts of the partnership and could be required to pay more than her agreed maximum payment of £100,000. Fi would, however, be entitled to rely on the internal partnership agreement to limit her liability within the partnership. This would mean that although she could be liable to outsiders beyond the £100,000, she would be able to claim reimbursement of any payments made above that limit from the other two partners, always assuming that they were in a position to make such a payment.

Chi has clearly used her powers for an unauthorised purpose. Unfortunately for the other partners, they cannot repudiate her transaction with the bank, even although it was outside her actual authority. The reason being, that it is within his implied authority as a partner to enter into such a transaction. As a trading partnership, all the members have the implied authority to borrow money on the credit of the firm and the bank would be under no duty to investigate the purpose to which the loan was to be put. As a result the partnership cannot repudiate the debt to the bank and each of the partners will be liable for its payment. It has to be stated, however, that Chi will be personally liable to the other partners for the £10,000 and as a further consequence of her breach of his duty not to act in any way prejudicial to the partnership business, the partnership could be wound up.

Di's purchase of the books was also clearly outside of the express provision of the partnership agreement. However, nonetheless the partnership would be liable as the transaction would be likely to be held to be within the implied authority of a partner in a gallery business (*Mercantile Credit v Garrod* (1962)). Once again, Di, the partner in default of the agreement, would be liable to the other members for any loss sustained in the transaction.

As regards any partnership debt owing, that is clearly within the ambit of the partnership and the members are all liable for non-payment.

If the partnership cannot pay the outstanding debts then the individual partners will become personally liable for any outstanding debt. Although under s.9 of the Partnership Act 1890 partnership debts are said to be joint, the Civil Liability Act 1978 provides that a judgement against one partner does not bar a subsequent action against the other partners. Once the debts owed to outsiders have been dealt with, only then the internal financial relationships of the partners amongst themselves will be dealt with according to the partnership agreement.

ACCA marking scheme	
	Marks
This question refers to key issues relating to the powers, authority and liability of partners.	
Candidates will exhibit a thorough knowledge of partnership law together with the ability to analyse the problems contained in the question.	8–10
Candidates will exhibit a sound knowledge of partnership law together with the ability to recognise the issues contained in the question. Knowledge may be less detailed or analysis less focused.	5–7
Identification of some of the central issues in the question and an attempt to apply the appropriate law. Towards the bottom of this range of marks there will be major shortcomings in analysis or application of law.	3–4
Very weak answers that might recognise what the question is about but show no ability to analyse or answer the problem as set out.	0–2

10   GILT LTD

This question raises issues relating to the duties owed by company directors to their companies and the consequences of any breach of such duties. Before the Companies Act 2006 directors' duties were considered as an aspect of the fiduciary relationship that existed between those directors and their companies. Certain duties follow from a person being fixed as a fiduciary, and these fiduciary duties are analogous to the duties owed by a trustee to a beneficiary under a trust.

Under the previous regulation, directors were required to act honestly and with good faith for the benefit of the company in discharging their duties. This general duty to the company was sub-divided into the three further heads: the duty to act *bona fide* in the best interests of the company, the duty to exercise their powers for a proper purpose, and the duty not to allow his personal interests to conflict with his duties to the company.

Those common law rules/equitable principles have now been given statutory effect under the provisions of chapter 2 of the Companies Act 2006. Somewhat paradoxically, although subsection 171(3) of that Act clearly states that the statutory rules replace the previous rules, nonetheless subsection 171(4) provides that the statutory rules have to be interpreted and applied in the same way as the previous common law and equitable rules/principles from which they were derived, and thus retains those previous rules and principles.

There are two particular issues that emerge from the problem scenario. The first relates to the fact that Harry has taken a facility fee from Itt plc and the second relates to the fact that the board of directors has used its general power to allot shares to pursue the particular end of assuring the successful takeover of their company.

These issues will be considered in turn below.

(i)   *Harry's facility fee*

The rule that directors should not allow a conflict of interest to arise was strictly enforced by the courts in the United Kingdom and it can be clearly stated that directors were forbidden from entering into any arrangement which would involve, even the possibility of, a conflict between their personal interests and the interests of their company. The simplest statement of the rule is that directors were not permitted to profit personally from their position without full disclosure and the prior approval of the company (*Regal (Hastings) v Gulliver* (1942) and *Boardman v Phipps* (1967)).

There can be no clearer instance of a conflict of interest than the situation of a director taking a bribe. This general prohibition has been given specific statutory form in s.176 of the Companies Act 2006, which sets out the categorical duty of directors not to accept benefits from third parties (s.176 CA 2006).

Under s.176, a director must not accept a benefit from a third party, which is conferred by reason of his being a director or his doing, or not doing anything as director. For the purposes of s.176 CA 2006 a third party is any person other than the company, an associated company or a person acting on behalf of the company or the associated company.

By virtue of s.176(4), however, there is no breach of duty if the acceptance of the benefit by the director cannot reasonably be regarded as likely to give rise to a conflict of interest. As a result, immaterial benefits and those which are entirely unrelated to the affairs of the company will not be covered by s.176. The statute retains the previous civil law remedies available under the common law or equity, as specifically stated in s.178 so directors in breach of the provision will be held liable to account to the company for any benefit received.

Applying the foregoing to Harry, it is unarguable that s.176 applies to his situation, as, no matter how the payment is referred to, it is nonetheless a benefit from a third party, Itt plc, to induce Harry to use his influence as a director to further the merger. As a result he has breached his duty to Gilt Ltd and not only will he be liable to be dismissed from the board by a simple majority vote (CA 2006 s.168), but he may also be required to pay any money received to Gilt Ltd.

(ii)   *The allotment of shares to Itt plc*

Once again the Companies Act 2006 restates a previous fiduciary duty in statutory form, with s.171(b) setting out the long-standing common law rule that directors' powers should be used only for the purposes for which they were conferred. This rule is known as the 'proper purposes doctrine' and was developed by the courts in order to ensure that directors use their powers for the purpose for which those powers were given to them and not for any ulterior or improper purpose. Most of the cases on this point have related to the exercise by directors of their power to issue new shares in an attempt to assist or, alternatively to prevent, potential takeover bids for their companies. Thus in *Howard Smith v Ampol Petroleum* (1974) directors preferred one takeover bid as opposed to another, which was supported by the majority shareholding. In order to defeat the bid they disliked, the directors issued new shares, effectively reducing the existing majority to a minority holding in the company, incapable of blocking their preferred takeover bid. This was clearly an abuse of the directors' powers and a breach of their duty to act bona fide in the interests of the company (See also *Hogg v Cramphorn* (1966) and *Bamford v Bamford* (1969)).

Another aspect of this general fiduciary duty is that directors must not act in such a way as will fetter the exercise of their discretion in relation to decisions that affect the operation of the company. For example, directors might enter into a contractual agreement with some outsider to use their vote in a particular way at board meetings. Once again, such an agreement is a clear breach of their fiduciary duty, although it must be recognised that if directors enter into contract on behalf of the company, which they genuinely consider to be in the company's best interests, then they may bind themselves to vote in favour of any subsequent resolutions necessary to achieve the successful completion of the contract.

Applying the above to the facts of the problem, it is apparent that the board of directors have contravened the provision of s.171 of the Companies Act 2006 in that they have used their power to allot shares, not for the primary purpose of raising capital for their company, but for the ulterior purpose of facilitating the take-over. As a result, although their exceeding their powers could be ratified by a vote at a subsequent general meeting, nonetheless without that ratification, May could apply to the court to have the share allocation declared invalid and Itt plc's use of those shares to vote in favour of the takeover bid would also be invalidated. In any subsequent vote to ratify the improper use of the directors' powers, Itt plc would not be permitted to vote.

ACCA marking scheme	
	Marks
This question refers to issues relating to the directors' duties and in particular the duty not to accept personal benefits and what is referred to as the 'improper purpose rule'. Candidates will exhibit a thorough knowledge of the law as set out in the Companies Act 2006 together with the ability to analyse the problems contained in the question. It is likely, but not necessary, for candidates to make reference to the previous non-statutory rules. likely that reference will be made to case authorities.	8–10
Candidates will exhibit a sound knowledge of the law together with the ability to recognise the issues contained in the question. Knowledge may be less detailed or analysis less focused.	5–7
Identification of some of the central issues in the question and an attempt to apply the appropriate law. Towards the bottom of this range of marks there will be major shortcomings in analysis or application of law.	3–4
Very weak answers that might recognise what the question is about but show no ability to analyse or answer the problem as set out.	0–2

Section 7

PILOT PAPER EXAM QUESTIONS

1 DELEGATED LEGISLATION

Explain the meaning and effect of delegated legislation, and evaluate its advantages and disadvantages, and how it is controlled by both Parliament and the courts.

(10 marks)

2 TYPES OF TERMS

In relation to the contents of a contract explain the following:

(a)	terms	**(2 marks)**
(b)	conditions	**(3 marks)**
(c)	warranties	**(3 marks)**
(d)	innominate terms.	**(2 marks)**

(Total: 10 marks)

3 NEGLIGENCE – DUTY OF CARE

In relation to the tort of negligence explain the meaning of 'duty of care'.

(10 marks)

4 REGISTRATION OF PUBLIC COMPANY

State the documents necessary and the procedure to be followed in registering a public limited company and enabling it to start trading.

(10 marks)

5 TYPES OF MEETINGS

In relation to company law explain and distinguish between the following:

(a)	annual general meeting	**(5 marks)**
(b)	general meeting	**(2 marks)**
(c)	class meeting.	**(3 marks)**

(Total: 10 marks)

6 MEANING OF CORPORATE GOVERNANCE AND RELATIONSHIP BETWEEN EXECUTIVE AND NON-EXECUTIVE DIRECTORS.

(a) Explain briefly what is meant by 'corporate governance'. **(4 marks)**

(b) Within the context of corporate governance examine the role of, and relationship between executive directors and non-executive directors. **(6 marks)**

(Total: 10 marks)

7 REDUNDANCY

In relation to employment law, explain the operation of the rules relating to redundancy.

(10 marks)

8 OFFER, INVITATION TO TREAT AND ACCEPTANCE

Al operates a small business manufacturing specialist engine filters. In January he placed an advertisement in a car trade magazine stating that he would supply filters at £60 per filter, but would consider a reduction in the price for substantial orders. He received a letter from Bash Cars plc requesting his terms of supply for 1,000 filters. Al replied, offering to supply the filters at a cost of £50 each. Bash Cars plc responded to Al's letter stating that they accepted his offer but that they would only pay £45 per filter. Al wrote back to Bash Cars plc stating that he would supply the filters but only at the original price of £50. When Al's letter arrived, the purchasing director of Bash Cars plc did not notice the alteration of the price and ordered the 1,000 filters from Al, which he supplied.

Required:

Analyse the situation from the perspective of contract law and in particular advise Al what price he is entitled to claim from Bash Cars plc.

(10 marks)

9 ISSUE OF SHARES AT A DISCOUNT

Flop Ltd was in financial difficulties. In January, in order to raise capital it issued 10,000 £1 shares to Gus, but only asked him to pay 75 pence per share at the time of issue. The directors of Flop Ltd intended asking Gus for the other 25 pence per share at a later date. However, in June it realised that it needed even more than the £2,500 it could raise from Gus's existing shareholding. So in order to persuade Gus to provide the needed money Flop Ltd told him that if he bought a further 10,000 shares he would only have to pay a total of 50 pence for each £1 share, and it would write off the money owed on the original share purchase.

Gus agreed to this, but the injection of cash did not save Flop and in December it went into insolvent liquidation, owing a considerable amount of money.

Required:

Explain any potential liability that Gus might have on the shares he holds in Flop Ltd.

(10 marks)

10   INSIDER DEALING

In January the board of directors of Huge plc decided to make a take over bid for Large plc. After the decision was taken, but before it is announced the following chain of events occurs.

(i)   Slye a director of Huge plc buys shares in Large plc.

(ii)   Slye tells his friend Mate about the likelihood of the take-over and Mate buys shares in Large plc.

(iii)   at a dinner party Slye, without actually telling him about the take-over proposal, advises his brother Tim to buy shares in Large plc and Tim does so.

Required:

Consider the legal position of Slye, Mate and Tim under the law relating to insider dealing.

(10 marks)

Section 8

ANSWERS TO PILOT PAPER EXAM QUESTIONS

1 DELEGATED LEGISLATION

This question asks candidates to explain both what delegated legislation is and its importance in the contemporary legal system. It specifically requires a consideration of the way in which Parliament and the courts seek to control it.

Within the United Kingdom, Parliament has the sole power to make law by creating legislation. Parliament, however, can pass on, or delegate, its law making power to some other body or individual. Delegated legislation is of particular importance in the contemporary legal context. Instead of general and definitive Acts of Parliament, which attempt to lay down detailed provisions, the modern form of legislation tends to be of the enabling type, which simply states the general purpose and aims of the Act. Such Acts merely lay down a broad framework, whilst delegating to ministers of state the power to produce detailed provisions designed to achieve those general aims. Thus delegated legislation is law made by some person, or body, to whom Parliament has delegated its general law making power. The output of delegated legislation in any year greatly exceeds the output of Acts of Parliament and, therefore, at least statistically it could be argued that delegated legislation is actually more significant than primary Acts of Parliament.

There are various types of delegated legislation:

(i) **Orders in Council** permit the government, through the Privy Council to make law. The Privy Council is nominally a non party-political body of eminent parliamentarians, but in effect it is simply a means through which the government, in the form of a committee of Ministers, can introduce legislation without the need to go through the full parliamentary process.

(ii) **Statutory Instruments** are the means through which government ministers introduce particular regulations under powers delegated to them by Parliament in enabling legislation.

(iii) **Bye-laws** are the means through which local authorities and other public bodies can make legally binding rules and may be made under such enabling legislation as the Local Government Act (1972).

(iv) **Court Rule Committees** are empowered to make the rules, which govern procedure in the particular courts over which they have delegated authority under such Acts as the Supreme Court Act 1981, the County Courts Act 1984, and the Magistrates' Courts Act 1980.

(v) **Professional regulations** governing particular occupations may be given the force of law under provisions delegating legislative authority to certain professional bodies.

An example is the power given to the Law Society, under the Solicitors' Act 1974, to control the conduct of practising solicitors.

The use of delegated legislation has the following advantages:

(i)   **Time-saving**. Delegated legislation can be introduced quickly where necessary in particular cases and permits rules to be changed in response to emergencies or unforeseen problems. The use of delegated legislation, also saves Parliamentary time generally. It is generally considered better for Parliament to spend its time in a thorough consideration of the principles of enabling legislation, leaving the appropriate minister, or body, to establish the working detail under their authority.

(ii) **Access to particular expertise**. Given the highly specialised and extremely technical nature of many of the regulations that are introduced through delegated legislation, the majority of Members of Parliament simply do not have sufficient expertise to consider such provisions effectively. It is necessary therefore, that those authorised to introduce delegated legislation should have access to the external expertise required to make appropriate regulations. In regard to bye-laws, local knowledge should give rise to more appropriate rules than general Acts of Parliament.

(iii) **Flexibility.** The use of delegated legislation permits ministers to respond on an ad hoc basis to particular problems as and when they arise.

There are, however, some disadvantages in the prevalence of delegated legislation:

(i)   **Accountability**. A key issue involved in the use of delegated legislation concerns the question of accountability. Parliament is presumed to be the source of statute law, but with respect to delegated legislation government ministers, and the civil servants, who work under them to produce the detailed provisions, are the real source of the legislation. As a consequence, it is sometimes suggested that the delegated legislation procedure gives more power than might be thought appropriate to such un-elected individuals.

(ii) **Bulk**. Given the sheer mass of such legislation, both Members of Parliament, and the general public, face difficulty in keeping abreast of delegated legislation.

The potential shortcomings in the use of delegated legislation considered above are, at least to a degree, mitigated by the fact that the courts have the ability to oversee and challenge such laws as are made in the form of delegated legislation.

Parliamentary control of delegated legislation

Since 1973, there has been a *Joint Select Committee on Statutory Instruments*, whose function it is to scrutinise all statutory instruments. The Joint Committee is empowered to draw the special attention of both Houses to an instrument on any one of a number of grounds specified in the Standing Orders (No.151 of the House of Commons and No. 74 of the House of Lords)) under which it operates; or on any other ground *which does not relate to the actual merits of the instrument or the policy it is pursuing*.

The House of Commons has its own *Select Committee on Statutory Instruments* which is appointed to consider all statutory instruments laid only before the House of Commons. This committee is empowered to draw the special attention of the House to an instrument on any one of a number of grounds specified in Standing Order No. 151; or on any other ground. However, as with the joint committee, it is nor empowered to consider the merits of any statutory instrument or the policy behind it.

Judicial control of delegated legislation

A validly enacted piece of delegated legislation has the same legal force and effect as the Act of Parliament under which it is enacted; but equally it only has effect to the extent that its enabling Act authorises it. Consequently, it is possible for delegated legislation to be challenged, through the procedure of judicial review, on the basis that the person or body to whom Parliament has delegated its authority has acted in a way that exceeds the limited powers delegated to them or has failed to follow the appropriate procedure set down in the enabling legislation. Any provision in this way is said to be *ultra vires* and is void.

Additional powers have been given to the courts under the Human Rights Act 1998 (HRA) with respect to delegated legislation. Section 4 of the HRA expressly states that the courts cannot declare *primary* legislation invalid as being contrary to the rights protected by the Act and limits them to issuing a declaration of incompatibility in such circumstances (*Bellinger* v *Bellinger* (2003)). It is then for Parliament to act on such a declaration to remedy any shortcoming in the law if it so wishes. However, such limitation does not apply to secondary legislation, which the courts can now declare invalid on the grounds of not being compatible with the HRA.

ACCA marking scheme	
	Marks
This question asks candidates to explain both what delegated legislation is and its importance in the contemporary legal system. It specifically requires a consideration of the way in which Parliament and the courts seek to control it.	
A thorough answer which explains the meaning of delegated legislation and how it is introduced. The perceived advantages and disadvantages should be considered and all aspects of control should be mentioned. For full marks reference should be made to the Human Rights Act 1998.	*6–10*
A less complete answer, perhaps lacking in detail or unbalanced in that it does not deal with some aspects of the question.	*0–5*
Max	**10**

2 TYPES OF TERMS

(a) **Contractual terms**, are statements which form part of the contract. Parties to a contract will normally be bound to perform any promise that they have agreed to and failure to perform will lead to an action for breach of contract, although the precise nature of the remedy will depend upon the nature of the promise broken. Some statements do not form part of a contract, even though they might have induced the other party to enter into the contract. These pre-contractual statements are called representations. The consequences of such representations being false is an action for misrepresentation not an action for breach of contract, and leads to different remedies. It is important, therefore, to decide precisely what promises are included in the contract. Once it is decided that a statement is a term, rather than merely a pre-contractual representation, it is further necessary to decide which type of term it is, in order to determine what remedies are available for its breach.

Terms can be classified as one of three types.

(b)   **Conditions**

A condition is a fundamental part of the agreement – it is something which goes to the root of the contract. Breach of a condition gives the injured party the right either to terminate the contract and refuse to perform their part of it, or to go through with the agreement and sue for damages. The classic case in relation to breach of condition is *Poussard* v *Spiers & Pond* (1876) in which the plaintiff had contracted with the defendants to sing in an opera they were producing. Due to illness she was unable to appear on the first night, or for some nights thereafter. When Mme Poussard recovered, the defendants refused her services as they had hired a replacement for the whole run of the opera. It was held that her failure to appear on the opening night had been a breach of a condition, and the defendants were at liberty to treat the contract as discharged

(c)   **Warranties**

A warranty is a subsidiary obligation which is not vital to the overall agreement, and in relation to which failure to perform does not totally destroy the whole purpose of the contract. Breach of a warranty does not give the right to terminate the agreement. The injured party has to complete their part of the agreement, and can only sue for damages. As regards warranties, the classic case is *Bettini* v *Gye* (1876) in which the plaintiff had contracted with the defendants to complete a number of engagements. He had also agreed to be in London for rehearsals six days before his opening performance. Due to illness, however, he only arrived three days before the opening night, and the defendants refused his services. On this occasion it was held that there was only a breach of warranty. The defendants were entitled to damages, but could not treat the contract as discharged.

For some time it was thought that these were the only two types of term possible, the nature of the remedy available being prescribed by the particular type of term concerned. This simple classification has subsequently been rejected by the courts as too restrictive, and a third type of term has emerged: the innominate term.

(d)   **Innominate terms**

In this case, the remedy is not prescribed in advance simply by whether the term breached is a condition or a warranty, but depends on the consequence of the breach.

If the breach deprives the innocent party of 'substantially the whole benefit of the contract', then the right to repudiate will be permitted; even if the term might otherwise appear to be a mere warranty.

If, however, the innocent party does not lose 'substantially the whole benefit of the contract', then they will not be permitted to repudiate but must settle for damages, even if the term might otherwise appear to be a condition. The way in which the courts approach such terms may be seen in *Cehave* v *Bremer (The Hansa Nord)* (1976). In this case a contract for the sale of a cargo of citrus pulp pellets, to be used as animal feed, provided that they were to be delivered in good condition. On delivery, the buyers rejected the cargo as not complying with that provision, and claimed back the money they had paid to the sellers. Subsequently the same buyers obtained the pellets, when the cargo was sold off, and used them for their original purpose. It was held that since the breach had not been serious, the buyers had not been free to reject the cargo, and the sellers had acted lawfully in retaining the money paid.

ACCA marking scheme	
	Marks
Thorough explanation of the meaning of terms generally together with an explanation of the three categories of terms with reference to appropriate cases or examples.	*8–10*
Reasonable treatment of terms generally and one or even two of the types of terms, or a less complete treatment of all the elements.	*5–7*
Very unbalanced answer, focusing on only one aspect of the question and ignoring the others, or one which shows little understanding of the subject matter of the question.	*0–4*
Max	**10**

3 NEGLIGENCE – DUTY OF CARE

A tort is a wrongful act against an individual which gives rise to a non-contractual civil claim. The claim is usually for damages, although other remedies are available. Liability in tort is usually based on principle of fault, although there are exceptions. Negligence is recognized as the most important of the torts, its aim being to provide compensation for those injured through the fault of some other person. However, an individual is not automatically liable for every negligent act that he or she commits and in order to sustain an action in negligence it must be shown that the party at fault owed a duty of care to the person injured as a result of their actions. Consequently, the onus is on the claimant to establish that the respondent owed them a duty of care.

The test for establishing whether a duty of care exists was initially set out in *Donoghue* v *Stevenson* (1932), the snail in the beer bottle case, in which the House of Lords established that a manufacturer owes a duty of care to the ultimate consumer of their goods. Irrespective of any lack of contractual relationship the manufacturer must exercise reasonable care to prevent injury to the consumer.

In putting forward the test to establish a duty of care Lord Atkin stated that:

> 'You must take reasonable care to avoid acts and omissions which you could reasonably foresee would be likely to injure your neighbour. Who, then, in law is my neighbour? ... any person so closely and directly affected by my act that I ought reasonably to have them in contemplation as being so affected when I am directing my mind to the acts and omissions which are called in question.'

It can be seen that this neighbour test for deciding the existence of a duty of care is an objective, rather than a subjective one. It is not a matter of what the respondent actually considered, but what they ought to have considered. Nor does the test require the contemplation of the resultant effect on the specific individual injured, but merely requires that identity of a class of individuals who might be injured as a consequence of the respondent's lack of care.

The test in *Donoghue* v *Stevenson* was subsequently extended in *Anns* v *Merton LBC* (1978), Lord Wilberforce introducing a two stage test for establishing the existence of a duty, as follows:

– Is there a sufficient relationship of proximity or neighbourhood between the alleged wrongdoer and the person who has suffered damage such that, in the reasonable contemplation of the former, carelessness on his part may be likely to cause damage to the latter?

- If the first question is answered in the affirmative, are there then any considerations which ought to negate, reduce or limit the scope of the duty or the class of persons to whom it is owed or the damages to which a breach of duty may give rise?

The impact of *Anns* led to the expansion of negligence, as the policy reasons acted only to limit liability once a duty had been found to exist, as opposed to limiting the existence of the duty itself. However, there was gradual criticism of, and retreat from the approach taken by Lord Wilberforce. Thus in *Peabody Donation Fund* v *Sir Lindsay Parkinson & Co Ltd* (1984), it was stressed that the proximity test had to be satisfied before a duty of care could be found to exist.

The decision in Anns was eventually overruled by *Murphy* v *Brentwood DC* (1990), where it was held that local authorities owed a duty of care to a building owner to avoid damage to the building, which would create a danger to the health and safety of the occupants. The duty arose out of the local authority's powers to require compliance with building regulations. However, as the damage was held to be pure economic loss, it was irrecoverable.

The present position, appears to be that in establishing the existence of a duty of care in negligence, an incremental approach must be taken. The claimant must show that the defendant foresaw that damage would occur to the claimant, that is, that there was sufficient proximity in time, space and relationship between the claimant and the defendant. In practical terms, foreseeability of damage will determine proximity in the majority of personal injury cases. The courts will then, where appropriate, consider whether it is just and reasonable to impose a duty and whether there are any policy reasons for denying or limiting the existence of a duty, for example, under the floodgates argument. The courts will not necessarily consider these in all cases.

The final retraction from *Anns* and support for the incremental approach was seen in *Caparo Industries plc* v *Dickman* (1990), where the application of a three stage test for establishing a duty of care was recommended. This requires consideration of the following questions:

- Was the harm caused reasonably foreseeable?

- Was there a relationship of proximity between the defendant and the claimant?

- In all the circumstances, is it just, fair and reasonable to impose a duty of care?

It is apparent that the courts' current position is to continue to retreat from Anns to a more 'category-based' approach, as referred to in the ratio of *Donoghue* v *Stevenson*.

This was clearly summed up by Lord Hoffmann in *Stovin* v *Wise* (1996), as follows:

The trend of authorities has been to discourage the assumption that anyone who suffers loss is *prima facie* entitled to compensation from a person ... whose act or omission can be said to have caused it. The default position is that he is not.

ACCA marking scheme	
	Marks
Thorough explanation of the meaning of duty of care with appropriate references to cases.	*8–10*
Reasonable duty of care but perhaps lacking in detail or cases authority.	*5–7*
Very unbalanced answer, lacking in detailed understanding.	*0–4*
	—
Max	**10**
	—

4   REGISTRATION OF PUBLIC COMPANY

Incorporation under the Companies Act 2006 requires companies to register certain documents with the Registrar of Companies. These documents are as follows:

Memorandum

This document must be signed by all the subscribers. It states that one or more persons wish to form a company, that they agree to become members of that company and to take at least one share in the company each.

Application

The application form must include the proposed name of the company; whether, and if so how, the liability of the members is to be limited; a statement as to whether the company is private or public; the details and address of the registered office.

Articles of Association

The articles of association, form part of the company's internal constitution, along with other agreements or special resolutions (s.17).

They set out the manner in which the company is to be governed and regulate the relationship between the company and its shareholders.

If no articles are submitted, the company will be governed by the model articles prescribed by the Secretary of State.

Statement of capital and initial shareholdings

This must state the number of shares, their aggregate nominal value and how much has been paid up on each share.

Statement of proposed officers

This gives details of the first directors and company secretary, if applicable, and their consent to act.

Statement of compliance

This provides confirmation that the provisions of Companies Act 2006 have been complied with.

Under s.14, the registrar will not register a company unless satisfied that all the requirements of the Companies Act in respect of registration have been complied with. Where, however, a certificate of incorporation has been given, then under s.15, it is conclusive evidence that the requirements of the Companies Acts have been complied with.

Trading certificate

A private company can commence trading immediately. However, a public limited company cannot commence trading until the registrar has issued a trading certificate (s.761 CA 2006). To obtain a trading certificate, there must be at least £50,000 of allotted share capital with at least one quarter of the nominal value and all of the premium being paid up.

It is a criminal offence for a plc to carry on a business without a certificate. If it does so, the company and any officers are liable to a fine.

Companies originally registered as private may be converted to public companies at a later date. The procedure under s.90 CA 2006 achieves the same ends as s.761.

Finally, if a public company does not obtain a trading certificate within one year of its registration, the court (Insolvency Act 1986, s.122) may wind up the company.

ACCA marking scheme	
	Marks
Answers will show a thorough understanding of the registration process, listing the documents required, and will make clear reference to the trading certificate in relation to public companies.	*8–10*
A sound understanding of the area, although perhaps lacking in detail.	*5–7*
Some understanding of the area but lacking in detail, perhaps failing to deal with the need for a trading certificate.	*2–4*
Little or no knowledge of the area.	*0–1*
Max	**10**

5 TYPES OF MEETINGS

In theory, the ultimate control over a company's business lies with the members in a general meeting. One would obviously conclude that a meeting involved more than one person; and indeed there is authority to that effect in *Sharp* v *Dawes* (1876) in which a meeting between a lone member and the company secretary was held not to be validly constituted. It is possible, however, for a meeting of only one person to take place in the following circumstances:

(i) in the case of a meeting of a particular class of shareholders and all the shares of that class are owned by the one member

(ii) by virtue of s.306 of the Companies Act 2006 the court may order the holding of a general meeting at which the quorum is to be one member.

Types of meetings

There are three types of meeting:

(a) **Annual general meeting.** By virtue of s.336 CA06, every public company is required to hold an annual general meeting (AGM) once a year, within the six months following the accounting reference date. (Private companies are no longer required to hold an AGM).

If a public company fails to hold an AGM then every officer in default may be fined.

S.307 CA06 states that 21 days' notice is normally required unless 95% of those members entitled to attend and vote agree to a shorter period. The usual business of an AGM includes consideration of the accounts, appointment of the auditors, election of the directors and the declaration of dividends.

Members can force the inclusion of a resolution on the agenda if they hold 5% of the voting rights or 100 members each hold an average of £100 of the paid up share capital: s.338 CA06.

(b) A **general meeting** can be held whenever required. At least 14 days' notice must be given and the person who requisitions the meeting may set the agenda.

In the case of a public limited company, a general meeting must be held if a serious loss of capital has occurred: s656 CA06. This is defined as the assets falling to half or less than the nominal value of the called up share capital.

(c) A **class meeting** is one held by a class of shareholders or debenture holders, usually to consider a variation of their class rights. A quorum for a class meeting is two persons holding, or representing by proxy, at least one-third in nominal value of the issued shares of the class in question: s.334 CA06.

Meetings may be convened in a number of ways by various people:

(i)   by the directors of the company.

(ii)   by the members using the power to requisition a meeting under s.303 CA 2006.

(iii) by the auditor of a company under s.518, which provides for a resigning auditor to require the directors to convene a meeting in order to explain the reason for the auditor's resignation.

(iv)   the court may order a meeting under s.306, where it is impracticable otherwise to call a meeting.

ACCA marking scheme	
	Marks
A good treatment of all three types of meeting, probably, although not necessarily, with reference to statutory provisions.	*8–10*
A sound understanding of the area, although perhaps lacking in detail.	*5–7*
Some understanding of the area, but lacking in detail, perhaps failing to deal with one type of meeting.	*2–4*
Little or no knowledge of the area.	*0–1*
Max	***10***

6   MEANING OF CORPORATE GOVERNANCE AND RELATIONSHIP BETWEEN EXECUTIVE AND NON EXECUTIVE DIRECTORS

(a)   Corporate governance refers to the way in which companies are run and operated. According to the Organisation for Economic Co-operation and Development:

Corporate governance is the system by which business corporations are directed and controlled. The corporate governance structure specifies the distribution of rights and responsibilities among different participants in the corporation, such as, the board, managers, shareholders and other stakeholders, and spells out the rules and procedures for making decisions on corporate affairs. By doing this, it also provides the structure through which the company objectives are set, and the means of attaining those objectives and monitoring performance.

Although these interrelated issues have always been of concern in the way companies function, it cannot but be recognised that the increase in the attention placed on matters of corporate governance has been a result of the perceived weakness in company regulation which has been apparent in some of the recent scandals involving such large companies as Enron and Worldcom in America and Marconi and Parmalat in Europe.

In order to ensure an effective corporate governance framework it has been deemed necessary to set out defined rules and regulations, including voluntary codes. In the United Kingdom one such code is the Combined Code On Corporate Governance, which is the result of the review of the role and effectiveness of non-executive directors conducted by Derek Higgs and a review of audit committees conducted by Sir Robert Smith. This new combined code has applied to listed companies since

November 2003. Companies have either to confirm that they comply with the Code's provisions or, where it does not, to provide an explanation of their non-compliance. Whilst listed companies are expected to comply with the Code's provisions most of the time, it is recognised that departure from its provisions may be justified in particular circumstances. Every company must review each provision carefully and give a considered explanation if it departs from the Code provisions.

(b) As regards the structure of the board of directors, the Combined Code requires that the board should include a balance of executive and non-executive directors (and in particular independent non-executive directors) such that no individual or small group of individuals can dominate the board's decision taking.

Executive directors usually work on a full time basis for the company and may be employees of the company with specific contracts of employment. Section 228 Companies Act (CA) 2006 requires that the terms of any such contract must be made available for inspection by the members. Section 188 renders void any such contract, which purports to be effective for a period of more than two years, unless it has been approved by a resolution of the company in a general meeting. In fact the Combined Code on Corporate Governance recommends that the maximum period for directors' employment contracts should be one year.

Non-executive directors do not usually have a full-time relationship with the company, they are not employees and only receive directors' fees. The role of the non-executive directors, at least in theory, is to bring outside experience and expertise to the board of directors. They are also expected to exert a measure of control over the executive directors to ensure that the latter do not run the company in their, rather than the company's, best interests. As the Combined Code puts it:

> 'As part of their role as members of a unitary board, non-executive directors should constructively challenge and help develop proposals on strategy. Non-executive directors should scrutinise the performance of management in meeting agreed goals and objectives and monitor the reporting of performance. They should satisfy themselves on the integrity of financial information and that financial controls and systems of risk management are robust and defensible. They are responsible for determining appropriate levels of remuneration of executive directors and have a prime role in appointing, and where necessary removing, executive directors, and in succession planning.'

It is important to note that there is no distinction in law between executive and non-executive directors and the latter are subject to the same controls and potential liabilities as are the former.

ACCA marking scheme	
	Marks
A good explanation of the meaning of corporate governance generally and the roles of the two types of directors in particular. Reference might well be made to the OECD or the Combined Code.	*8–10*
A sound understanding of the area, although perhaps lacking in detail.	*5–7*
Some understanding of the area, but lacking in detail, perhaps failing to deal the relationship of the two group of directors.	*2–4*
Little or no knowledge of the area.	*0–1*
Max	**10**

7   REDUNDANCY

This question requires candidates to explain the main features of the law relating to dismissal from employment on the basis of redundancy, paying particular regard to the way in which redundancy payments are calculated.

There are two major purposes behind the law relating to redundancy. The first purpose is to encourage employers to consider alternatives to dismissing their employees, and the second is to ensure that where employees have been dismissed on the grounds of redundancy that they should have at least a minimum level of payment to tide them over until hopefully they can regain employment. The law relating to redundancy is currently to be found in the Employment Rights Act 1996 (ERA). The determination of redundancy depends on the qualifying rules stated in that Act, and in order to be awarded redundancy payment individuals must follow the procedures stated therein.

Redundancy is defined in s 139(1) of the ERA as being: 'dismissal attributable wholly or mainly to:

(a)   the fact that his employer has ceased, or intends to cease, to carry on the business for the purposes of which the employee was employed by him, or has ceased, or intends to cease to carry on that business in the place where the employee was so employed, or

(b)   the fact that the requirements of that business for employees to carry out work of a particular kind, or for employees to carry out work of a particular kind in the place where they were so employed, have ceased or diminished or are expected to cease or diminish.'

It should be noted that even where a dismissal clearly falls within the above categories, an individual will not be able to claim redundancy payments unless they meet the qualification requirements, the most important of which relates to length of service. In order to qualify for redundancy payments an employee must have been continuously employed by the same employer or associated company for a period of two years. (The decision to reduce the length of service in relation to a claim for unfair dismissal to one year has not been extended to redundancy claims (*R* v *Sec State for Employment ex p Seymour Smith* (2000)).

Redundancy as a consequence of cessation of business is relatively straightforward and unproblematic although it should be noted that it applies to temporary as well as permanent cessation as seen in *Gemmell* v *Darngavil Brickworks Lid* (1967).

Problems do tend to arise in relation to the closure and relocation of the place of business. If the employer offers the employee a similar job at the new location, *which involves the employee in no added inconvenience*, then the employee cannot claim redundancy (see Managers (*Holborn Ltd* v *Hohne* (1977)). Where the employee does suffer additional inconvenience then they cannot be required to move unless they have an express mobility clause in their contract of employment, which require them to move with their job. An example of the former maybe seen in *O'Brien* v *Associated Fire Alarms* (1969) in which the plaintiff successfully claimed redundancy when he was dismissed for refusing to move from Liverpool to Barrow in Furness. However in *Rank Xerox Lid* v *Churchill* (1988) an employee with a mobility clause was not allowed to claim redundancy when required to move location of employment.

At the outset of redundancy proceedings the onus is placed on the employee to show that they have been dismissed, which they do by demonstrating that they are covered by s 136 of ERA, which provides four types of dismissal. These are:

(i)   the contract of employment is terminated by the employer with or without notice;

(ii)   a fixed term contract has expired and has not been renewed;

(iii)   the employee terminates the contract with or without notice in circumstances which are such that he or she is entitled to terminate it without notice by reason of the employer's conduct;

(iv)   the contract is terminated by the death of the employer, or the dissolution or liquidation of the firm.

Normally employees who resign are not entitled to claim redundancy but type (iii) above provides for what is known as constructive dismissal in recognition of the situation where the unreasonable action of the employer has been tantamount to forcing the employee to resign. It is of course possible for the employee to behave in an unreasonable manner, and where they have refused to take up 'suitable' alternative employment offered to them by their employer they cannot claim redundancy. The difficulty arises in deciding what constitutes suitable alternative employment and can really only be decided on the facts of each case.

Once dismissal has been established a presumption in favour of redundancy operates and the onus shifts to the employer to show that redundancy was not the reason for the dismissal.

Employees who have been dismissed by way of redundancy are entitled to claim a redundancy payment from their former employer. Under the ERA the actual figures are calculated on the basis of the person's age, length of continuous service and weekly rate of pay subject to statutory maxima. Thus employees between the ages of 18 and 21 are entitled to ½ weeks pay for each year of service, those between 22 and 40 are entitled to 1 weeks pay for every year of service, and those between 41 and 65 are entitled to 1½ weeks pay for every year of service.

The maximum number of years service that can be claimed is 20 and as the maximum level of pay that can be claimed is £310, the maximum total that can be claimed is £9,300, (i.e. $1.5 \times 20 \times 310$).

Disputes in relation to redundancy claims are heard before an industrial – tribunal and on appeal go to the Employment Appeal Tribunal.

There is also a statutory requirement for an employer to consult a recognised trade union or elected employees' representatives in good time to consider ways in which any redundancies can be avoided.

ACCA marking scheme	
	Marks
A complete answer, demonstrating an understanding of what is meant by redundancy and the legal procedures controlling its operation, but must also be able to describe the way in which any payments are calculated.	*8–10*
An accurate recognition of the issues relating to redundancy and the calculations, but perhaps lacking in detail.	*5–7*
An ability to recognise some, although not all, of the key issues, or perhaps a recognition of the area of law but no attempt to apply that law.	*2–4*
Very weak answer showing no, or very little, understanding of the question.	*0–1*
Max	**10**

8   OFFER, INVITATION TO TREAT AND ACCEPTANCE

This question requires candidates to analyse the problem scenario from the perspective of contract law paying particular regards to the rules relating to: invitation to treat, offers, counter offers and breach of contract.

An offer is a promise to be bound on particular terms, and it must be capable of acceptance. The person who makes the offer is the offeror; the person who receives the offer is the offeree. The offer sets out the terms upon which the offeror is willing to enter into contractual relations with the offeree. An offer may, through acceptance by the offeree, result in a legally enforceable contract. However, it is important to distinguish what the law will treat as an offer from other statements which will not form the basis of an enforceable contract. The original advertisement in the magazine was not an offer; it was merely an invitation to treat. As such it is not an offer to sell but merely an invitation to others to make offers. The point of this is that the person extending the invitation is not bound to accept any offers made to them. The classic case in this area is *Partridge* v *Crittenden* (1968) in which a person was charged with offering a wild bird for sale contrary to the Protection of Birds Act 1954, after he had placed an advert relating to the sale of such birds in a magazine. It was held that he could not be guilty of offering the bird for sale as the advert amounted to no more than an invitation to treat.

The original letters Al received from Bash Cars plc was a request for information and did not amount to offers to purchase filters from Al (*Harvey* v *Facey* (1893)). The first offer was made by Al when he wrote to both Bash Cars plc stating his terms of supply. Bash Cars plc was at liberty to accept Al's offer to supply the 1,000 filters at £50 each and thus enter into a binding contract, which Al would have had to perform or stand liable to pay damages for any breach of the contract. However, Bash Cars plc did not accept the original offer, stating that it was only willing to pay £45 per filter. That letter amounted to a counter offer, which made Al the offeree rather than the offeror, as he had originally been. The effect of such counter offers was to destroy Al's original offer, so that it could no longer be accepted (*Hyde* v *Wrench* (1840)) without further negotiations. Al's next letter restating his original terms represented a further counter-offer to the companies own counter-offer. That letters restored Al to his position as the offeror with Bash Cars reassuming the role of offerees, who could accept or reject the terms as it wished.

By sending the order for the filters, the purchasing director of Bash Cars accepted Al's offer and therefore entered into a binding contract on Al's terms, which require the company to pay £50 per filter.

ACCA marking scheme	
	Marks
A complete answer, highlighting and dealing with all of the issues presented in the problem scenario. It is most likely that cases will be referred to, and they will be credited.	*8–10*
An accurate recognition of the problems inherent in the question, together with an attempt to apply the appropriate legal rules to the situation.	*5–7*
An ability to recognise some, although not all, of the key issues and suggest appropriate legal responses to them. A recognition of the area of law but no attempt to apply that law.	*2–4*
Very weak answer showing no, or very little, understanding of the question.	*0–1*
Max	*10*

9 ISSUE OF SHARES AT A DISCOUNT

This question requires candidates to consider various issues relating to the issuing of shares by companies, the requirement for those shares to be paid for by shareholders and shareholders' potential liabilities for the debts of their companies.

The first issue relates to the shares taken by Gus in January. United Kingdom law requires that the capital of any company having share capital must be divided into shares of a designated and fixed amount (s.2(5)). The nominal value of the shares represents the extent of a shareholder's potential liability (*Borland's Trustees* v *Steel* (1901)).

There is, however, no requirement that companies issue shares to the full extent of their authorised capital, nor indeed is there any requirement that the company require its shareholders to immediately pay the full value of the shares.

The proportion of the nominal value of the issued capital actually paid by the shareholder is called the paid up capital. It may be the full nominal value, in which case it fulfils the shareholders responsibility to outsiders; or it can be a mere part payment, in which case the company has an outstanding claim against the shareholder. It is possible for a company to pass a resolution that it will not make a call on any unpaid capital. However, even in that situation, the unpaid element can be called upon if the company cannot pay its debts from existing assets in the event of its liquidation.

Consequently, there was nothing unlawful in the issue of the shares as partly paid up, but the remaining, unpaid, part, can always be called upon if the company requires it to pay off its debts.

The foregoing point is further strengthened by rules preventing companies from issuing shares at a discount. It is a long established rule that companies are not permitted to issue shares for a consideration that is less than the nominal value of the shares together with any premium due. The strictness of this rule may be seen in *Ooregum Gold Mining Co of India* v *Roper* (1892). In that case the shares in the company, although nominally £1, were trading at 12.5p. In an honest attempt to refinance the company, new £1 preference shares were issued and credited with 75p already paid (note the purchasers of the shares were actually paying twice the market value of the ordinary shares). When, however, the company subsequently went into insolvent liquidation the holders of the new shares were required to pay a further 75p.

The common law rule is now given statutory effect in s.580 Companies Act 2006 and is supported by s.582 which states that shares are only treated as paid up to the extent that the company has received money or money's worth. If a company does enter into a contract to issue shares at a discount it will not be able to enforce this against the proposed allottee. However, anyone who takes shares without paying the full value, plus any premium due, is liable to pay the amount of the discount as unpaid share capital, together with interest at the appropriate rate (s.580(2) CA2006). Also any subsequent holder of such a share who was aware of the original underpayment will liable to make good the shortfall (s.588 CA 2006).

Applying the foregoing to Gus's situation in relation to his shareholdings in Flop Ltd he cannot avoid liability to pay up to the full value of the shares he has taken in it. Thus in relation to the first lot of shares he will be liable to pay a maximum of £2,500 (25 pence × 10,000) shares and in relation to the second lot he will be liable to pay a maximum of £5,000 (50 pence × 10,000 shares). The extent of his liability will depend on the actual debts owed but cannot exceed the nominal value of the shares.

ACCA marking scheme	
	Marks
A complete answer, highlighting and dealing with all of the issues presented in the problem scenario. It is most likely that cases and statutory provisions will be referred to, and they will be credited.	*8–10*
An accurate recognition of the problems inherent in the question, together with an attempt to apply the appropriate legal rules to the situation.	*5–7*
An ability to recognise some, although not all, of the key issues and suggest appropriate legal responses to them. A recognition of the area of law but no attempt to apply that law.	*2–4*
Very weak answer showing no, or very little, understanding of the question.	*0–1*
Max	*10*

10 INSIDER DEALING

Dealing in shares, on the basis of access to unpublished price sensitive information, provides the basis for what is referred to as 'insider dealing' and is governed by part V of the Criminal Justice Act 1993 (CJA).

Section 52 of the CJA sets out the three distinct offences of insider dealing:

(i)   an individual is guilty of insider dealing if they have information as an insider and deal in price-affected securities on the basis of that information

(ii)   an individual who has information as an insider will also be guilty of insider dealing if they encourage another person to deal in price-affected securities in relation to that information

(iii)   an individual who has information as an insider will also be guilty of insider dealing if they disclose it to anyone other than in the proper performance of their employment, office or profession.

The CJA goes on to explain the meaning of some of the above terms as follows:

(i)   Dealing is defined in s.55 CJA, amongst other things, as acquiring or disposing of securities, whether as a principal or agent, or agreeing to acquire securities. Section 52 makes it clear that only such activity in a regulated market is covered by the Act.

(ii)   Inside information is defined in s.56 as:

        –   relating to particular securities,

        –   being specific or precise,

        –   not having been made public and

        –   being likely to have a significant effect on the price of the securities.

(iii)   Section 57 states that a person has information as an insider only if they know it is inside information and they have it from an inside source. The section then goes on to consider what might be described as primary and secondary insiders. The first category of primary insiders covers those who get the inside information directly through either:

        –   being a director, employee or shareholder of an issuer of securities; or

        –   having access to the information by virtue of their employment, office or profession.

        The second category of insiders includes those whose source, either directly or indirectly, is a primary insider, as defined above.

Applying the general law to the problem scenario, one can conclude as follows:

(i)   Slye is an 'insider' as he receives inside information from his position as a director of Huge plc. The information fulfils the requirements for 'inside information' as it relates to: particular securities, the shares in Large plc; is specific, in that it relates to the takeover; has not been made public; and is likely to have a significant effect on the price of the securities. On that basis Slye is clearly guilty of an offence under s.52 when he buys the shares in Large plc.

(ii)   When Slye tells his friend Mate about the likelihood of the take-over he commits the second offence of disclosing information he has as an insider. Mate then becomes an insider himself and is guilty of dealing when he buys shares in Large plc.

(iii)   When Slye advises his brother Tim to buy shares in Large plc, he commits the third offence under s.52 of encouraging another person to deal in price-affected securities in relation to inside information. Tim on the other hand has committed no offence for the reason that, although he has bought shares in Large plc, he has not received any specific information and therefore cannot be guilty of dealing on the basis of such information.

ACCA marking scheme	
	Marks
A good analysis of the scenario with a clear explanation of the law relating to the insider dealing, with detailed reference to statutory provisions.	*8–10*
Some understanding of the situation but perhaps lacking in detail or reference to the statutes.	*5–7*
Weak answer lacking in knowledge or application, with little or no reference to the statute.	*0–4*
Max	**10**